The Indian Ocean in Global Politics

About the Book and Editors

The Indian Ocean in Global Politics
edited by Larry W. Bowman and Ian Clark

This up-to-date analysis of the major political issues associated with the Indian Ocean region examines recent developments in South Asia, the Gulf, and Africa and their effect on Indian Ocean security matters and politics. Regional perspectives on the problems of the area are assessed, as are the roles played by the major external powers with regional interests—the United States, the Soviet Union, and France—and such international organizations as the United Nations.

Nine of the chapters grew out of the International Conference on Indian Ocean Studies held in Perth, Australia, in August 1979. Three additional chapters were commissioned to ensure a comprehensive view of the issues discussed. This collaboration by recognized authorities is sure to become a standard reference in the field.

Dr. Bowman is associate professor of political science at the University of Connecticut; he has written widely on Western policy in the southern Africa and Indian Ocean regions and is editor of Westview's series entitled Nations of Contemporary Africa. Dr. Clark, lecturer in politics at the University of Western Australia, is coauthor of *The Politics of Intrusion: The Super Powers and the Indian Ocean* (1979).

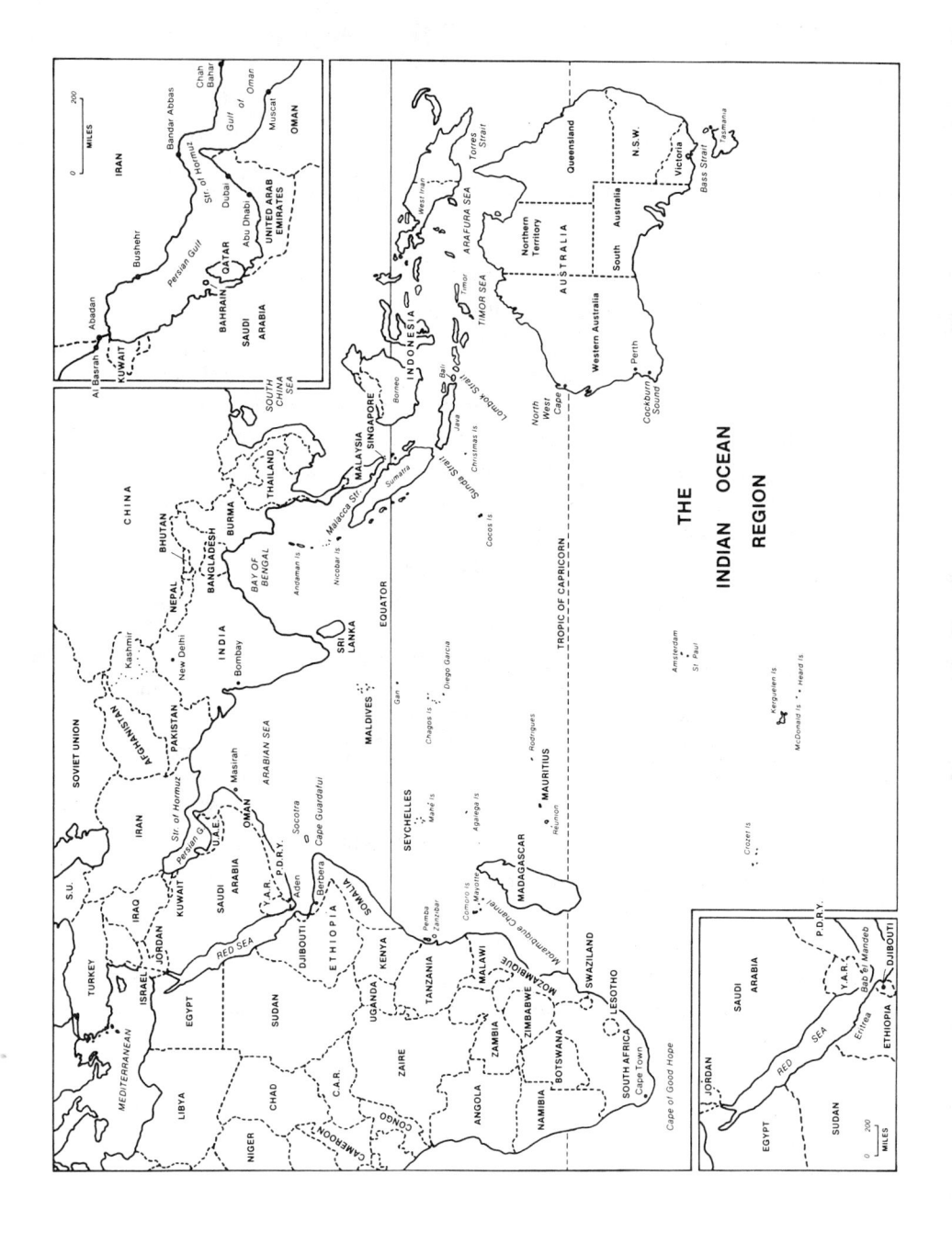

THE INDIAN OCEAN REGION

The Indian Ocean in Global Politics

edited by
Larry W. Bowman and Ian Clark

Westview Press • Boulder, Colorado
University of Western Australia • Nedlands, W.A.

This volume is included in Westview's Special Studies in International Relations.

All rights reserved. No part of this publication may be reproduced or transmitted in any form or by any means, electronic or mechanical, including photocopy, recording, or any information storage and retrieval system, without permission in writing from the publisher.

Copyright © 1981 by Westview Press, Inc.

Published in 1981 in the United States of America by
  Westview Press, Inc.
  5500 Central Avenue
  Boulder, Colorado 80301
  Frederick A. Praeger, Publisher

Published in 1981 in Australia by
  University of Western Australia Press
  Nedlands, Western Australia, 6009

  Agent: Eastern States of Australia and New Zealand:
  Melbourne University Press, Carlton South, Vic. 3053

Published in 1981 in India by
  Young Asia Publications
  7, Ansari Road
  New Delhi–110002

Library of Congress Catalog Card Number: 80-18298
ISBN (U.S.): 0-86531-038-6; 0-86531-191-9 pbk.
ISBN (Australia): 0-85564-182-7

Printed and bound in the United States of America

Contents

Map of Indian Ocean Region......................frontispiece
Preface..ix

Introduction, *Larry W. Bowman* 1

Part 1. Regional Powers in the Indian Ocean

1. The Strait of Hormuz: The Global Chokepoint,
   Rouhollah K. Ramazani..................................7
2. New Patterns of India's Relations
   with Indian Ocean Littoral States, *Dieter Braun* 21
3. India's Nonalignment and Superpower
   Naval Rivalry in the Indian Ocean, *Joel Larus* 41
4. Australia and the Indian Ocean, *Henry S. Albinski* 59
5. African Conflict and Superpower Involvement in
   the Western Indian Ocean, *Larry W. Bowman* 87

Part 2. External Powers in the Indian Ocean

6. The October War, the 1973–1974
   Arab Oil Embargo, and U.S. Policy
   on the Indian Ocean, *Kim C. Beazley* 107
7. Carter's Diplomacy and the Indian Ocean Region,
   Ashok Kapur 131

8. Soviet Arms Supplies and Indian Ocean Diplomacy,
   Ian Clark 149
9. Soviet Naval Policy in the Indian Ocean,
   Geoffrey Jukes................................... 173
10. France and the Indian Ocean, Jean-Pierre Gomane 189

Part 3. International Organizations in the Indian Ocean

11. The United Nations Ad Hoc Committee on the
    Indian Ocean: Blind Alley or Zone of Peace?
    Philip Towle 207
12. Demilitarization Proposals for the Indian Ocean,
    George W. Shepherd, Jr........................... 223

The Editors and Contributors 249
Index 253

Preface

This book has its origins in the International Conference on Indian Ocean Studies (ICIOS) held in Perth, Australia, from August 15 to 22, 1979. Almost 250 people from around the world gathered for this conference, which was primarily sponsored by UNESCO and the state government of Western Australia. UNESCO's interest in ICIOS grew out of a 1974 meeting in Mauritius at which a UNESCO-sponsored group of experts called for the development of interregional and international study of the Indian Ocean. The state government supported ICIOS as part of its year-long celebration of the 150th anniversary of the founding of Western Australia. The conference was organized and hosted by the three institutions of higher education in the Perth area: Murdoch University, the Western Australian Institute of Technology, and the University of Western Australia.

Seven sections composed the agenda of the conference: environment and resources, trade and development, the history of commercial exchange and maritime transport, cultural exchanges and influences, comparative education, archives and resources for study, and international politics. Dr. Ian Clark, lecturer in politics at the University of Western Australia, became the secretary for the international politics section. Although he did not know it at the time, the work he was to do from mid-1978 onward as he organized the section was to lay the groundwork for the present volume.

At the conference itself, sixteen papers were given in the international politics section. During the eight days of the conference, each paper was presented in a formal session, critiqued, and discussed within the section. This was a rich and stimulating experience in itself and provided the basis on which the decision was made to move forward to publication.

At the end of the conference the two editors selected nine of the papers for inclusion in this volume. They also invited three active members of the section—Jean-Pierre Gomane, Geoffrey Jukes, and Philip Towle—to prepare new papers that would fill in gaps in the overall coverage of Indian Ocean international issues. Prior to leaving Perth, the twelve authors committed themselves to the book. Following the conference, the papers were either newly written or revised in light of conference comments. In Connecticut, Larry W. Bowman did the overall editing and preparing of the manuscript for publication.

On the last day of the conference, the delegates passed a series of resolutions. They noted that the ICIOS meeting had represented an important and unique opportunity for the peoples of the Indian Ocean littoral and island states to jointly discuss and share their cultures, economic plans and goals, environmental concerns, history, current problems, and future aspirations. The participants pledged to work to keep alive the idea of international Indian Ocean studies and urged that a second ICIOS be held within five years of the Perth meeting. It was also urged that every effort be made to publish the results of the conference in permanent form. Seen in this light, the willingness of Westview Press to publish the work of the international politics section is particularly appreciated.

Several people, organizations, and institutions have been very helpful in bringing this overall project to fruition. In Perth, Mrs. J. Cook and Mrs. P. Carruthers of the Department of Politics at the University of Western Australia (UWA) did typing for Dr. Clark. The assistance of the staffs of both the Department of Politics and the Centre for South and Southeast Asian Studies at UWA were instrumental in providing the institutional support for the entire ICIOS effort.

In the United States, the University of Connecticut Research Foundation and in particular the director of the Research Foundation, Hugh Clark, made an early financial commitment to help assist Bowman's trip to Perth. Further assistance to Bowman was provided by the American Universities Field Staff based in Hanover, New Hampshire; the associate director of the Field Staff, John M. Thompson, was especially helpful.

Preface

Once the manuscript began to take shape, the University of Connecticut Research Foundation was again most helpful by supporting the preparation of the final manuscript, and Pam Hodge of West Willington, Connecticut, deserves special thanks for her prompt typing of the entire manuscript as the chapters came in from the far corners of the globe. Ray Blanchette of the University of Connecticut publications staff prepared a new map for the book. Finally, the entire project would never have taken shape so promptly without the early support and commitment provided by Lynne C. Rienner, associate publisher at Westview. For her enthusiasm, patience, and trust, we are most grateful.

Larry W. Bowman
Ian Clark

Introduction

Larry W. Bowman

It is almost prosaic in 1980 to reiterate the importance of the Indian Ocean region. Throughout the last decade developments both on the Indian Ocean and in the littoral and island states of the region have repeatedly drawn world attention. Only the most obvious need be mentioned here in order to underline how crucial the regional developments are to the rest of the world.

Oil issues provide the most compelling concern. The emergence of the Organization of Petroleum Exporting Countries (OPEC), the oil embargo of 1973–74, the continuing stark dependency of the developed world on access to Gulf oil, and the need for assured and steady transport of that oil across the Indian Ocean suggest the variety of challenges that must be met. The Iranian revolution and its aftermath and the seizure of the Great Mosque in Mecca are two recent reminders of the precariousness of oil supply questions.

As if the issue of oil were not enough to rivet attention on the region, other issues can be added. There have been three India-Pakistan wars in the past generation, the last in 1971. There remain vast ongoing tensions in the subcontinent, now complicated by the reality of nuclear proliferation. Along the western Indian Ocean, in the Horn of Africa, and in southern Africa, the forces of nationalism, liberation, and racism continue to vie for influence and ascendancy against the background of vast income disparities and the need for economic development. The recent invasion of Afghanistan by the Soviet Union has again drawn attention to the region and sparked a renewed debate both in the West and elsewhere about Soviet intentions on and around the Indian Ocean.

The decision of Pres. Jimmy Carter to respond to the Soviet invasion by upgrading U.S. military capabilities in the Indian ocean raises new questions about the overall role of the superpowers in this area. It also reminds us of the difficulties inherent in developing arms control and demilitarization proposals for the region. With all of this, it is little wonder that the area is often described as an arc of instability.

If there is a single dimension of Indian Ocean analysis that a book of this breadth quickly confronts, it is that it is exceedingly difficult to clearly differentiate between the domestic, regional, and international events that occur; the interdependencies are just too great. To give just a few simple examples, any problem in the Strait of Hormuz that would threaten oil tanker traffic could scarcely be contained as an issue of importance to only Iran and Oman. Much the same thing could be said for the Strait of Bab el Mandeb or anywhere else where open sea lines of communication were threatened; the reverberations of any trouble would instantaneously spread throughout the world. In much the same way, domestic political changes in several key states (India, Iran, Saudi Arabia, South Africa) could scarcely fail to have international and regional consequences. Similarly any superpower confrontation in the Indian Ocean would be difficult to confine to that region alone.

The twelve chapters in this book collectively point out, analyze, and stress the extreme complexity of Indian Ocean developments. They provide a sophisticated and varied appraisal of the multifaceted dimensions of politics throughout the area. Nonetheless, no single book can hope to be comprehensive and cover the entire range of issues and actors that have an impact on the Indian Ocean region. As an indicator of the interest in the region, no less than forty-four nations were represented at the July 1979 meeting of the littoral and hinterland nations of the Indian Ocean, and fifteen other countries sent observer delegations. Although in principle all of those countries and their particular concerns with Indian Ocean matters are of interest, they cannot reasonably all be addressed.

What we have tried to present in *The Indian Ocean in Global Politics* is a comprehensive survey of the main international issues that affect the nations of the Indian Ocean region. Throughout the chapters there is a constant analysis of the military, strategic, political, economic, and arms control issues that affect the behavior of both regional and external actors.

Introduction

Part 1 of the book emphasizes the regional dimensions of international politics in the region. Whether considering southern Africa, the Horn of Africa, the Gulf, India and the subcontinent, or Australia, there are countless regional issues that command attention and pose enduring problems. Many regional issues pose the threat of conflict, and the causes can be as diverse as competing nationalisms, religious rivalries, the aftereffects of colonialism, or competition for military, strategic, political, or economic advantage. In all these situations there exists the possibility of involvement by actors external to the region. However, as many authors point out, regional disagreements would generally go on regardless of external attention, and the degree to which external powers can manipulate regional conflicts to their advantage is often very limited.

Part 2 of the book considers the activities in the region of three external actors—France, the Soviet Union, and the United States. The French case is somewhat unique because of the long history of France's activity in the Indian Ocean and its continued maintenance of both troops and dependent territories in the area. As far as the two superpowers are concerned, readers will quickly discover that there is no uniformity of opinion either among the countries of the region or among the authors of the chapters about the nature, purpose, and importance of superpower activity in the region. Some consider it benign; others, a stabilizing presence; and still others, a threat to the independence of the littoral states. One point that comes out, however, is that there is far more to superpower activity than simple attentiveness to one another. There are profound local and regional issues that undergird the determination of the superpowers to be active on and under the Indian Ocean and in the littoral states.

Part 3 provides an analysis of international efforts to encourage arms control, demilitarization, and the establishment of a Zone of Peace in the Indian Ocean. Considerable difference of opinion is expressed as to the need for, value of, and prospects for any of the various proposals. What becomes clear in the discussion, however, is that the negotiations are extremely complex and that there is considerable room for doubt that either regional actors or external powers are seriously committed to any form of arms restraint.

The strength of this book lies in the comprehensive attention it pays to the international issues that confront the region and in the historical perspective it provides to the drama of current developments. A broad context is provided through which regional rivalries, external involvements, and trends and developments during the 1980s can be viewed. As readers will quickly recognize, there is no effort made to force a single orientation to these developments. What is provided instead is an analysis of developments from southern Africa right around the littoral to Australia. The chapters offer a variety of interpretations and quite different critical assessments of the dynamics of regional politics and the impact of external actors. It is to be hoped that the reader will gain some appreciation of the stakes in the region and a sharpened awareness of the roles played by various actors. Given the range of current crises in the region, the book could scarcely be more timely.

Part 1

Regional Powers in the Indian Ocean

1
The Strait of Hormuz: The Global Chokepoint

Rouhollah K. Ramazani

Ensuring the uninterrupted flow of Persian Gulf oil to world markets through the Strait of Hormuz is an economic, a political, and a strategic imperative. Yet fears and suspicions as to how this basic goal might be achieved tend to complicate both the identification of the problems involved and the proposals for overcoming them. Shah Mohammed Riza Pahlavi used to exaggerate the vulnerability of the strait in order to demonstrate the indispensability of his regime to the maintenance of the strait's security with the assistance of the United States. The Iranian revolutionary regime seems to exaggerate the invulnerability of the strait in order to show that regime's independence from the United States. Within the Western world there are those who overestimate the vulnerability of the strait as a means of pushing military contingency plans for quick reaction to Persian Gulf crises, and others underestimate its vulnerability in order to discourage plans for U.S. military intervention.

This chapter will attempt to steer away from these preconceived notions. There must be room for a rational and objective discussion of this admittedly important subject. It will argue that the Strait of Hormuz is potentially the world's most important economic chokepoint and that it can be transformed into an active chokepoint by a variety of conflict situations. It will also seek to propose that the uninterrupted flow of Gulf oil to world markets through the strait might be aided by cooperative efforts such as the creation of a Common Patrol Authority as well as unilateral and bilateral arrangements aimed at minimizing threats of disruption. Finally, it will speculate that the establishment of such an authority might, in the long run, aid further efforts toward regional cooperation and, it is to be hoped, ease superpower tensions in and around the strategic Strait of Hormuz.

The Importance of the Strait

A complex of geographic, economic, and legal factors combine to characterize the Strait of Hormuz as a potential global chokepoint. To begin with, the strait is wider than the other major Indian Ocean straits that are traversed by oil tankers. Nowhere in its 104-mile length is it narrower than the Strait of Bab el Mandeb at the entrance to the Red Sea, the Strait of Tiran at the entrance to the Gulf of Aqaba, the Strait of Malacca, or the Strait of Singapore. This should be no cause for comfort, however, because (a) none of those other straits carries as much tanker traffic as the Strait of Hormuz; (b) the more favorable width of the strait does not necessarily mean that all of its waters are navigable; and (c) the strait itself and its northern terminus that forms the entrance to the Persian Gulf are studded with numerous islands. Although the strait's entrance to the Gulf of Oman is more than fifty nautical miles wide, it narrows to slightly over twenty miles at its northeastern end between Larak Island on the Iranian side and the Quoins on the Omani side. The oil tanker traffic is, in fact, heavily concentrated in Omani territorial waters where the deeper navigational channels exist.

The economic stakes in the Strait of Hormuz are global in nature. Although it connects the high seas through the Gulf of Oman to only a semienclosed sea, rather than to other high seas, it is the world's most important international oil highway, because the Persian Gulf happens to be the world's largest known site of oil reserves and production. Concern about oil prices tends to focus world attention on the OPEC countries as a cartel at the expense of an adequate appreciation of the overriding importance of the Gulf states as the main suppliers of the world's oil. The six Gulf states of OPEC (Saudi Arabia, Iran, Iraq, Kuwait, the United Arab Emirates, and Qatar) produce roughly 30 million barrels of oil daily, and the seven non-Gulf states of OPEC (Libya, Venezuela, Algeria, Nigeria, Indonesia, Gabon, and Ecuador) produce only 3 million barrels a day. This means that 57 percent of the world oil trade must pass in oil tankers through the Strait of Hormuz to world markets at the rate of one every eleven minutes.

Given this overwhelming share of the Gulf states in the total OPEC supplies, the vital importance of the Strait of Hormuz to the major oil-consuming nations becomes obvious. Japan receives almost 90 percent of its oil imports from OPEC; Western Europe, about 80 percent; and the United States, approximately 70 percent. Although the United States is the world's single largest producer of oil (about 10.3 million barrels a day), it is simultaneously the world's largest single consumer of it—about 19 million barrels a day in 1979. The Tokyo-agreement ceiling of over 8 million barrels of oil imports a day through 1985 would hardly begin to dent the pressure of the U.S. demand on the world oil supply. President Carter's ambitious goal of cutting U.S. imports in half over a decade still leaves open the immediate and continuing problem of U.S. dependence on foreign oil, even assuming total success for U.S. projected efforts at conservation and its search for alternative sources of energy, as well as stepped-up U.S. exploration for oil in the United States.

The Strait of Hormuz is even more vitally important to the Gulf states themselves. Given the fact that oil revenues constitute the backbone of the Gulf economy, oil exports through the strait must be maintained. Even Iraq, which exports a higher percentage of its oil through pipelines than any other Gulf state, is heavily dependent on the uninterrupted flow of oil exports through the strait. Furthermore, all Gulf states are vitally dependent on non-oil seaborne trade. The flow of capital goods for economic development, food supplies, and arms from the outside world is on the rise, despite the drop in Iran's arms imports since the fall of the shah's regime.

At the moment the Strait of Hormuz is less significant to the Soviet Union and the states belonging to COMECON (Council for Mutual Assistance). The trade of socialist states with Iraq is important, but it is by no means as significant as the overall trade of the West with Iraq. The trade of prerevolutionary Iran was important to Moscow, but the bulk of the Iranian trade with the Soviet Union takes place overland rather than through the strait. However, there are strong indications that the Soviet Union is already feeling the energy squeeze because of shortfalls in its planned oil production, and it may well become a competitor of the major non-Communist oil customers of the Gulf states in the near future.

In contrast to the socialist states, the less developed countries

(LDCs) are significantly dependent on oil tanker traffic through the Strait of Hormuz. Between fifty and sixty LDCs import Gulf oil, and in 1977 it was estimated that LDCs would receive over 5 million barrels a day from the Persian Gulf area. Although the OPEC nations dislike hearing about the so-called South-South dichotomy between the oil-rich and the oil-poor nations of the underdeveloped world, a disruption of the oil flow from the Gulf would adversely affect many Brazils and Thailands of the Third World, as every oil price rise does. The World Bank program of technically aiding the LDCs to produce their own oil might make them self-sufficient in a decade, although at the moment that is more a matter of hope than of prediction. In the meantime they—like the Gulf states, Japan, and the Western industrialized world—will be dependent on an uninterrupted flow of oil through the Strait of Hormuz.

The uncertainty of international legal norms compounds the problems of such an uninterrupted flow of oil through the strait. If most coastal states of the world extended their territorial sea limit from the traditional three to the current twelve miles, some 116 international straits would be brought under sovereign jurisdiction of coastal states. The Strait of Hormuz is no exception. Both Iran and Oman, the two Persian Gulf states bordering the strait, claim twelve miles of territorial sea. As a result, the narrow section of the strait that falls roughly between thirty degrees to fifty degrees north latitude and thirty degrees to twenty degrees east longitude would lie completely within their claimed sovereign jurisdiction, and therefore there would be no high sea in that area of the strait and no free airspace above it. Even if this were not the case, there would still be the problem that the vessels entering the strait customarily proceed within Omani waters where the main channels of navigation exist.

The uncertainty about general international legal norms and the unilateral extension of the Iranian and Omani territorial sea limits parallel the absence of any particular agreement governing the Strait of Hormuz. Prior to the Iranian revolution, Oman and Iran agreed (March 7, 1974) to ensure the safety of navigation by joint patrol. Although legally Oman was a participant in patrolling the strait, in actual practice only Iran had the requisite naval capacity to maintain the safety of navigation. The revolutionary situation in Iran has raised questions about the status of the Omani-Iranian agreement.

The Strait of Hormuz

Unlike the Turkish straits that are governed by the Montreux Convention, no legal regime as yet has been determined for the Strait of Hormuz. In light of the vital, global economic significance of this international waterway, the absence of any governing legal norms in general or agreement among the Gulf states in particular adds to the uncertainty of freedom and safety of navigation.

Potential Threats to the Strait

Conflict situations might transform the Strait of Hormuz from a potential to an active global chokepoint. These situations generally fall into three broad categories: interstate conflicts, domestic crises, and acts of nonstate entities. Interstate conflicts fall into three subcategories: conflict between the superpowers, between the Gulf states and major oil-consuming nations, and among regional states.

In a general nuclear or conventional war between the United States and the Soviet Union the blockage of the Strait of Hormuz must be assumed. Given its vital economic significance to the industrialized democracies and its close geographic proximity to the Soviet Union, the strait would probably be mined by the Soviet Union in order to cripple the West. In peacetime it is unlikely that the Soviet Union would bluntly cut the flow of oil supplies through the strait unless the USSR was prepared to risk a nuclear war with the NATO countries.

The second type of interstate conflict that might make oil tanker traffic hazardous through the Strait of Hormuz would be hostile military intervention by the United States in the Persian Gulf oil fields. It is often suggested that such intervention would be countered by retaliatory destruction of oil installations. But such a drastic course of self-inflicting action would probably be less acceptable to the Gulf states than the closure of the strait, which in the short term would hurt the United States more than the Gulf states. A retaliatory course of action, however, would hurt not only the interventionist power, but every country in the world that is dependent on Gulf oil supplies and all Gulf states that are dependent on imports. Quite apart from the risks of such retaliatory measures, possibly unacceptable military risks, such as Soviet military intervention, or the infeasibility of successful operations have been cited as arguments against U.S. military intervention in the Gulf oil fields. In any event, the creation of a quick-reaction military strike force was still in the planning stage in late 1979, despite the fact that the idea of such a force had been discussed in the Pentagon as early as the late 1960s.

The third type of interstate conflict that might render the oil tanker traffic through the Strait of Hormuz hazardous would be armed conflict in the regions adjacent to the Persian Gulf area. Until the conclusion of the Egyptian-Israeli peace treaty, the most obvious such conflict was the Arab-Israeli one. Even if no oil embargo were to be imposed in any new Arab-Israeli war, the strait would be blocked as a consequence of a rapid spread of hostilities to the Gulf area. The Arab states of the Gulf would participate in a new war against Israel, partly because both opportunities and capabilities for arms transfer from the Gulf states to the "confrontation states" of the Middle East increased after the 1973 Arab-Israeli war. But the peace treaty between Egypt and Israel may well have decreased the chances of disruption of oil tanker traffic through the strait to the extent that the treaty has reduced the threat of an outbreak of a new war.

Besides interstate conflicts, internal wars might disrupt the oil flow through the Strait of Hormuz. At the moment the only case in point is the possible revival of the civil war in Oman. The insurgency in the Omani province of Dhofar was declared crushed by Sultan Qabus bin Said in December 1975, largely as a result of successful Iranian-Omani joint military operations. Subsequently Iran's military presence in Oman was actually terminated in the course of Iran's revolution. As early as 1971 the Popular Front for the Liberation of Oman and the Arabian Gulf (PFLOAG) guerrillas attempted to occupy the Omani enclave at the tip of Musandam Peninsula overlooking the Strait of Hormuz. With the Iranian military withdrawal from Oman and the abandonment of air and naval outposts in the region, the Dhofari rebellion was expected to revive. However, as late as September 1979 when I visited Oman, there was no major sign of concern about the revival of the Dhofari rebels. Sultan Qabus lost his major Gulf ally when the shah fell, and the sultan has become all the more aware of the threat that the rebels could pose to the strait as well as to his regime. Clearly, the fall of Oman to forces hostile to Western interests could pose a serious threat to the safety of navigation through the strait. During my visit

The Strait of Hormuz

to the Musandam Peninsula, I was told of two plans undertaken by Oman for the better protection of the safety of navigation through the strait. One plan, which reportedly went into effect on November 1, 1979, was to move the inbound and outbound shipping channels to safer and deeper waters north of the traditional channels by establishing a new separation zone. The other plan was to improve navigational safety by completing facilities on the island of Ghanam, near the village of Khassab at the tip of the peninsula. Presumably these efforts would reduce the chances of terrorist attacks on oil tankers.

The prospect of successful terrorist attacks on oil tankers, however, is hotly debated for two reasons. First, it is argued that many bypasses in the strait are beyond the effective range of most weapons on the shore. Second, it is pointed out that armed guerrillas would find it difficult, if not impossible, to attack oil tankers without a base from which the guerrillas could operate. Nevertheless, the U.S. Department of State warned about the possibility of terrorist attacks on oil tankers in July 1979, and Sheikh Ahmad Zaki Yamani, the Saudi Arabian oil minister, stated the problem as follows:

> The Palestinians are growing ever more desperate, and I wouldn't be surprised if one day they sank one or two supertankers in the Strait of Hormuz, to force the world to do something about their plight and Israel's obstinacy. This would block the channel through which pass 19 million barrels daily. This would make the present crisis seem like child's play.[1]

Assuming that terrorist attacks could take place, which I doubt, it is unlikely that the sinking of "one or two" tankers could actually block the strait. Nevertheless, it could produce great fears about the vulnerability of the strait's channels.

A more hazardous situation could arise, however, if instead of an attack on oil tankers by tactical rockets from the shore the navigable channels of the strait were seeded with mines. This kind of action is apparently more within the realm of possibility. Both Iran and Saudi Arabia are equipped with minesweepers; thus the Gulf states themselves have some capacity for such action should the need arise. The revolution in Iran has by no means lessened Iran's interest in the safety of navigation through the strait, although the Iranian naval authorities today, as contrasted with the period before the fall of the shah's regime, are far more skeptical about the prospects of terrorist attacks on oil tankers.

Protecting the Strait

What could reasonably be done to minimize the potential threats to the uninterrupted flow of oil to world markets through the Strait of Hormuz? As noted, such threats would most likely arise from regional wars, internal wars, or terrorist acts rather than from U.S. military intervention in Gulf oil fields or from a direct, deliberate interdiction of oil tankers by the Soviet Union. Apparently for the purposes of assuring Saudi Arabia and other friendly Arab states of U.S. support in the aftermath of the shah's downfall, of putting the Soviet Union on notice that the United States is determined to defend its vital interests in the region, and of preparing for swift military action in the event of a real and clear threat to U.S. vital interests, the Carter administration agreed on June 21–22, 1979, to undertake a modest increase in the U.S. military presence in the Indian Ocean–Middle East area. This was believed to mean that one or two destroyers would be added to a small flagship and two destroyers. It also meant that (1) the number of regular U.S. task force deployments in the Indian Ocean would increase from three to four a year; (2) U.S. air force combat aircraft would stage more routine "demonstration" visits into Arab countries; and (3) a new emphasis would be placed on military sales and high-level contacts with Oman and the smaller sheikhdoms of the Persian Gulf.[2]

These recommendations formed part of a continuous review of U.S. options in the area, particularly in light of the ripple effects of the Iranian revolution on the security of the Persian Gulf. The recommendations were the early results of the process set in motion in February 1979 when U.S. Defense Secretary Harold Brown visited the Middle East. In an appraisal of Secretary Brown's proposals to the Middle East leaders at the time, I evaluated the advantages and disadvantages of his formula and suggested alternatively the necessity and the feasibility of security cooperation between the countries of the Organization for Economic Cooperation and

Development (OECD) and the Persian Gulf states.[3] My principal concern was that the United States might be inclined to proceed alone, without appropriate consultation with other OECD countries and particularly without taking adequate note of the sensibilities of the local states and the lessons of the Iranian revolution. I argued that "the vital interest of the industrialized democracies and those of the Gulf states, which are basically compatible, must be protected by means of any combination of skillful multilateral and alliance diplomacy."[4] If the modest and symbolic increase in U.S. military presence is not intended to exclude U.S. security cooperation with regional and OECD states, it may well aid such cooperation in the foreseeable future for the security of the Persian Gulf area in general.

In the light of this chapter, however, there is the more specific need to protect the international oil tanker traffic through the Strait of Hormuz. As a global chokepoint, the security of this strategic waterway must be accorded the highest priority. For the bulk of the Persian Gulf oil to reach world markets without interruption, the security of the oil tanker traffic through the strait must be assured. Even when all other major chokepoints of the Indian Ocean—such as the Strait of Bab el Mandeb, the Mozambique Channel, the Strait of Malacca, and others—are secure, that security will be no cause for comfort as long as there are still potential threats to the safety of navigation through the Strait of Hormuz.

The protection of oil tanker traffic must be the business of the local states as well as of the interested and capable external powers. There is not a single local state that would benefit from the interruption of the oil flow through the strait, and more importantly, all the Gulf states have shown that they are vitally interested in maintaining the freedom of navigation through the strait as a matter of principle. The immediate need for the protection of oil tanker traffic through the strait, however, cannot wait for the universal adoption of that principle through the extremely slow process of the Law of the Sea Conference. The littoral states have repeatedly stated that because of the particular characteristics of the Persian Gulf and the Strait of Hormuz, they would prefer bilateral or regional arrangements (not necessarily to the exclusion of a universal agreement) as a means of creating legal norms governing maritime security, safety of navigation, prevention of pollution, fisheries, and the exploration and exploitation of resources. They have already signed an important convention for the prevention of pollution (April 24, 1978) with the help of the United Nations, and there is reason to believe that they can also agree on the maintenance of the freedom of navigation through the Strait of Hormuz. Although the Iranian-Omani bilateral agreement (March 7, 1974) provided for the security of the strait, it failed to enjoy the acceptance of the other Gulf states because, in effect, Iranian power dominated the strait as British power had previously.

A Gulf-wide agreement on the regime of the Strait of Hormuz could aid the safety of international navigation there. Like the Montreux Convention governing the Turkish straits, such an agreement among the Gulf states would ensure a degree of predictability. At the moment the Strait of Hormuz is not only unguarded, but its status is shrouded in ambiguity. The clarification of legal norms governing the status of the strait would obviously not automatically assure security for oil tanker traffic, but it could be a first step toward that goal.

To achieve that goal, however, any agreement on the regime of the Strait of Hormuz must be backed by power. Given the vital interests of the major oil-consuming nations in the freedom of navigation through the strait, it would seem unreasonable to expect them to refrain from unilateral measures, including improvement of their military presence, to protect their vital interests. This is especially true as long as the Gulf states themselves are unwilling or unable to agree either on the governing principles or on the requisite power to support them. This is exactly why the often-stated ideal of "local security by local powers" has had a hollow ring to it to date. In the long run that ideal would have a better chance of realization if the regional states could first cooperate among themselves and later combine their efforts with those of interested external powers as a means of enhancing the prospects of effective protection of the safety of navigation. Given the suspicion of some Gulf–Indian Ocean states about the Western powers' motives, it would be advisable not to prejudice such an effort by planning to involve the oil-consuming nations of the West at the very outset. This might have been the main reason for the rejection of the Omani proposals by

Iraq in the summer of 1979, although the foreign minister of Oman denied that his country had suggested Western participation.

Unfortunately, the deterioration of relations among the Gulf states since the Iranian revolution would seem to reduce the prospects of cooperation among them. The pronouncements and actions of some Iranian clerical leaders have stirred deep concern in Bahrain and Kuwait about the intentions of the revolutionary regime, despite repeated assurances that Iran does not plan to export its revolution, opposes interference in the affairs of other states, and denies the revival of its territorial claim to Bahrain. Iraq's denunciation of its 1975 Shatt-al-Arab agreement with Iran has the potential of reversing all the hopeful signs of accommodation among the Gulf states that had followed that agreement. Nevertheless, one would hope that enlightened self-interest would make the Gulf states realize that their goal of economic and political self-reliance cannot be aided by the increase in tensions and conflict situations. On the contrary, such circumstances have historically made the Gulf states more vulnerable to foreign manipulation, interference, and intervention.

Future Prospects for the Strait

It is to be hoped that eventual cooperation between the regional and interested external powers for the protection of the oil tanker traffic through the Strait of Hormuz will produce significant positive effects on the wider concerns of the Indian Ocean states and the superpowers. The notions of a Zone of Peace, nuclear free zone, demilitarization, Asian Collective Security System, Asian Common Market, and the like have been bandied about for a long time. Regardless of their merits or demerits, they have one thing in common. They are too broad, too ambitious, and largely unrealistic. There is nothing wrong with dreaming big dreams, but one must care about their realization.

The idea of common efforts for the protection of oil tanker traffic through the Strait of Hormuz does not have the high-sounding effects of any of those other ideas, but it is more concrete and perhaps more practicable. It should be much easier, for example, to organize a small common patrol authority to supervise the passage of oil tankers through the strait than to provide a universal security arrangement for the entire Persian Gulf–Indian Ocean area.

There is every reason to believe that such a modest and concrete cooperative effort in a matter of vital importance to all concerned could act as a catalyst for larger long-term goals of cooperation among the Indian Ocean states. For example, the idea of a Common Patrol Authority for the Strait of Hormuz could be expanded to a Common Patrol Authority for the Indian Ocean if it proved attainable and effective in practice. Obviously the creation of a larger authority for the Indian Ocean would require the cooperation of states bordering the other major chokepoints in the Indian Ocean, and it would be unrealistic to start with such a grand idea. It is more vital, urgent, and feasible to begin with the idea of an authority for the strait and hope that the idea will catch on as a model for cooperation in the Indian Ocean as a whole. Furthermore, cooperation on one complex set of problems, such as the protection of oil tanker traffic through the Indian Ocean chokepoints, may well have a salutary effect on interested leaders for working together on other common problems. This sectoral approach to the problem of regional cooperation has already been attempted successfully in the Persian Gulf area with respect to prevention of pollution, delimitation of the continental shelf, peaceful settlement of disputes, research on solar energy, reclamation of desert lands, water conservation, and medical care.

High-sounding but unrealistic proposals are not, of course, the monopoly of regional academicians and practitioners. The goal of superpower cooperation in the general area of the Indian Ocean has not been helped in the past by such dramatic pronouncements as President Carter's call for "complete demilitarization" of the Indian Ocean (March 16, 1977). The Soviet Union has no vital economic interest in the Strait of Hormuz at the present time, although it has considerable political and strategic interests in the general Indian Ocean–Persian Gulf area. One need not view these Soviet interests from a doctrinaire geopolitical perspective of a Soviet design for land and naval encirclement of the entire Eurasian landmass to realize their nature. The actual behavior of the Soviet Union reveals that ever since the end of World War II Moscow has sought to expand its power and influence – at the expense of the West in general and the United States in particular—in a widening circle of regional states lying south of the Soviet Union's borders. The Soviet thrust into the northern tier, the eastern Mediterranean, and finally into the Indian Ocean–Persian Gulf has concentrated in each case on a chokepoint—the Turkish straits, the Suez Canal, and the Strait of Hormuz, respectively. In none of these regions have instruments of Soviet policy been confined to the deployment of naval arms, although Soviet naval power has increased enormously in the Indian Ocean area since 1968. In that area Soviet instruments have included the encouragement of the nationalization of Western oil companies, acquisition of oil and gas privileges for the Soviet Union, propaganda attacks on Western military sales, transfer of Soviet arms, encouragement of Communist participation in national-front governments, support of Communist coups and national liberation movements, and massive infusion of Soviet and Cuban arms supplies and military personnel.

Soviet-U.S. competition in the Indian Ocean–Persian Gulf area has increased substantially since the Iranian revolution. President Carter strengthened U.S. naval forces in the area in March 1979, dispatching the 80,000-ton carrier *Constellation* and several escorting warships. The Soviet navy sent the 40,000-ton *Minsk*, two powerful guided-missile cruisers, and the *Ivan Rogov*, the biggest warship ever built by the Soviet Union. This Soviet move brought superpower naval muscle flexing to the northwest quadrant of the Indian Ocean for the first time.

The creation of a Common Patrol Authority for the Strait of Hormuz proposed in this chapter may well reduce Soviet-U.S. competition at this vital chokepoint. Any common action that ensures the uninterrupted flow of Gulf oil to world markets would minimize global unease in time of crisis. Furthermore, one would hope that the reduction of tensions between the two superpowers at this potential global chokepoint would eventually enable the United States and the Soviet Union to enter into calm and realistic negotiations aimed at the long-term objectives of the mutual reduction of arms supplies to regional powers, mutual limitations on naval deployment and use of base facilities in areas adjacent to the Strait of Hormuz, and mutual acceptance of restraints on direct and indirect intervention in local conflicts in the Indian Ocean.

Notes

1. See the text of Yamani's interview with Senior Editor Arnaud de Borchgrave, *Newsweek*, July 9, 1979, p. 21.
2. *Washington Post*, July 1, 1979.
3. R. K. Ramazani, "Security in the Persian Gulf," *Foreign Affairs* 57, no. 4 (Spring 1979):821-835.
4. Ibid., p. 835.

2
New Patterns of India's Relations with Indian Ocean Littoral States

Dieter Braun

This chapter is meant to be a contribution to the ongoing political and academic debate on the changing character of relations among developing countries, connected with the notion of "collective self-reliance."[1] Whereas it remains debatable as to how such a new interdependence among Third World countries might evolve or whether it is a practical proposition at all, there is no doubt that in the Southern Hemisphere political and economic links are rapidly increasing. Consequently, a new kind of relationship is emerging, and it fits into the more general framework of South-South relations as distinct from North-South or East-West relations.[2]

South-South Relations and the Indian Ocean Region

There are many reasons why the process is gaining momentum, both on the bilateral and the multilateral levels. Foremost among them is the Third World quest for unity in order to collectively pressure the industrial North for a better economic deal. One southern demand is for the opening of northern markets to the increasingly sophisticated, and therefore competitive, goods from the South. As a simultaneous endeavor, however, the southern countries could help themselves absorb their new manufacturing capacities by establishing market systems together, probably with preferential conditions for Third World exchange.

In this respect, the most promising approach is the regional one, and there are several regional and subregional systems in operation in Latin America, Africa, and Asia. Other regional systems have been tried and abandoned, largely on political grounds. Although geography remains the most compelling factor in furthering economic cooperation, politics provide much of the necessary underpinning; there must be a minimum of parallel interests and priorities among potential partners regarding both domestic and foreign policies.[3]

In recent years, the countries bordering the Indian Ocean, which together constitute a sizable part of the Third World, have realized both common interests vis-à-vis outside powers (see, for example, the Indian Ocean peace zone proposal) and increased interdependence. After the OPEC price hike (of 1973-74), new forms of cooperation among the newly rich and some of the very poor have developed. Complementarities, such as a lack of or an abundance of manpower, have been put to mutual advantage, and special skills and resources have been exchanged.

But apart from such side effects of the oil boom, a new pattern of mainly economic and technological cooperation is discernible along the Indian Ocean littoral. Because of its location, size, potential, and, last but not least, the direction of its policy, India has in many respects become the hub of this development. This chapter will evaluate this proposition. In the process, the past will be mentioned only insofar as it has had a direct bearing on the current situation, which, as far as India's capacity to acquire a new role in the region is concerned, has developed since about 1975.

India's Changing Image

After gaining independence, and primarily during Jawaharlal Nehru's period of stewardship, India displayed considerable ambition to perform on the international stage. Apart from questions related primarily to the East-West conflict, the thrust was in the direction of Afro-Asian common interests and aspirations. Although India did succeed in strengthening the consciousness of countries that were to be later termed the Third World, it failed to convince those countries of its own leadership qualities. This became clear even before the Himalayan debacle of 1962. At Bandung (1955) it was China—invited at India's insistence—that impressed the assembled Asian and African leaders as a potential power factor, rather than India with its predominantly moral appeal.⁴

Up to 1971, India was bogged down by domestic difficulties and by its fixation on the rivalry with Pakistan. After the fall of Dacca, India's position as the de facto hegemonic power in its subregion was increasingly recognized both within and outside South Asia. Nonetheless two significant handicaps remained: India's links with the Soviet Union were too close to free Asians in adjacent regions from the suspicion that India was acting as Moscow's agent, and India's economic performance was not sufficient to offer attractive stimuli to its smaller neighbors, let alone to more distant countries.

By the mid-1970s, however, several factors had combined to strengthen India's capacity to win and influence others. New patterns of cooperation with the countries of oil-rich West Asia had evolved and were deliberately pursued by both Indian entrepreneurs and the government; the shah of Iran, by proposing his own ambitious plans, accorded India a special partnership role in an Asian Common Market scheme; India took political initiatives (in the direction of the United States and China) to broaden its options vis-à-vis the major global powers; the Indian economy, after years of frustrating near-zero growth rates, recovered, and there was a considerable breakthrough both in agriculture and in nontraditional exports. To some extent, the increase in exports was the result of New Delhi's early and persistent policies of import substitution and, subsequently, of export diversification. Perhaps most important of all, India pursued a credible policy of befriending its neighbors and thus laid the foundation for extended regional activities, mainly along the littoral of the Indian Ocean—its "privileged zone for exercising influence."⁵

Subsequent changes of government in New Delhi did not alter these trends and priorities. During 1977–78, some were even reinforced and accelerated. Relations with the United States, China, Nepal, and Bangladesh improved rapidly, and in addition, it was realized that not enough attention had been paid to Southeast Asia.

The most important of these factors—the consolidation of relevant parts of the economy—can hardly be attributed to either recent Congress party or successive Janata party initiatives. Neither the good monsoons nor the high remittances from Indians working abroad (mainly in the Gulf area) had been part of India's fifth five-year plan.[6] The achievements were the result of a long gestation period, full of trial and error. Yet the fact remains that India, after 1975, had begun to perform in many practical, tangible ways. India now is a "developed developing country"[7] with remarkable capabilities that have already succeeded in changing its former image in many Third World countries, particularly around the Indian Ocean.

Sectoral Economic Improvements

In a predominantly agricultural country, such as India, economic progress must have its base in the agricultural sector, which accounts for 45 percent of India's GNP. Up to 1974-75, India had required annual food imports in considerable quantities. Since 1975, it has increased production to such an extent that it has accumulated sizable grain reserves, enabling it to give wheat and rice to needy countries on a credit basis (Vietnam, Afghanistan, Mauritius). Likewise, Indian fresh fruit and vegetables are being flown regularly to Gulf countries on a commercial basis.[8]

There is agreement among experts, both Indian and foreign, that this progress is only partly attributable to favorable weather; to an increasing degree, it is the result of greatly improved cultivation methods and of agricultural technology. One such feature is increased irrigation, making more land independent of the rains. For instance, in 1978 India claimed a world record in newly irrigated land, 2.6 million hectares. On the other hand, the barely curbed population growth offsets much of the surplus.

Independence from food imports has also contributed to India's much-improved foreign exchange reserves. Since 1975, these have risen fivefold and grew to $7 billion by early 1979.[9] The most important single factor has been remittances from Indians abroad, mainly in the Gulf countries. The government has used this situation to liberalize some of its import policies, thus exposing some sections of Indian industry to the rigor of international competition for the first time.

This liberalization further adds to a long-standing export strategy aimed at increasing the contribution of nontraditional goods to India's total exports. Since the early 1970s, exports of Indian engineering goods and other technical products have risen by jumps rather than steps. Even in 1978 when total exports declined, the growth of engineering goods—compared to the figures of the previous year—was 13 percent.[10] As a result, the pattern of Indian exports has significantly changed, helping to create India's new image of a developed developing country.

An increasing portion of such exports is destined for construction of complete plants abroad, designed and executed by Indian firms. In this field, they are already competing with Western and Japanese firms and have gained experience regarding their relative strengths and weaknesses. The latter result partly from a developing country's structural inability to keep abreast of far-advanced technologies, which require the input of costly and constant research and development efforts. Strengths, on the other hand, result from a developing country's ability to produce more cheaply (low wage levels), to have enough trained people available and willing to work under difficult circumstances (e.g., construction work in Arabian sands without alcohol), and to apply technology specially suited for conditions in developing countries.

Indeed, India's competitiveness is highest where the demand is not for the most advanced but for the most appropriate labor-intensive technology, required for civil engineering, infrastructure, railways, transmission lines, power stations, and cement or sugar plants. Today, India is in a position to offer complete services from consultancy on a particular project (often as a joint venture) to turn-key construction (including maintenance for an agreed period and training of indigenous personnel).[11] It is obvious that developing countries in particular demand such a set of offers; consequently, India has geared its efforts in this direction, making legitimate use of "collective self-reliance" slogans.

India's Role as an Aid Giver

Although India is reaping straight economic benefits from its refined technological and managerial capabilities, there is another aspect of South-South relations that initially means a financial burden. India operates a development assistance program, which, in essence, is hardly different from the aid efforts of the industrial countries. In the performance of this task, India displays both strength and weakness; the latter is mainly dictated by financial restrictions, and the former derives from mental and material affinities with the aid receiver.

India started early to assist other countries in their development. In the 1950s, Nepal depended heavily on India for its basic infrastructure, and Indian technicians, teachers, and administrative personnel were soon active in other neighboring countries such as Bhutan, Sri Lanka, and Afghanistan; later they became active in Bangladesh and, more recently, in the Maldives. Another area in which Indian experts were in early demand was East Africa (Ethiopia, Kenya, Tanzania) and southern Africa (mainly Zambia).

There are various types of Indian assistance, and again they are similar to developing programs in the North-South context – technical and managerial aid and training, scientific and educational assistance, and military assistance. Taken together, many thousands of foreign trainees, students, and specialists have so far made use of Indian offers for advice, training, or teaching, either in their home countries or in India.

A large portion of such Indian activities has been paid for by other sources: the Colombo Plan, Commonwealth funds, United Nations Development Programme (UNDP) and other UN agencies, or bilaterally by foreign governments. The Indian budget has annually indicated the extent to which its own public funds have been used for such purposes. To give an example, one scholarship granted to a foreign student of medicine is estimated to cost the Indian government 100,000 rupees (approximately $13,000). In 1978 there were eighty such students studying in India – and hundreds of applications were awaiting decision by the Indian authorities.[12]

It is obvious that political considerations play a predominant role when major financial burdens are involved; this is surely true for a poor country, more so than for a rich one. One clear trend in India's rapidly increasing assistance program is a concentration on those areas of Asia and Africa where, geographically, India occupies a central position – the Indian Ocean littoral and its hinterland. There are obvious reasons for this concentration: proximity and short transport routes; historical links, both ancient and colonial; ethnic connections; and strategic interests. India has recently gained where it had failed in the 1950s and 1960s. Today, instead of moral exhortations, it offers assistance, expertise, and tangible values. Some of these activities will now be examined in more detail.

Bilateral Cooperation: South Asia

India's insoluble dilemma in its own subregion has its roots in India's size and concomitant natural superiority in all areas that constitute power. For the smaller neighbors, this emphasizes the necessity of keeping a distance in order to survive and to preserve an identity. India, for its part, needed a long time to understand such reflexes and to react accordingly. The Janata government even made it an article of faith to "have abandoned high-mindedness, arrogance and imperiousness" in "dealing with nationalisms and sensitivities nearer home."[13]

Apart from perception, another necessary precondition for good relations among unequal partners is an ability and willingness on the part of the larger one to assist the other in a meaningful way. In this context, India's neighbors have asked for more favorable terms of trade and better access to Indian markets. In straight terms, the request is for Indian efforts to install industrial and other indigenous capabilities on a credit (and partly grant) basis, thus helping India's smaller neighbors attain self-sufficiency. At a later stage, India's neighbors hope to sell surplus products to India in order to balance bilateral trade.

Only recently have political relations between India, on the one hand, and Nepal and Sri Lanka, on the other, sufficiently improved to make such deals mutually acceptable; with Bangladesh and, above all, with Pakistan such a stage has not yet been reached. Apart from politics, India also needed the resources to shoulder the economic burdens involved in financing numerous joint-venture projects with poorer countries. In late 1978, the *Statesman*, a leading Indian daily, felt obliged to encourage its government to shed old habits vis-à-vis its weaker neighbors. The paper stated that India's economy was sufficiently strong to pursue a policy of generosity instead of narrow self-interest. This policy could lead toward regional cooperation.[14]

India has recently concluded agreements with Nepal to assist in the construction of various basic industries: machinery, cement, paper, and mining. India is to provide finance, know-how, and personnel; it has also pledged to assist in the setting up of training centers where at least 700 Nepali can be trained annually for operating these projects.[15] If these agreements are implemented, it would signify a qualitative change in the pattern of Indian-Nepali economic relations.

With Sri Lanka, too, it is India's task to achieve a structural change in economic relations. Up to now, the trade balance has been strongly tilted in India's favor because of the smaller partner's inability to export suitable goods. In 1978, India's Engineering Export Promotion Council sanctioned participation in joint ventures amounting to $30 million; the Industrial Bank of India agreed to finance the purchase of Indian machinery and equipment. Quotas of Indian imports from Sri Lanka were raised, and preferential clauses, as well as buy-back arrangements, were introduced. The state visits of both the Sri Lankan president to India (late 1978) and India's prime minister to Sri Lanka (early 1979) were dominated by economic and trade subjects. India showed its willingness to cooperate beyond previous limits, and Sri Lanka clearly welcomed that willingness.

For some time aid, rather than trade, will continue to characterize India's relations with Afghanistan, which traditionally has been regarded by New Delhi as a "neighbor."[16] The historical notion of Afghanistan being a "buffer" between India and Russia is still present in the minds of Indian diplomats, and the takeover in Kabul (April 1978) by a Marxist regime, tilted strongly toward the Soviet Union, has caused considerable—though unofficial—concern. However, India's widespread development efforts, supported by substantial training programs, have not been interrupted; on the contrary, except for military programs, they have been intensified. India clearly wants to keep a foot in the door of a country that India regards as part of its area of special interest and responsibility.

Regarding Pakistan, there has been progress since 1972 in the direction of normalization and cooperation, but the time does not yet seem ripe for a breakthrough. The problem-ridden Islamic republic, whose foreign policy options have been drastically reduced since early 1977, keeps looking westward toward the Arab-Islamic world for orientation, assistance, and partnership. India's earlier hopes for a fruitful economic cooperation—shared by some Pakistani businessmen—have not materialized.[17] At present, trade is completely out of balance; India could swamp the Pakistani market with cheap engineering goods. In particular, Pakistan shies away from any agreement that might entail dependence on India's superior resources (coal or iron ore for Pakistan's incipient steel production); on the other hand, India is not prepared to lower its barriers to admit competitive Pakistani goods (medical instruments, carpets, textiles, etc.).

It seems that India is biding its time until Pakistan realizes that it cannot opt out of the subcontinent. Events in Iran and possible policy shifts in certain Arab states could contribute to such a realization. On the other hand, Pakistan's very existence as a nation-state is jeopardized by domestic troubles. This is a matter of concern to several parties both in the region and outside it, but India — after the shifts in Afghan policy — should now have a special stake in Pakistan's stability.

Bilateral Cooperation: The Gulf Region

In recent years, India's growing economic involvement in the Gulf region has been a major success story. The setbacks that have occurred might be attributed to the learning process, especially when one considers the speed with which new patterns of interregional relations evolved after the 1973-74 "energy crisis." At that time, predictions regarding the consequences for an oil-importing developing country, such as India, had in general been gloomy; in retrospect, however, the new economic power concentrated along the shores of the Gulf has released dynamic elements and created opportunities of which India has made ample use.

Whereas between 1973 and 1978 oil prices rose — roughly — fivefold, India increased its exports into the Gulf region by about the same factor. In the process, India developed new economic structures and trade patterns, exploited and processed some of its raw materials with the help of foreign capital, and found employment for several hundred thousand Indians, which resulted in the already mentioned favorable foreign exchange balance.[18]

Within a few years, India's image in the Gulf countries changed considerably, in fact more than anywhere else, because there was a sudden presence where formerly there had been next to none. In early 1976, Bombay's *Economic and Political Weekly* complained that in the Middle East India had "no image" for its goods or its knowhow.[19] Indicative of a new assessment is that in late 1978, a joint Arab delegation from chambers of trade, industry, and agriculture visited India to explore fresh areas for joint ventures and other technological cooperation as well as India's capacity to export agricultural products.[20]

Between 1973 and 1978, three phases of India's economic relations with the Gulf states can be distinguished. First, between 1973 and 1975, Iran was India's most important partner, and the shah proved to be generous with credits and offers for joint ventures. Second, between 1975 and 1977, India's "export" of labor to the Arab Gulf states reached its peak and became an important factor for the Indian economy; and, third, after 1977 the emphasis shifted to Indian offers of industrial turnkey projects, mainly to Iraq, Kuwait, and the United Arab Emirates (UAE). This branch of activity will probably be the most promising for some time to come.

Partnership with Iran held out shining prospects for India, because the two economies seemed to be particularly complementary. When the shah visited New Delhi in February 1978, hopes in India were high that some very substantial projects (iron ore, aluminum, irrigation) could be implemented, that Iranian crude oil could be safely counted upon to cover about 40 percent of India's import needs, and that Indian firms and experts would be in further demand in Iran.[21] Because of the breakdown of the shah's regime, the joint communiqué of 1978 will remain paper only; it still shows, however, the degree to which India had been attuned to this promising bilateral relationship.

The new importance of Iraq as India's main source of crude oil correlates with the general upgrading of bilateral economic relations that had started some years ago. India's incentives to earn Iraqi money have once more increased as the oil bill weighs heavily on the trade scale.

In this respect, 1978 was a promising year because Iraq doubled its imports from India. In 1977–78, Indian firms were already entrusted with projects in Iraq totaling about $250 million. In addition, the Indian public-sector company Engineering Projects (India)— EPI—secured construction contracts worth $186 million in late 1978,[22] Indian consultancy firms are actively working out feasibility studies for further projects, Iraq promised another doubling of its imports from India for 1979, and apart from industry, there is also increasing cooperation in agriculture and in the military sector.[23]

It appears that Iraq and India share some basic political convictions, of which close links with the USSR are but one indicator. Other indicators point in different directions: Each country is interested in keeping its army free from Communist influence; their approaches to nonaligned and to North-South policies in general seem to be similar; and Iraq has expressly supported South-South relations as a counterweight to undue influence of industrialized countries in the Third World. In this context, Iraq has voiced its preference for cooperation with a developed developing country such as India.[24]

There is less of a common political background in the other Arab Gulf states and emirates; in Saudi Arabia, in particular, Pakistani influence has been, and to an extent continues to be, very strong. But India's economic and technological potentials have been increasingly recognized and put to use. Labor-intensive plants are of little interest to rich countries with sparse populations. However, for certain installations and construction projects—electrification or housing, for example—Indian company bids to do the job with a few hundred or even a few thousand personnel, brought in for the purpose and afterward withdrawn, are attractive. Their prices also are competitive. There have been problems with Indian workers feeling discriminated against, which has led to strikes and unrest, but the firms and governments concerned are learning from such experiences. The Indian labor minister visited Iraq, Kuwait, Bahrain, and the UAE in early 1979 "to study the working conditions of the Indians." On that occasion, some figures were published. For example, 16,000 Indian workers were employed on projects in Kuwait, and that figure does not include experts provided under bilateral agreements or medium-level personnel working in businesses, banks, hotels, and hospitals.[25]

On balance, India's presence in the Gulf is firmly established, and it seems there will be ample opportunity during the 1980s to maintain and even enlarge it. Geographical proximity across the Arabian Sea makes for easy access, and Bombay has become attractive to visiting Gulf Arabs.[26] India thus has its modest share of the oil wealth, although its citizens have to work very hard for it.

Bilateral Cooperation: Africa and the Islands

India's relations with the African littoral countries and island-states in the western Indian Ocean display a rather different pattern. Four factors seem to be relevant: a common heritage of colonial history, of which today's Commonwealth membership of Kenya, Tanzania, Zambia, Mauritius, and the Seychelles is a more than symbolic relic;[27] successive generations of Indian immigrants that constitute ethnic minority populations in many countries (a majority in Mauritius); the racial conflict in southern Africa, about which India's attitude since gaining independence has been unambiguous; and a level of development that makes Indian assistance, expertise, and partnership relevant and welcome.

In contrast to the Middle East, India's political and economic links with eastern and southern Africa date back to the 1950s and 1960s, to India's first efforts to secure a special position in Afro-Asian affairs, both before and after those African countries became independent. In 1963 an Indo-African Development Association was founded, and a large number of joint ventures, mainly in light industry, were planned or partly implemented. However, the failure rate was high, and only a small number were actually completed. Apart from African instabilities and a lack of qualified personnel, Indian firms were not in a position to back their ventures with sufficient capital.[28]

After the Lusaka nonaligned summit of 1970, India made a special effort to support the liberation movements in southern Africa with various forms of assistance, mainly in terms of technical and medical aid as well as educational support. Indian engineers, doctors, and secondary school teachers were also in growing demand in countries such as Kenya and Ethiopia.

After 1975–76, India was in a position to raise the level of its engagements in trade, technical assistance, and joint ventures, but with regard to the last, financial constraints still remain a handicap. The same applies to government credits because, for instance, India is still unable to match China's generosity; interest rates are not favorable, and credits are tied to the purchase of Indian machinery and equipment. However, the number of joint ventures has still risen. In addition, the Indian capacity to train indigenous personnel has significantly increased, and more sophisticated technology has been introduced.

Whereas strong trade links with Kenya have always existed, and whereas Indian experts in Zambia are more numerous than anywhere else in Africa (some 3,500 in 1978),[29] relations with Tanzania have acquired a unique quality based on common policies and philosophy. Both countries are searching for a middle road between capitalist and Marxist models with, however, a strong emphasis on "socialism" according to indigenous conditions; both place an emphasis on South-South relations as a means to diminish dependence on the industrialized world; both have nearly identical views on nonalignment and the new international economic order; and both have a common approach to the racial conflict in southern Africa.[30]

Economically, India's share in the development of Tanzania has become very substantial, because India's various intermediate and "appropriate" technologies seem to be particularly relevant for Tanzania's development model.[31] In 1978, there were about 900 Indian experts in Tanzania, the largest contingent there from any country; generally, an expert stays for a five-year period, which is longer than elsewhere. At the same time, there are more Tanzanian students and trainees in India than from other African countries; at one technical college (Rourkee), 180 engineering students were to finish a special four-year course in 1979.[32]

Indian geologists discovered natural gas on an island belonging to Tanzania, and the national Indian oil company (ONGC), together with its Tanzanian counterpart, is exploiting these finds. Trade has reached a high level; in Africa south of the Sahara, Tanzania has become the biggest market for Indian goods, a position formerly held by Kenya. Since Tanzania has recently shed some ideological rigidity, it has also become interested in private investment, and the Indian private sector is presently evaluating various possibilities for joint ventures. A joint commission, established in 1975, meets annually under the aegis of cabinet ministers to examine the state of cooperation and to define areas for its extension.

Bilateral relations thus seem to be on an even keel. The same applies to the relationship with Zambia,[33] but in Kenya, Ethiopia, and also Mozambique, India is in the process of strengthening its presence, regardless of ideological differences. The New Delhi government is prepared to spend sizable funds in the area, mainly for technical and educational assistance. Today, those parts of Africa seem to be more accessible to India than any other area outside the subcontinent.

Bilateral Cooperation: Southeast Asia

In a historical and cultural perspective, Southeast Asia, rather than Africa, should have qualified for lasting links with India. However, in the postcolonial period South and Southeast Asia drifted apart—the former increasingly looking toward Iran and the Arab world, and the latter, toward Pacific Asia.[34]

Before the end of Indira Gandhi's first stewardship, some efforts were made to counteract this tendency. When the Janata government took over, it repeatedly pointed out that throughout independent India's history, Southeast Asia had been neglected and that this state of affairs must be changed.[35] However, as far as the area of the Association of South-East Asian Nations (ASEAN) is concerned, Indian advances have usually been met with some reservations. There is a psychological barrier that is difficult for India to overcome, even with much improved economic and technological offers, because India's negative image is still evident. It is perceived as a backward country of uncomfortable dimensions, too close to both the USSR and Vietnam and consequently at cross-purposes with both the United States and China. The common reaction of ASEAN countries is, therefore, caution.

In 1977, when ASEAN's capitals had absorbed the shock of Saigon's takeover and the attitude toward Vietnam had softened, India hoped for an opportunity to bring to the fore its asset of good relations with both parties, Communist and non-Communist alike. Because of "the flexibility and non-exclusiveness of its approach," India alone enjoyed the confidence of both sides.[36] Subsequently such an overoptimistic equation has lost all validity. With events in Kampuchea and the Chinese/Vietnamese border area, new complications have arisen, and mediation by India is not on the agenda.[37]

In spite of political impediments, there has been some recent progress in the economic and technological fields. In late 1978, a delegation of the Indian Chamber of Industry and Commerce toured the ASEAN countries to explore new venues for Indian investment, in this case mainly from the private sector. Indian companies offered advanced technologies that were labor intensive, export oriented, and utilized indigenous raw materials.[38]

Indonesia exemplifies a former sluggishness in its relations with India as well as a willingness for a new approach. When its minister of industry visited New Delhi in early 1979, he described relations of the previous decade as having been "a bit dormant."[39] Indeed, a comprehensive trade agreement concluded in 1966 had been allowed to expire in 1970 without renewal; not until 1978 was a new agreement signed.[40] By the end of 1978, seven joint ventures were in production and nine were in preparatory stages.[41] Total Indian investment in Indonesia stood at nearly $80 million, and it is now expected to rise considerably. As yet, however, there is no Indian bank operating in Indonesia.[42] According to recent government agreements, cooperation is envisaged in the fields of agriculture, science (including nuclear science), and various technical disciplines. There is also some military cooperation, mainly between the navies.

The one exception to the still not very substantial amount of activity between India and the Southeast Asian states that border the Indian Ocean is Malaysia. There have been regular official exchanges, an occasional high-level visit,[43] and Malaysia and India have supported each other on a number of political issues.[44] Of all the joint ventures set up by India since the early 1960s, those in Malaysia were the most numerous and have shown the lowest rate of failure.

Many factors account for this smoother relationship. By far the highest number of ethnic Indians in the Indian Ocean area live there as Malaysian citizens (about one million); the countries' common British heritage has led to similar institutions, which makes cooperation easier; and there has been a certain similarity in economic policies (e.g., import substitution, labor-intensive production, and caution vis-à-vis foreign investment). Also, there has always been a large number of Malaysian students at Indian universities (in 1976 about 5,000, in 1978 about 6,000), albeit many of them are of Indian ethnicity, and Indian experts and consultancy firms had an early start in Malaysia.

The Indian government's restrictive financial policies are having a negative impact on business relations with Malaysia. International competition is stiff, and where an Indian firm would be in a position to make the cheapest bid, some Western or Japanese company might outdo it by offering more accommodating conditions of payment. Even for well-established joint ventures, the Indian firms have encountered great difficulties in obtaining capital transfer from India other than in the form of machinery or spare parts.[45] Results from a new Indian liberalization policy are still being awaited.

The varying features of bilateral relations were certainly discussed during the visit of Malaysia's Prime Minister Datuk Hussein bin Onn to India in January 1979. On the Indian side, all important cabinet ministers were involved, and discussions on economic and technological cooperation played a predominant role and led to a comprehensive agreement at the end of the visit. Malaysia was seeking Indian participation mainly in the fields of metallurgy, energy, industry, science, and agriculture. Back in Kuala Lumpur, the Malaysian prime minister "stressed that India was far more advanced than was apparent from poor publicity and promotion."[46] This judgment comes from the only Southeast Asian country that over the years has maintained close contacts with India.

Conclusion

"Poor publicity and promotion" on the part of India is, indeed, the main reason why the world at large has hardly been aware of the fact "that India is far more advanced than is apparent." For a nation that belongs to a special global category because of its size, population, mass poverty, and huge social problems, it is certainly wiser to keep a low profile than to try to throw its weight about. India seems to have learned some lessons from its past. Undoubtedly, too, mounting domestic problems will prevent it from seeking an overly ambitious international role, because that would not be credible.

On the other hand, by raising its sights from the subcontinent, India cannot fail to realize that it has a role to play in the larger region of the Indian Ocean. There, rapidly increasing contacts and exchanges among Third World countries of widely differing stages of development and political convictions are bound to bring India's potential into proper focus. The process is already well under way, and it will probably continue along the lines indicated, with particular emphasis on economic and technical cooperation.

To the degree that India will be capable of assisting others and of benefiting from its partners' assets, it will also gain political influence. This sequence – mutual benefits first, politics later – might be conducive to the main requirement of each country in this troubled Afro-Asian region: stability through change.

Notes

1. This term was introduced at the Lusaka nonaligned summit in 1970; the subject was particularly elaborated on at the 1976 Colombo summit.

2. See, for instance, Bradford Morse, "South-South Technical Cooperation, Collective Self-Reliance and the UNDP," *Development Dialogue*, no. 1 (1977).

3. See S. K. Asante, "Politics of Regional Economic Integration: The Case of the Economic Community of West African States (ECOWAS)," *Vierteljahresberichte der Friedrich-Ebert-Stiftung* (December 1978).

4. C. H. Heimsath and S. Mansingh, *A Diplomatic History of Modern India* (Bombay: Allied Publishers, 1971), p. 236.

5. Alain Lamballe, "L'Inde et l'Ocean Indien," *Projet* (February 1978): 160.

6. The plan was terminated in 1978, one year ahead of schedule.

7. The Indian minister of finance at the World Bank meeting, September 1978.

8. It is outside the scope of this paper to comment (a) on distributive policies within India with regard to the poorest layers of society and (b) on the social tensions that have built up in recent years as a concomitant to the rise in food production.

9. *Financial Times,* February 28, 1979, p. 4.

10. *Financial Times Survey: India,* February 5, 1979, p. vi.

11. India's main problem with joint ventures—there are more than three hundred either operating or in various stages of preparation—is a lack of financial credit facilities. Thus India's contribution is mainly restricted to supplying material and know-how.

12. Based on interviews by the author in New Delhi in late 1978.

13. Foreign Minister A. B. Vajpayee, *India News* (Indian Embassy, Bonn), August 23, 1978.

14. *Statesman,* November 3, 1978.

15. *Times of India,* September 30, 1978.

16. See the classification in the annual reports of the Indian Ministry of External Affairs.

17. There was a high tide in 1976; see, for example, Mohammed Ayoob, "India and Pakistan: Prospects for Detente," *Pacific Community* (October 1976).

18. There are no reliable figures available. According to a special report in an Indian weekly, there were by late 1978 nearly 500,000 Indians in the Arab Gulf states (excluding Iraq), which is more than one-seventh of their total population (*Illustrated Weekly of India,* December 3 and 10, 1978).

19. *Economic and Political Weekly* (Bombay), May 29, 1976, p. M-39.

20. *Monitor Service* (Deutsche Welle, Cologne), December 6, 1978.

21. In early 1979, there were still nearly 2,000 Indian doctors in Iran, many of whom wanted to leave as soon as possible (*Times of India,* February 27, 1979, p. 1).

22. *Newsweek,* October 30, 1978, p. 42.

23. India, however, lost a big railway project to Brazil.
24. *Middle East* (February 1979):108.
25. *Times of India*, February 8, 1979, p. 2.
26. In 1978, Air India operated nearly thirty flights a week (see Marcus F. Franda, "India, Iran and the Gulf," *American Universities Field Staff Reports*, no. 17, April 1978).
27. The last African visit of an Indian head of government was Mrs. Gandhi's 1976 trip to Tanzania, Zambia, Mauritius, and the Seychelles.
28. See *Economic and Political Weekly* (Bombay), May 29, 1976, and S. Sadiq Ali, "Continuite des relations indo-africaines," *Afrique Contemporaine* (March/April 1978):1-4.
29. S. Sadiq Ali, "Continuite des relations indo-africaines."
30. See A. Jumbe, "India and Tanzania," *India Quarterly* (January-March 1973). Mr. Jumbe was (and still is) the vice-president of Tanzania.
31. While touring Caribbean states in 1976, President Nyerere praised Indian technology as being particularly suitable for the Third World (see *Hindu*, October 19, 1976).
32. See Lamballe, "L'Inde et l'Ocean Indien," p. 169, and *Link* (New Delhi), July 9, 1978, p. 26.
33. Both Mr. Nyerere and Mr. Kaunda have recently received the Nehru Award for International Understanding.
34. Alastair Buchan, in his last book, also identified this trend: *The End of the Post-War Era* (London: Weidenfeld and Nicolson, 1974), p. 281.
35. See addresses to the assembled Indian ambassadors to East and Southeast Asia in New Delhi (Autumn 1977) and Mr. Desai addressing his Malaysian counterpart visiting New Delhi, January 1979 (BBC Summary of World Broadcasts, FE/5606/A 3/3 [September 5, 1977] and FE/6026/A 3/10 [January 26, 1979]).
36. *Times of India*, August 23, 1977, p. 1; this is a rather typical Indian self-interpretation.
37. In fact, in the first half of 1979, India tried to mediate between ASEAN and Indochina. The effects were highly negative for India's reputation in ASEAN capitals.
38. *Times of India*, November 13, 1978, p. 2.
39. *Times of India*, February 16, 1979, p. 5.
40. *Times of India*, June 5, 1978, p. 6.
41. The seven in production were textiles, machine tools, automotive parts, steel products, synthetic fibers, pharmacopoeia, bicycles.
42. *Financial Times Survey: India*, February 5, 1979, p. vi.
43. In 1979 the Malaysian prime minister visited India; this was the first visit in seventeen years.

44. For instance, during the *konfrontasi* period, after the creation of Bangladesh and following India's nuclear explosion.
45. *Times of India,* June 3, 1978, p. 7.
46. *Far Eastern Economic Review,* February 9, 1979, pp. 14–15.

3
India's Nonalignment and Superpower Naval Rivalry in the Indian Ocean

Joel Larus

Introduction

A number of foreign policy issues could be used to illustrate how India interprets and applies its nonalignment concept to superpower affairs, but the issue of U.S.-Soviet naval rivalry in the Indian Ocean has special importance for New Delhi. India has been modest in outlining its future naval posture in the Indian Ocean, but its determination to be the preeminent power in the region would be weakened, if not destroyed, if Washington and Moscow carry out a prolonged, increasingly spirited naval arms race there. Since the late 1960s when the United States and the Soviet Union first began deploying warships in the Indian Ocean, Indian leaders have characterized the superpowers' naval presence as a threat to the peace of the littoral and hinterland states, a move toward neocolonialism, and a reopening of the era of gunboat diplomacy. India has protested innumerable times about the militarization of the ocean by outside powers and has disputed their right to disregard the declared policies of the local states. The presence of the U.S. and Soviet fleets, accordingly, has been a concern of Indian governments for nearly twenty years.

This chapter will examine how the administration of Indira Gandhi and later that of Morarji Desai interpreted and applied the nonalignment concept to the naval competition between the United States and the Soviet Union in the Indian Ocean.

The Gandhi Era

Nonalignment has been a prominent feature of India's foreign policy since independence, but it is a concept that even the Indians themselves have difficulty defining with precision and consistency.[1] Because nonalignment postulates broad general principles of interstate conduct, one Indian regime has not always interpreted and applied the concept as its predecessor did. To ascertain the elements of nonalignment that a particular Indian government favored and those it discounted, it is necessary to determine how top-level leaders interpreted the concept and then show how it was applied to concrete foreign policy issues.

Throughout her years as prime minister, Mrs. Gandhi frequently spoke about her dedication to India's nonaligned status, and she detailed her version in her speeches and writings. In 1972, for example, she contributed an essay, "India and the World," to the fiftieth anniversary issue of *Foreign Affairs,* in which she offered a succinct statement of what she considered to be the essence of a nonaligned state's foreign policy. Nonalignment, she wrote, did not imply that her country was not involved in world politics or that it was committed to a neutralist foreign policy. "It was and is an assertion of our freedom of judgment and action." India would not hesitate to express its views on any major controversy relating to world peace, nor would her government fail to support causes it considered to be just. She maintained that the Treaty of Peace, Friendship, and Cooperation that her government had concluded with the Soviet Union the previous year did not lessen or destroy India's nonaligned status. Those who argued to the contrary, she continued, and who believed the treaty placed India within the Soviet bloc were incorrect. India's commitment to the traditional principles of nonalignment remained unaffected and unswerving.

Then directing her observations at Washington and those U.S. officials who had sharply criticized her government for its pro-Soviet biases and sympathies, Mrs. Gandhi added, "Successive U.S. administrations have ignored the fact that India must see her problems and her relationships in a different perspective. They have insisted on interpreting our *nonalignment* within the confines of a neutralism which they imagined to be *slanted in favor of Russia.*"[2]

The underscored words in the prime minister's summary statement—taken out of context—characterize her government's policy regarding the naval rivalry of the superpowers in the Indian Ocean. From the late 1960s until the 1977 election, the Gandhi regime consistently maintained that India was a nonaligned state, even as its ocean policies became more and more "slanted in favor of Russia." The pro-Soviet nonalignment of the Gandhi era in ocean affairs was the result of a combination of political and military factors, and its evolution can be divided into three periods.

Period 1

In November 1965, Great Britain announced the creation of a new British Indian Ocean Territory (BIOT), and within months Washington and London had concluded an agreement concerning the availability of Diego Garcia, a coral atoll in the Chagos Archipelago approximately 1,200 miles south of India's Cape Comorin. According to the original program of development announced by the U.S. Defense Department, the eleven-mile island was to become a limited, austere communication station for units of the fleet that were to be sent into the Indian Ocean. It was to be a minimum support site, the Pentagon repeatedly maintained, and was needed to fill a gap in the U.S. worldwide communication system and to provide logistic support for U.S. naval operations.

Insofar as Washington was concerned, Diego Garcia was an ideal military site. It was centrally located in the Indian Ocean, and from there U.S. naval and air power could be deployed to any quadrant of the Indian Ocean in a reasonable amount of time. Except for some 1,200 natives who were relocated after the British-U.S. agreement was concluded, the atoll was uninhabited. Once the natives were moved, there was no possibility whatsoever that a local, anti-American protest movement would take place there or that a Moscow-inspired coup would force the ouster of U.S. personnel and a termination of U.S. naval rights. The United States had a guaranteed fifty-year legal right to use and develop the island. According to the terms of the lease agreement, Great Britain and the United States were to share defense facilities set up on Diego Garcia until the year 2016. Pentagon officials, understandably, were pleased with the arrangement.

The initial response of the Gandhi administration to the announcement about Diego Garcia was temperate, but it did not mask India's displeasure that U.S. naval power was to be deployed permanently in the region. The lease, New Delhi emphasized, was of questionable propriety: Two outside countries negotiating about territory in the Indian Ocean was uncomfortably similar to nineteenth-century imperialism. Furthermore, Washington and London were disregarding the objections of local states.

When the issue was raised in the Lok Sabha in November 1968, the prime minister informed the country that her government was opposed to the Pentagon's plans for Diego Garcia and that Washington had been notified of India's position. U.S. authorities, she reported, were not planning to station troops on the atoll, and in the absence of U.S. troops, Washington had categorically denied that the island could be considered a "base." It was India's position, the prime minister continued, that a naval site, even one without assigned military personnel, was a base and that the U.S. position was without merit. "We are opposed to the establishment of foreign military bases," Mrs. Gandhi stated, "and believe the Indian Ocean should be an area of peace, free from any kind of military base."[3]

At approximately the same time that the U.S. navy was concerned with plans for Diego Garcia, the Soviet Union was similarly engaged in trying to locate and secure a suitable naval site for its fleet in the Indian Ocean. Moscow's task was considerably more difficult because of a hostile political climate. In 1966 when units of the Soviet fleet first appeared in the Indian Ocean and after 1968 when they began to maintain a naval presence there, the USSR was without a regional ally and had yet to come to the aid of any local, pro-Marxist revolutionary groups. Under such circumstances, Soviet opportunities for negotiating a long-term treaty giving its fleet an ocean port as its base of operations or otherwise securing a strategically attractive harbor were nonexistent. To overcome its disadvantage, the Soviet navy was at first compelled to set up a network of floating bases or berthing stations on the high seas to provide its warships with necessary repair facilities and other essential support services. Only in 1969, when a pro-Soviet government in Somalia came to power and established a close relationship with Moscow, did the Soviet navy undertake a sizable construction program at Berbera, a deep-water port in the northwest region of the country overlooking the entrance to the strategically important Red Sea. For the next eight years Russian warships had special rights and privileges at Berbera, and the construction program was begun.

India's initial response to the Soviet program of making Berbera the Soviet fleet's primary facility in the Indian Ocean differed from its reaction to Diego Garcia. New Delhi called attention to the fact that Somalia was a sovereign state and entitled to authorize the use of its ports by whatever navy it wished, including the warships of a non–Indian Ocean state. Also, India did not equate the Somalian-Soviet agreement as an example of neocolonialism, as it did the U.S.-British lease of Diego Garcia. The former was a traditional arrangement between two independent states; the latter was the result of a diplomatic bargain between two outside states, and it smacked of imperialism. These early distinctions were the roots of nonaligned India's pro-Soviet leanings.

Several times between 1968 and mid-1970, members of the Lok Sabha questioned Congress party leaders about Soviet naval power in the Indian Ocean and its significance to the country's national defense position.[4] They expressed concern about reports of a growing number of Soviet warships in the region as well as concern about Soviet plans to lease a naval base from one of the littoral states. To such inquiries, the Gandhi officials were noncommittal, evasive, or less forthright than in replying to similar questions concerning U.S. plans in the Indian Ocean. They denied they had any information about Soviet naval movements or ship strength in the Indian Ocean or about Moscow's plans to acquire naval facilities from a regional state. The government promised to keep watch on naval developments in the region that might affect India's interests, a statement that did not please the Lok Sabha members who were anxious about Russian long-range objectives in the Indian Ocean. The Foreign Office was not willing to be as critical or suspicious of Soviet naval deployment in the Indian Ocean as it was of U.S. fleet movements.

In the first period of U.S.-Soviet naval rivalry in the Indian Ocean, therefore, India's pro-Moscow leanings were very modest, albeit noticeable. Its tolerance for the Soviet naval presence was only slightly greater than its annoyance with Washington for acquiring a regional base. Strong anti-Americanism was not yet a feature of India's Indian Ocean policy, nor was there unqualified support for the

Soviet Union's policy. Those aspects of Mrs. Gandhi's policy evolved in the next two periods.

Period 2

At the September 1970 conference of the heads of state of the nonaligned nations at Lusaka, a resolution was passed calling on the attending nations to consider and respect "the Indian Ocean as a Zone of Peace from which great power rivalries and competition, as well as bases conceived in the context of such rivalries and competition either army, navy, or air force, are excluded."[5] India was one of the principal advocates of the proposal, and it has been a leader in the several campaigns since Lusaka to have the Zone of Peace concept accepted and implemented by the principal naval powers of the world, particularly the Soviet Union and the United States.

Within weeks after passage of the resolution, the Gandhi government noticeably hardened its stand concerning the U.S. naval presence in the Indian Ocean. More than ever before, Indian officials began making a clear-cut distinction between a naval base under the exclusive jurisdiction of a superpower (i.e., Diego Garcia) and a naval port facility made available on a limited basis to a superpower with the host state extending limited rights and privileges (i.e., Berbera). The former arrangement, India maintained, was an example of the worst type of neocolonialism and intolerable to local states. It threatened the peace of the Indian Ocean.

In the first Lok Sabha debate on the Indian Ocean question after Lusaka, the government's distinction between a naval base and a naval port facility became an issue. On November 19, 1970, some members who were concerned about the growing U.S.-Soviet naval arms race raised questions about the reported establishment of Soviet naval sites in the Indian Ocean. The government was asked to respond to reports that the Russians were attempting to acquire and develop a port from which their fleet could operate.

Swaran Singh, the minister of external affairs, side-stepped the questions from the floor. Had Mauritius given facilities to the Soviet fleet? Had a secret agreement been concluded making the Pakistani port of Gwadar available to the Soviets? Did the government have information about a Soviet naval presence on the island of Socotra? In each instance Mr. Singh spoke at some length about India's objective of working to have the Indian Ocean free of naval bases under the jurisdiction of outside powers. It was the position of the Gandhi government, the foreign minister continued, that the acquisition of port facilities by a naval power is a "normal international arrangement."[6]

Mr. Singh attempted to prevent further discussion of the issue by adding that the administration was of the opinion that "no useful purpose is served by spelling out that this country [i.e., the Soviet Union] has got the port facilities." His effort failed. One opposition member accused the Congress party of being "soft with Russia" whenever its naval presence in the Indian Ocean was under examination in Parliament. Another member believed that Mr. Singh had failed to define the scope and strategic importance of the Soviet fleet in regional affairs, and then he added the comment that the administration was going "out of the way to withhold information or to give sketchy or inadequate information about the exercises and about the presence of the Soviet naval power in the Indian Ocean."

The foreign minister persisted in holding to the distinction between a base and a port facility. Several times during the ensuing question-and-answer exchange, Mr. Singh categorically stated that the Soviet Union did not have a naval base in the region, and he indicated that other port arrangements made with local littoral states were of no concern to the Indian government. "The question asked was as to whether the Soviets have got any military base in the Indian Ocean area," he said in his summary statement, "[and] my reply is No. If they have not got one, I cannot say they have got a naval base here."

India's growing pro-Soviet attitude became more apparent in January 1971. At the Commonwealth Heads of Government Conference in Singapore, Mr. Singh discounted the buildup of Soviet naval power in the Indian Ocean while speaking spiritedly about the threat to regional peace from U.S. naval power. At his closing press conference, he tilted India's nonalignment somewhat more in the Russian direction. The Soviet Union, unlike the United States, had not accquired jurisdiction over a local port and had not set up a naval base for its fleet in the Indian Ocean. Since the Russians lacked such an installation, India had concluded that the Soviet naval presence was not a matter for India's concern either politically or militarily. Diego Garcia, in contrast, epitomized U.S. imperialistic tendencies and neocolonial policies.[7]

By mid-1971, the end of the second period, the Gandhi regime continued to affirm its dedication to the nonalignment concept, but its policies were about to become more tilted toward the Soviet Union. The Bangladesh issue was reaching crisis proportions, and the government in New Delhi concluded it needed overt Soviet support to protect the country's national security interests against any eventuality. The decision was made to place India's nonaligned status in limbo in order to realize an added measure of backing from Moscow.

Period 3

Two events took place in the closing months of 1971 that turned New Delhi's foreign policy against the United States. In August, the Russo-Indian Treaty of Peace, Friendship, and Cooperation was signed. Although Article 4 stated that the Soviet Union respected India's policy of nonalignment, questions were raised in India and abroad about the political consequences of a bilateral agreement that pledged the signatories to enter into mutual consultations in the event of an attack or a threat on either one of them. Many argued that the irreducible minimum of nonalignment was the need to avoid being aligned with either superpower by formal treaty and that India had infringed this key element.

The second event that intensified India's hostility to the U.S. fleet presence in the Indian Ocean was the dispatch of a U.S. task force, including the nuclear carrier U.S.S. *Enterprise,* into the Bay of Bengal during the Bangladesh War in a poorly concealed, crude attempt by Washington to pressure New Delhi and influence India's military operations. India reacted very strongly to the U.S. action: It charged the U.S. fleet with conducting gunboat diplomacy and being a pernicious influence in the Indian Ocean. With the Nixon administration's tilt toward Pakistan, as well as its pro-Peking policies and its hostile actions at the United Nations, the anger of New Delhi officials reached a record height.

India moved to a policy of open and vigorously pursued anti-Americanism. For the next several years, the Gandhi government continued to claim that India remained a nonaligned power, but its pro-Soviet policies disturbed many who had difficulty squaring New Delhi's positions with its commitment to the nonaligned cause.

Hostility toward the United States was particularly noticeable with regard to the U.S. naval presence in the Indian Ocean. India excused, justified, or ignored the naval power of the Soviet Union, but the U.S. navy and, more particularly, its base at Diego Garcia became the government's special scapegoat. As Washington added to its naval capabilities in the Indian Ocean, India's vilification against the United States increased. In early 1973 the Pentagon announced that Diego Garcia was in operation, and New Delhi received the news as an additional indication of a growing U.S. imperialism in South Asia as well as another indication of Washington's hostility toward India. Late that same year, when a U.S. aircraft task force was dispatched into the Indian Ocean as a precautionary move related to the impending Middle East crisis, officials in the Foreign Office became more outspoken. The task force was not withdrawn promptly after the end of the Israeli-Egyptian fighting, and the gulf between New Delhi and Washington widened.

Some of India's most acerbic statements about the U.S. naval presence were made during a Lok Sabha debate on November 12, 1973.[8] When questioned about the various operations of the U.S. fleet, Mr. Singh told the House that the government had been offered a variety of reasons why Washington believed it necessary to maintain a strong contingent of ships in the Indian Ocean. Discarding the guarded language of diplomacy, the foreign minister charged the U.S. authorities with deliberate deception or worse. In reviewing the recent history of Diego Garcia and how it grew from a minimum support site into an important U.S. naval base, Mr. Singh noted that the State Department and the Pentagon had offered and "altered one reason after another" to explain U.S. naval policies in the Indian Ocean. There was, Mr. Singh admitted, "a reasonable doubt" among Indian officials "about the credibility of these various reasons that they have given."

At the same time, India looked upon the Soviet naval presence with greater approval and tolerance than at any time in the past. Not only did the Soviet fleet not threaten the independence of any local state, New Delhi maintained, but it counterbalanced U.S. naval power. India now became the Soviet Union's principal supporter in South Asia and the leading partisan for Russian naval power in the region. Some of the arguments the Gandhi administration employed to explain its position were unusual, if not bizarre. New Delhi officials, for example, are reported to have contended that the Soviet Union was "nearly a littoral state" of the Indian Ocean, and thus it was entitled to deploy naval power to whatever levels it considered necessary.[9]

Between 1971 and 1977, therefore, India's nonaligned status was questioned in many Western countries. How its extreme pro-Moscow policy negated the country's nonaligned status — or at least how a leading Western diplomat interpreted events — was succinctly noted by Sir Alec Douglas-Home in 1974 when he was secretary of state for Foreign and Commonwealth Affairs. India, he said, applied a double standard in judging Indian Ocean naval affairs. The Russian fleet had been growing more powerful in the area since the closing years of the 1960s, but "there has not been a squeak" from New Delhi. As a nonaligned state, India had the responsibility of demonstrating a comparable understanding of the West's need to maintain its power in South Asia, he added, but such balance was not in evidence.[10]

Advocating an Indian Ocean policy that reflected a balanced appreciation of the security needs of both Moscow and Washington was contrary to the Gandhi administration's interpretation and application of the nonalignment concept. That standard became the goal of the Gandhi government's successor.

The Desai Response

In a dramatic upset in March 1977, the Janata party led by Morarji Desai defeated Indira Gandhi's Congress party. Many observers both in India and abroad believed that the new prime minister and his Foreign Office would revitalize the country's nonalignment policies because of their campaign promises. During the preelection debate when the relationship of India to the superpowers was discussed, Mr. Desai unequivocally declared that, if elected, his administration would return India to "true nonalignment."[11] It would deal with the United States and the Soviet Union "with evenhandedness" and would make a concerted effort to display "equal friendship" to both Washington and Moscow.[12]

Following his inauguration, the prime minister explained in greater detail how India's nonalignment had been corrupted during the preceding several years. He categorized Mrs. Gandhi's nonalignment policies as "anti-Western" and "spurious" and hinted at forthcoming changes. The Janata party, he predicted, expected to "carry out a policy of proper nonalignment, fully nonaligned, and with no suspicions of any alliance with anybody."[13]

The new minister of external affairs, Atal Bihari Vajpayee, reaffirmed and elaborated upon the country's need for a revitalized nonaligned foreign policy. In his maiden speech to Parliament as a member of the government, the foreign minister stated that his ministry would never say or do anything that would give rise to the belief that India tilted toward a particular bloc. Specifically, the incoming administration was agreed that India's foreign policy should end its pro-Moscow bias. The country's national interest required a more objective, less close relationship with the Soviet Union.[14]

Questioned in the Lok Sabha as to why he and Prime Minister Desai were so critical of the former administration's interpretation and application of the nonalignment concept, Mr. Vajpayee responded, "If anything that we say or do give rise to the feeling that we have leaned towards a particular bloc and have surrendered our sovereign right of judging issues on their merit, it will be a deviation from the straight but difficult path of nonalignment. The Janata Government would never allow this to happen."[15]

Within days of its victory, the Janata party's campaign promise about substituting a genuine nonalignment policy for the spurious version of the past several years was given definition. One of the first major foreign policy issues the government had to resolve after taking control was whether or not to terminate the 1971 treaty with the Soviet Union. Many expected such an announcement to be forthcoming since they were unable to equate balanced nonalignment with a treaty linking India to the Soviet Union. They were disappointed. Four days after Mr. Desai became prime minister, the Foreign Office announced that the treaty would remain in force. Simultaneously, however, Indian leaders began to signal Washington that they were interested in improving relations and opening talks to discuss the several issues disturbing U.S.-Indian relations.

Thus outlined, the Janata party's policy of evenhanded nonalignment was not an exact duplication of the version that Mrs. Gandhi's government had favored. The 1971 treaty remained in force, but the new administration was committed to reducing India's close association to the Soviet Union as well as to strengthening India's relations with the United States. In the next several weeks the government began to introduce policy changes that indicated how it proposed to apply genuine nonalignment to the continuing naval rivalry of the superpowers in the Indian Ocean.

Since the Carter presidency had begun in January, there was considerable optimism in India and abroad that U.S.-Soviet naval arms limitation talks would result in a slowing down, if not the termination, of the arms race in the Indian Ocean. The Desai administration decided India had much to gain if the superpower efforts were successful, and it inaugurated an important change in India's ocean policies.

On June 16 members of the Lok Sabha questioned the government for the first time about its position on Diego Garcia. Rather than singling out Washington for its neocolonial policies or continuing the Gandhi regime's distinction between a naval base and a naval facility, the foreign minister made the promised "concerted effort" to display "equal friendship" to both superpowers. His responses to parliamentary inquiries were moderate in tone, balanced, and optimistic. Mr. Vajpayee never once mentioned Diego Garcia by name, nor did he denounce Washington for seeking imperialistic objectives in the Indian Ocean. He appealed to both outside powers to "eliminate foreign military presence and the resulting tensions from the region."[16] Several times he emphasized the benefits regional states would realize if the Indian Ocean were free of superpower rivalry.

Mr. Vajpayee's moderate answers did not please some members of the Lok Sabha who wanted India to continue its "special relations" with the Soviet Union. One hostile member, anxious to obtain assurance that there would be continuity in the country's foreign policy and that Mrs. Gandhi's programs would not be discarded, pointedly asked whether the Desai government had requested Washington to dismantle Diego Garcia. The foreign minister's answer again was different both in tone and in emphasis from replies given to similar inquiries in the past. The incoming regime, he stated, did not "regard Diego Garcia as a bilateral problem between India and the United States." His brief comment was a hint that the government hoped that the Diego Garcia issue, as well as the entire problem of naval rivalry in the Indian Ocean, would be resolved at the bilateral talks being conducted by the superpowers or at the United Nations where the Zone of Peace proposal was then pending.

Two weeks later New Delhi offered Washington another hint that it had reinterpreted nonalignment. In a lengthy address on June 29 that prefaced his ministry's demands for grants for 1977–78, the foreign minister reviewed in some detail the leading political and military problems that faced the country. Mr. Vajpayee did not specifically mention Diego Garcia, nor did he berate the United States for maintaining a naval presence in the region.

Once again because of his restrained approach, the foreign minister was attacked by an opposition member who maintained that "the United States had no business to maintain a base on Diego Garcia."[17] Then, seeking to draw out specific details concerning the incoming administration's position regarding the U.S. fleet, he added that "the Indian Ocean must be a free zone. There should not be any dilly-dallying on this point." Mr. Vajpayee declined to respond.

Soon after taking over as prime minister, Mr. Desai stated his position concerning the activities of the Soviet Union in Indian Ocean affairs. His comment was in no way similar to those expressed earlier by Mrs. Gandhi. "It is wrong to say that the Soviet Union has no base whatsoever," he told Parliament on July 14, "it has spheres of influence in the Indian Ocean, and this could not be denied."[18]

When President Carter visited New Delhi in January 1978, the joint communiqué issued at the close of the visit contained no mention whatsoever of the different positions the two countries maintained regarding Indian Ocean affairs.[19] Six months later when Mr. Desai visited Washington, the two leaders again showed moderation. The June communiqué first reported that Mr. Carter "described the state of talks between U.S.A. and U.S.S.R. on the stabilization of their military presence in the Indian Ocean."[20] The prime minister was then quoted as hoping that "these discussions would continue and result in the eventual removal of all great power military presence in the Indian Ocean."

In Parliament the Janata party's less pro-Soviet application of nonalignment remained a point of attack by some opposition party members, particularly those extremely hostile to the United States.

In March 1978 a group that opposed evenhanded nonalignment took issue with Mr. Vajpayee's policy of deemphasizing India's hostility toward U.S. naval power in the region, as well as with the Foreign Office's lessened pro-Soviet orientation. They were concerned, they announced, that the government had not been sufficiently forceful the previous month when it had not formally protested the Pentagon's decision to reinforce U.S. fleet strength during the Ethiopian-Somalian crisis. Invited to explain the government's public silence, the foreign minister again steered clear of pro-Soviet extremism. "The government would like foreign bases, including Diego Garcia, to be eliminated and wound up," he responded.[21]

The answer was attacked by opposition members who did not support a lessened pro-Soviet tilt to India's foreign policy. Referring with a measure of sarcasm to the Janata party's commitment to genuine nonalignment and to its promise of avoiding special relations with both superpowers, one Lok Sabha member accused the administration of "moving closer to the U.S. position" in Indian Ocean affairs. Another announced the government was maintaining silence about U.S. naval power in South Asia "because of the dollar dole promised by U.S. multilateral corporations." Mr. Vajpayee replied that "the policy of the previous government was being pursued without any shift or tilt toward the United States."

Throughout its remaining months in office, the Desai administration worked to realize a balanced nonalignment policy. Its evenhanded approach was particularly noticeable at the meeting of the littoral and hinterland states of the Indian Ocean, a UN conference held in July 1979, only days before the collapse of the Desai government. The meeting was the outgrowth of the General Assembly's declaration of 1971, which sought to establish a Zone of Peace in the Indian Ocean. India was one of the original advocates of the zone proposal and throughout the Gandhi period had been one of its strongest proponents, particularly backing those sections that called upon the outside powers to end their naval programs in the area.

At the July meeting, the Indian ambassador to the United Nations, Brahesh Mishra, was the leadoff speaker following the opening remarks of the conference's president.[22] It was the opinion of some delegates that the ambassador's position had greater balance and showed more independence of Moscow than comparable statements on the Zone of Peace offered by Indian diplomats in the early 1970s and that it was another indication of how the Desai administration was attempting to apply its genuine nonalignment policies.[23]

Mr. Mishra began by speaking despairingly of "force or the threat of force against the littoral and hinterland states, reminiscent of the days of gunboat diplomacy."[24] Those acquainted with the language of India's Foreign Office translated this remark into a comment directed against Washington and its deployment of aircraft-carrier task forces in the region. Immediately thereafter, he went on to deplore the fact that the "great Powers" had increased their interference in the internal affairs of the local states "in total disregard of the principles of peaceful coexistence and of the inalienable right of every nation to decide its own political and social system." This observation, some diplomats decided, was New Delhi's way of protesting not only U.S. policies in the Middle East and Persian Gulf, but also recent Soviet interventions in the Horn of Africa area. According to one source, the Mishra statement was the type of evenhanded presentation that could not have been made when India's nonalignment had a pronounced pro-Moscow tilt.

Conclusion

As early as 1969 one Indian scholar noted that the nonalignment concept "can change, and in fact has changed, with the coming of new governments."[25] The summary review offered here of India's nonalignment policy during two administrations, insofar as it pertains to U.S.-Soviet naval rivalry in the Indian Ocean, supports Professor Misra's observation.

Under Mrs. Gandhi's leadership, nonalignment in Indian Ocean affairs was a policy that grew increasingly supportive of the Soviet's naval presence in the region. It became nonalignment with a pro-Soviet bias. Until early 1977 New Delhi either tacitly approved of or disregarded the Soviet Union's naval programs in the Indian Ocean and openly attacked Washington for carrying out comparable naval deployment. As Sir Alec Douglas-Home indicated, Gandhian nonalignment was slanted against the West.

The Desai government's Indian Ocean policies, in contrast, moved India away from the pro-Soviet standard Mrs. Gandhi favored.

Under the Janata party's leadership, there was a modest revitalization of nonalignment, a limited evenhandedness. The government showed less inclination to act as if Soviet naval power deployed in the Indian Ocean was ipso facto in India's national interest and had to be supported uncritically. The United States continued to be censored for its Indian Ocean naval presence, particularly for its programs at Diego Garcia, but the Foreign Office's criticism was noticeably less abrasive and less biased.

The sum total of the policy modifications that the Desai regime effected in India's nonalignment status did not result in a major shift in the country's Indian Ocean policies. They did succeed in improving relations with Washington concerning Indian Ocean affairs, seemingly without sacrificing Soviet backing. Desai's evenhandedness and independence gave India's nonalignment a new measure of respectability in world affairs. It remains to be seen if the country's next government will build upon this more balanced approach.

Notes

1. See, for example, K. P. Misra, "The Concept of Nonalignment: Its Implications and Recent Trends," in Misra, *Studies in Indian Foreign Policy* (New Delhi: Vikas Publications, 1969), pp. 90–106.
2. *Foreign Affairs* 51, no. 1 (October 1972):74 (underscoring added).
3. *Lok Sabha Debates,* November 13, 1968.
4. See *Lok Sabha Debates,* August 7, 1968; March 26, 1969; August 20, 1969; and May 6, 1970.
5. Cited in T. T. Poulose, "Indian Ocean: Prospects of a Nuclear-Free, Peace Zone," *Pacific Community* 5, no. 2 (1974):323–324.
6. *Lok Sabha Debates,* November 19, 1970.
7. *Times* (London), January 16, 1971.
8. *Lok Sabha Debates,* November 12, 1973.
9. The Indian officials who so argued are referred to in G. W. Choudhury, *India, Pakistan, Bangladesh, and the Major Powers* (New York: Free Press, 1975), p. 243.
10. *Times* (London), February 8, 1974.
11. *New York Times,* March 20, 1977.
12. Ibid., March 23, 1977; see also March 25, 1977.
13. Ibid., March 29, 1977.
14. *Lok Sabha Debates,* June 29, 1977.

15. Ibid.
16. Ibid., June 16, 1977.
17. Ibid., June 29, 1977.
18. *Statesman,* July 15, 1977.
19. *New York Times,* January 4, 1978.
20. Ibid., June 15, 1978.
21. *Lok Sabha Debates,* March 3, 1978.
22. United Nations Document A/AC.199/SR.2, July 5, 1979.
23. These conclusions were obtained by the author in interviews at the United Nations.
24. United Nations Document A/AC.199/SR.2, July 5, 1979.
25. Misra, "Concept of Nonalignment," p. 92.

4
Australia and the Indian Ocean

Henry S. Albinski

Australia's position as an Indian Ocean littoral state heavily colors its interest in the region. A third of its coastline, representing the underpopulated but mineral-rich state of Western Australia, fronts on the Indian Ocean. A comparatively high proportion—27 percent—of Australia's gross domestic product is tied to commerce, and over 50 percent of its overseas trade, as measured by tonnage, passes through the Indian Ocean. Australia values opportunities, such as those developing in the Middle East and Persian Gulf region, that will help it achieve a profitable export trade. Together with other industrially advanced nations Australia has a strong appetite for petroleum. Although it currently produces about 70 percent of its requirements, this figure will drop quickly in the 1980s. Australia's overseas oil supplies originate in the Middle East and the Gulf, and of course they are shipped across the Indian Ocean.

Australia's interest in the Indian Ocean basin is considerably more complex than the above economic factors themselves suggest. Australia is an island-continent, which is Western and affluent but underpopulated, located on the edge of Asia and far removed from the traditional European and North American centers and from major allies. These constraints have shaped Australia's responses to the international environment.[1]

This chapter will assess how Australia associates its geopolitical interests with the Indian Ocean basin. It will examine Australia's

---

This study was completed in February 1979 while the author was a senior Fulbright scholar and visiting Fellow in Strategic Studies at the Australian National University. A nearly identical version was published as an article in the May 1979 issue of *Australian Journal of Defence Studies*. Appreciation is expressed to the editors for permission to reprint.

perceptions of its capacity for influence and its policy choices. The chapter will not, however, attempt to assess the inherent validity of the Australian government's assumptions or to estimate likely, longer-term policy effects. An effort will be made to determine some broad conclusions about Australia's behavior as an international actor.

Australian Assumptions About the Indian Ocean

The present, Liberal–National Country party (L-NCP) government led by Malcolm Fraser came to office in December 1975, following three years of leadership by the Australian Labor party. The government has acknowledged the plurality of forces that shape international competition and condition security, but still, "there is no substitute for a system of balances which will make resort to disruptive behavior an irrational act. If this seems an old-fashioned solution, it is well to remember that in power terms we are still living in an old-fashioned world of nation states."[2] The government accuses the Soviets of bearing most responsibility for destabilization. Their military buildup is said to have been unwarranted and ominous. Alone or through surrogates, their interventions are alleged to be designed to confuse and to frustrate the West, and to weaken its resistance. Adventurism abroad and persecution of dissidents at home have made it difficult for others to believe that the Soviet leadership can be trusted. At large, the Soviets are perceived as bent on expanding their influence so as to achieve world primacy.[3]

Government expressions have at times failed to discriminate between Soviet intentions and Soviet capabilities, but the tendency has been to portray the Soviet Union's Indian Ocean role as symptomatic of the above assumptions. The government's warnings were especially stern during its first months in office. Emphasis was given to the eventual dangers posed to Australia and to its maritime interests by such evidence as the number of Soviet Indian Ocean ship-days and facilities like those at Berbera.[4]

By the latter part of 1976 the government seemed to modulate its pronouncements on the Indian Ocean. This change reflected the strategic assessment advice of its own advisers, and it reflected the measured conclusions of a parliamentary committee, which had just examined Indian Ocean issues, and the public remarks of the committee's chairman, Sen. J. P. Sim, a respected Liberal back-bencher.[5] It also reflected signals from the Ford administration in Washington. Despite its ongoing attempts to secure additional congressional funding for Diego Garcia and its reluctance to enter into force limitation negotiations with the Soviets, the Ford administration felt that anxieties expressed in some Australian government quarters were overstated.[6]

It is not the L-NCP government's conviction that Australia is foreseeably subject to a direct threat from Soviet naval power in the Indian Ocean, but Australia is persuaded that the Soviet presence there is not benignly inspired.[7] For instance, the Soviets might wish to interdict not only commerce enroute to Australia, but commerce on its way around the Cape and to Asia. More than half of the world's seaborne oil is carried on Indian Ocean routes, since the Middle East–Gulf region has been supplying 20 percent of American, 70 percent of European and over 75 percent of Japanese petroleum requirements. Alarmed by the 1973–74 Arab oil boycott and more recently by the shutdown of production in Iran, Australia has become sensitive to the delicate balance that – Australia argues – sustains the economic and defense capabilities of the non-socialist, developed world and therefore to Australia's own contribution to global and regional security balances. Australia has pictured NATO as a force for deterring the Soviets in Europe and the United States as a vital force worldwide, including underwriting security in Australia's neighborhood. Japan's economic health is seen as being linked to the avoidance of regionally destabilizing impulses to remilitarize. Japan is perceived as an asset to the modernization of China – the Soviet Union's arch opponent – and as a major aid, investment, and trade contributor to non-Communist Southeast Asia, with whose stability Australia is centrally concerned.

The government in Canberra has been unnerved by events on the Indian Ocean littoral such as in Afghanistan, the Gulf, and the Horn of Africa. Those events have been construed as part of a continuing drift of influence toward the Soviet side, and they have reinforced Australia's views about the Soviet drive for primacy and about deterioration in the strategic balance. Seeing the Indian Ocean as symptomatic of what is going wrong internationally underpins beliefs that, whatever friends may do to help, it is the United States that is "the only power that can balance the might of the Soviet Union. If America does not undertake the task it will not be done. If it is not done the whole basis of peace and security is unsupported."[8]

Australia and the United States

By exhortative and material means, Australia has exerted itself on behalf of an effective Western and especially a U.S. posture in the Indian Ocean. Australia has hoped for minimum Soviet capabilities in the area. At one time, before the Somali took action, Australia was especially eager to have the Soviet facility at Berbera removed. More specifically, Australia has argued for appropriate U.S. strike, surveillance, and other capabilities as part of the wider strategic effort and for more localized purposes, including approaches to Australia's western coast. In form, Australia has favored an Indian Ocean military balance at the lowest practical force level. Its inward preference, however, has been for a net U.S. advantage over the Soviets. Given Australia's desire for effective regular and reactive U.S. capabilities and suspicion of Soviet promises, it has been skeptical about Zone of Peace proposals. It has characterized them as premature and impractical, but has ornamented its position by speculating that the concept itself could serve as a restraint on the superpowers.[9] When President Carter entered office his declared objective of a "demilitarized" Indian Ocean was therefore especially unsettling to Australia. Assurances were obtained that the expression had been used as a rhetorical gambit to induce the Soviets to negotiate seriously on Indian Ocean as well as other issues.[10] A retired U.S. naval officer has suggested that Australia, and Fraser in particular during his June 1977 visit to Washington, may have been directly responsible for dissuading Carter from following a demilitarization objective.[11] However this interpretation is not substantiated by available internal evidence.

Australia's efforts to encourage an effective U.S. naval presence in the Indian Ocean began even before Carter was elected, or before naval limitation negotiations with the Soviets had begun. The Fraser government came to office on the heels of the Indonesian takeover of Portuguese East Timor, and although the L-NCP wished to continue the Australian tradition of seeking cordial relations with Indonesia, for various reasons it was critical of Jakarta's Timor policy. It refused to recognize the takeover and objected to the methods used and the lack of genuine self-determination offered to the inhabitants of East Timor. The United States cautioned Australia that its posture could cause political problems for Indonesia's friendly, anti-Communist government. Moreover, Western reliance on countering the Soviets in the Indian Ocean could be compromised. Indonesia could object to the submerged and undetected passage of U.S. submarines, including SSBNs, through the Ombai-Weter straits off Timor, and possibly through Indonesia's other waterways.[12] It was a consideration that, shortly thereafter, helped to modify Australia's reaction to the Timor question. In general, Australia has approached law-of-the-sea issues in ways intended to ensure unhindered merchant and naval traffic through the Indonesian straits. Soviet vessels tend not to use the southern Indonesia waterways, moving instead through the Malacca Strait, but U.S. vessels do. If an appropriate international regime would not ordinarily permit undetected passage by U.S. submarines, then an exception taken through bilateral agreement could accomplish much the same objective. In normal times, a diversion of over 3,000 miles around Australia would reduce on-station time for surface and submarine craft, and a delay in force projection could mean that a crisis situation could not be handled.[13]

Australia closely followed the Soviet-U.S. Indian Ocean arms limitation negotiations that began in 1977, and Australia was kept fully briefed by Washington. Australia made a number of representations to the U.S. side and caused the United States to retract and to ask the Soviets for a redrafting of some provisions previously agreed upon. The Soviets felt that Australia was exercising a negative influence, and when the United States suspended negotiations in February 1978, Moscow imputed some responsibility to Australia, but the charges were in fact overdrawn. On balance, however, the whole episode should be seen as an outstandingly successful Australian diplomatic effort.

The United States placed the talks in abeyance because of Soviet intervention on the Horn of Africa. The Soviets were accused of defaulting on an understanding that neither side would escalate its forces or involvement in the region while conversations were proceeding. Some months later, after Soviet naval deployments had returned to earlier levels, the United States was prepared to resume negotiations. However, other irritations in the Soviet-U.S. relationship plus divisions within official U.S. circles intervened.[14]

At time of writing, the conversations have not been resumed. Although some terms remain to be settled, U.S. spokesmen have revealed those parts of a package by which Washington is prepared to stand. It is helpful to notice how these and other known provisions very largely coincide with Australian preferences.[15]

The prospective agreement basically calls for a freeze on established facilities and forces. Regarding facilities, this means that the lost Soviet installation at Berbera cannot be replaced in kind. It also means that the United States can retain its own key installations, such as the North West Cape communication station in Western Australia and the Diego Garcia facility, which the Fraser government supported enthusiastically. It means that, as before, the United States can regularly deploy carrier task forces into the Indian Ocean. Submarines are presently not covered by the agreement, which is a net U.S. advantage. The United States has superior antisubmarine warfare (ASW) capabilities, is better able to conceal submarine deployments into the region, and has a better strategic reason than the Soviets to reserve the right, even on an occasional patrol basis, to deploy SSBNs into the Indian Ocean. Consistent with Australian wishes, land-based strike aircraft will not be prohibited from the region, but the scale of their permitted deployment remains unsettled. An arms limitation treaty would be of limited duration, and a major breach by the Soviets would permit the United States to counter by whatever means necessary.

If such terms imply "balance," then it is a balance that arguably favors existing U.S. force and facility levels and meets Australian criteria. Not only are Soviet capabilities kept manageable and short on base and replenishment facilities, but stabilization means that the United States is not likely to be drawn into a game of naval escalation. Should such a race occur it would surely mean a dilution of already strained force levels in the Pacific, Australia's primary security sector, in order to reinforce the Indian Ocean.

A bilateral Soviet-U.S. agreement would entirely exempt littoral states such as Australia. At this time, among the littoral states only India and Australia possess a distant-water naval capability. Under the prospective agreement's terms, Australia would fall short of its wish for an unconditional and unlimited U.S. right to surge forces into the Indian Ocean on the excuse of assisting Australia under ANZUS (a security treaty signed by Australia, New Zealand, and the United States in 1951). Nor could the ANZUS partners duplicate the amphibious "Kangaroo" exercises that are periodically staged to the east of Australia, since exercises off the west coast would represent an upward change in status quo practices. Under the same rationale, even if it wanted to, the United States could not utilize the newly commissioned facility at Cockburn Sound, HMAS Stirling, as a major naval base for itself. At bottom, however, Australia sought and obtained terms consistent with its geographically immediate security interests. A Soviet attempt to define the coverage of the Indian Ocean as extending northward across the Timor and Arafura seas and southward across the Great Australian Bight was rejected. Assurances were repeatedly made by Washington to Australia that, whether as an expression of the ANZUS alliance or otherwise, the United States would continue to exercise in the Indian Ocean with allies.

The Fraser government has consistently tried to sustain U.S. interest in Australia's environment. As a corollary, it has tried to widen the potential ambit of circumstances and sites in which the United States might be called upon to respond, especially in an Australian-defined emergency. Australia has tried to employ the ANZUS alliance as a foundation on which the United States would feel obligated to extend support. The United States has been sympathetic. One reason has been that since the various Asian-Pacific states have wondered about U.S. will and credit, maintaining a visible and viable ANZUS becomes a signal that the United States cares about trusted friends and allies.[16]

The language of the ANZUS treaty refers to possible assistance to the signatories in the event of "an armed attack on the metropolitan territory of any of the Parties, or on the island territories under its jurisdiction, in the Pacific, or on its armed forces, public vessels or aircraft in the Pacific."[17] In part, the parties found it convenient not to impose a rigid definition on what was subsumed under the "Pacific" rubric. Such definitions are still avoided. But the Fraser government in Australia has construed the pact, broadly, as extending into the Indian Ocean. The position was tersely stated in a 1976 joint submission by the Defence Department and the Joint Intelligence Organization during parliamentary committee hearings on the Indian Ocean. Australia "interprets the spirit of the ANZUS treaty as conferring obligations on all parties to include the Indian Ocean." Although "the ANZUS treaty is related specifically to the Pacific area or metropolitan territories of the respective signatories . . . it needs to be held in mind that a large segment of Australia's metropolitan territory is on the Indian Ocean. This may suggest some implications for desirable forms of cooperation among the treaty partners to assist the performance of their respective obligations to each other."[18]

An early Australian success along these lines took place at the July 1977 ANZUS Council meeting in Wellington, New Zealand. Largely at Australian urging, the final communiqué carried a clause stating that any U.S.-Soviet arms limitation agreement in the Indian Ocean "must be balanced in its effects and consistent with the security interests of the ANZUS partners."[19] Later in 1977, at the request of Australia, Secretary of State Cyrus Vance wrote to Foreign Minister Andrew Peacock that any Indian Ocean arms agreement "will not in any way qualify or derogate from the US commitment to Australia or limit our [U.S.] freedom to act in implementing our commitment under the ANZUS treaty," that the Soviets had been so advised, and specifically that joint exercises in the Indian Ocean under ANZUS aegis would not be affected.[20]

By the turn of 1977-78, the notion of a joint Indian Ocean exercise was being broached on an informal feasibility level by Australian service personnel with their U.S. counterparts, and some planning went forward. Eventually, the U.S. administration decided that politically it would make good sense to stage such an event. It would serve to notify the Soviets that their Indian Ocean buildup was being answered, and it would be a reassurance of U.S. bona fides to allies generally. For Australia, it would confirm the promise made in the Vance letter, and it would reassure Australia that the United States cared about ANZUS.

When Vice-President Walter Mondale arrived in Australia in early May 1978, he first informed the prime minister of the final decision to proceed with an exercise later in the year, named Operation Sandgroper, and then made the announcement publicly. In a way, the exercise was an extension of an array of ANZUS military exercises and other forms of defense cooperation, but Fraser was not far off the mark in his special recognition of it. The exercise was particularly welcome at the time. It was announced less than a month after a mission of senior Australian officials to Washington had sought further information and reassurances on the course of Soviet-U.S. Indian Ocean negotiations, which were then stalled. Australia, like the United States, was greatly exercised over growing Soviet influence in parts of the Indian Ocean littoral. Operation Sandgroper was something concrete from the United States, at least foreseeably linking ANZUS to the Indian Ocean.[21] The New Zealanders also joined in Operation Sandgroper. For them, although the Indian Ocean is very far from New Zealand and New Zealand's military resources were very lean, the principal rationale for participating was that it could and would be done in an ANZUS context, with the United States willing to acknowledge a wide ambit for the alliance.

Australia believes that its Indian Ocean interests can be furthered by material as well as verbal expressions. It wishes to enhance the capabilities of friendly forces and to cultivate an encouraging climate that will fortify U.S. will. It also wishes to engage the United States in and around Australia in ways that will continue to highlight its importance to Washington, thereby raising prospects for U.S. responses supportive of Australian interests, under the ANZUS umbrella or otherwise.

Some of the most important measures available to make such a presentation to the United States pertain to U.S. access to or use of Australian facilities. An early step taken by the Fraser government was to rescind the ban on the entry of nuclear powered vessels into Australian ports. The ban had originally been imposed in the closing stages of the former L-NCP government, and it had been retained by the Whitlam Labor government. The Fraser government knew full well that the United States felt inconvenienced by the ban, and that there was widespread feeling in Washington that the ban contradicted and therefore denigrated the ANZUS partnership. Reporting on its early 1976 visit to Australia and New Zealand a U.S. congressional delegation remarked, "How could the best of allies, Australia and New Zealand, count on the protection of the United States Navy without its presence? We emphasized this incompatibility and as a result, the delegation is most gratified that during the course of the trip the Governments of both New Zealand and Australia announced the lifting of the ban on visits by nuclear-powered ships."[22]

Continuing earlier practice, the Fraser government has made Western Australian facilities available to U.S. forces. The United States has no military base anywhere in Australia, but it has access to or jointly operates a large variety of facilities serving various defense-related functions.[23] In the Australian interior, at Pine Gap and Nurrungar, there are space tracking and communications installations. On the west coast is HMAS Stirling, which can accommodate a destroyer and submarine force and to which the U.S. navy has access. Because of Stirling's extreme southeasterly location on the Indian Ocean and the availability of other facilities, the United States has no reason to make use of Stirling except for occasional visits though more widespread utilization could be expected under drastically changed circumstances.

The United States makes regular use of the airfield at Learmonth, at Exmouth Gulf, to supply the North West Cape communication station there. The North West Cape facilities, which are also available to the Royal Australian Navy (RAN), contribute directly to U.S. strategic capabilities. The installation is linked to other communication stations, including Diego Garcia, in a global network. The North West Cape facility houses sophisticated equipment for ship-to-shore-to-ship message traffic and an especially potent very-low-frequency (VLF) capacity for distant communication with submerged craft. There has been speculation as to whether U.S. SSBNs have been deployed in the Indian Ocean and whether the North West Cape station has served their particular strategic function. This is not the place to review the argument, which on balance seems to support occasional SSBN deployments. An official Australian publication, produced about the time the station was commissioned, stressed that the VLF transmitter "is able to penetrate the surface of the oceans to provide communication for the United States Navy's most powerful deterrent force – the nuclear powered ballistic missile submarine."[24]

Australia also provides services outside its metropolitan territory for U.S. forces in the Indian Ocean. For some years U.S. military air traffic has been transiting through Singapore as Orion P-3 reconnaissance and some transport aircraft have flown back and forth between the Pacific and Indian oceans. The conducting of surface and submarine surveillance patrols in the Indian Ocean has been considerably facilitated by stopover rights in Singapore and by ground support given to the aircraft by Australian personnel stationed at Tengah Airfield. Those personnel primarily assist the development of the Singapore air force and provide support for the Five-Power Integrated Air Defense System at Butterworth in Malaysia. No U.S. personnel were permanently assigned to Singapore, and the Singapore government thought it politically indelicate to assign its own people to assist the U.S. flights, so the Australians were therefore a natural and welcome asset. By 1978, U.S. transit traffic was increasing, Singapore no longer felt it necessary to operate sotto voce, and its perceptions of regional security requirements had sharpened. It therefore made sense for Australia to enter into a public agreement with the United States to formalize the support services.[25]

Within the Indian Ocean itself, Australia has tried to enlarge the scope of its cooperation with the United States and to make the U.S. strategic effort there more effective. Early in the Fraser government, Defence Minister D. J. Killen announced a closer, bilateral defense effort in the area.[26] Much of the government's intention was simply to commit the United States to the area more substantially. One incidental motive was to mollify Western Australia's security concerns. In various ways, including port access to nuclear powered vessels, the U.S. presence in Western Australian waters became more apparent than it had been during the Labor government's time in office.

More particularly, U.S. access to the Australian Cocos Islands has become more regularized. The loss of U.S. military landing rights in Thailand placed a larger premium on Singapore and, as a backstop, on the Cocos. At present an estimated three dozen U.S. flights, all or nearly all of them by P-3 aircraft, stop at Cocos annually. As an Australian Department of Defence submission argued in 1975, the Cocos airfield "bestows considerable advantages of range and endurance in the approaches to the Indonesian Archipelago, and extends the range of surveillance aircraft in the Indian Ocean. Should it ever become necessary to sustain naval and/or air operations in the Indian Ocean, facilities at Cocos Island would greatly increase the surveillance of any Australian forces."[27]

Diego Garcia, the principal U.S. facility in the Indian Ocean, has consistently been endorsed by the Fraser government. The facility deploys numerous surveillance flights, provides fleet replenishment services, is tied into the U.S. communication network, and apparently can receive, process, and relay transmissions from aircraft and satellites overflying Communist nations.[28] Diego Garcia's capabilities could also serve to monitor a force reduction agreement in the region.

Diego Garcia's surveillance mission is not limited to U.S. aircraft. About one in four such deployments out of Deigo Garcia is believed to be by Australian P-3s, and Australian P-3s of course also utilize Cocos. Although the Labor government stepped up the Royal Australian Air Force's (RAAF's) long-range Indian Ocean surveillance in the second half of 1974, surveillance capabilities have risen further in recent years.

Still, Australia's surveillance and other defense force deployments in and around its Indian Ocean coast are modest. An argument continues over the appropriateness of diverting sophisticated, essentially military systems to civil tasks, including protection of the prospective 200-mile exclusive economic zone.[29] No Australian warships larger than patrol boats are permanently based in Western Australia, though a ship is usually to be found at Stirling. The Australian fleet is headquartered in eastern Australia, and its normal operational waters are in Southeast Asia and the Pacific, not in the Indian Ocean.[30] Because of the importance it attached to the exercise, Australia made a substantial air and naval contribution to Operation Sandgroper off Western Australia in 1978, including four destroyers and two submarines.[31] Ideally, the United States would prefer a larger Australian naval presence in the Indian Ocean, but it welcomes surveillance cooperation, access to Western Australian facilities, the operation of the North West Cape station, and Australian assistance in Singapore and the use of the Cocos. Taken in conjunction with diplomatic movements, these contributions illustrate considerable Australian effort to realize regional security objectives.

Australia, Southwest Asia, and the Gulf

Our assessment continues through a review of Australia's reactions to two flash-point areas on and near the Indian Ocean littoral, namely Southwest Asia and the Gulf and southern Africa. Both locations are thousands of miles from Australia, but their geographical importance and other factors have been keenly noticed, as have Soviet interest in and potential for influence in those areas. The Fraser government has frequently alluded to the interdependence of strategic developments and has identified the Indian Ocean basin generally as a legitimate Australian concern. In 1978 Southwest Asia was rent by political unrest. There was a coup in Afghanistan that produced a regime closely attached to the Soviet Union. The new government signed a treaty with the Soviets, which included a clause calling for continued cooperation in the military field. NATO planners were worried about Afghanistan, projecting a bad-case analysis in which "If Pakistan should fall apart the Russians would have a clear road to the Arabian Sea and the capability to build bases near the exit from the Persian Gulf through the Strait of Hormuz."[32] A short time before, the Soviets and Cubans had intervened massively on Ethiopia's behalf in the Horn of Africa. Soviet actions, which included increased naval and air activity in the area and a heavy supply effort from facilities in South Yemen, contributed directly to the U.S. postponement of Soviet-U.S. Indian Ocean arms limitation negotiations.

Events in Afghanistan and on the Horn suggested that the Soviets were searching for political targets of opportunity and that their influence was being consolidated to the east and to the west of the Persian Gulf. Then came months of turmoil in Iran and the eventual overthrow of the shah and his system. A close and reliable friend of the West, the self-professed policeman of the Gulf, was gone. A succeeding regime was bound to follow a far more neutral foreign policy, and sizable foreign economic interests were endangered. It was possible that continued instability could eventually produce a government sympathetic to the neighboring Soviet Union.

As the Iranian crisis deepened, Australian spokesmen issued concerned statements. There was worry about the chain of events in Southwest Asia, the Horn, and Iran, about the potentially adverse effects on the region's strategic balance, about the worldwide impact of disruptions in petroleum supplies, and about the possible spread of political infection to neighboring countries.[33]

What, however, did Australia do or counsel to arrest or minimize the allegedly disastrous fallout from the Iranian crisis? In the months toward the end of 1978 and the beginning of 1979 Australian policy faced hard choices. What was the appropriate mixture of diplomatic, economic, and military measures that should be taken or counseled so as to minimize the damage within Iran itself? What was the most promising posture that could be adopted vis-à-vis the Soviets? What kinds of demonstrations of support should be extended to neighboring states such as Saudi Arabia? In the event, Australia kept itself informed but took no initiatives and did not advise the Americans.

Australia's outwardly passive attitude appeared to conflict with its expressed anxiety about Gulf and Indian Ocean developments generally. It also seemed out of character with its vigorous efforts to engage an effective U.S. presence in the Indian Ocean. One consideration that governed Australia's approach was its assessment of Iranian politics. It seems clear that well before Washington came to grips with the strength of the discontent in Iran, Australia had concluded that the shah's popularity was thin and that his system was precarious. When Carter tried to shore up the shah by defending him publicly, Australia demurred. Later, when unrest turned to revolution, Australia was understandably disquieted. But it did not simplistically interpret the agitation just as a religious protest or as the work of Soviet-inspired radicals, but as reflecting "the political and economic aspirations of a large part of the Iranian people who had experienced a period of rapid economic and social change."[34] Hence it seemed prudent to let the turmoil run its course, to avoid intrusions that could offend sensitive opposition groups, to hope for a reasonably moderate outcome, and to limit the catch the Soviets might expect from fishing in troubled waters.

Early on, Australia accepted that it and others would have to learn to live with a government quite different from the shah's. At least implicit in Australia's approach was a concern about an early resumption of Iranian petroleum production for worldwide distribution. Only about 4 percent of Australia's annual crude oil requirements had been imported from Iran, and some alternative sources were available to compensate for this shortfall. Still, as previously mentioned, although Australia's domestic oil production satisfied 70 percent of its needs, a drop is soon to come, with only 40 percent expected from its own wells by 1986–87. At a time when the Fraser government was striving to contain inflation, oil prices were already rising sharply, and Australia's oil consumption was mainly in the area of transport, for which there was no alternative energy substitute ready.[35]

Iran's turmoil also threatened to jeopardize profitable trade. With prospects for overseas sales of Australian uranium declining, the government had hoped to sell enough uranium to Iran over fifteen years to earn, at current prices, about A$1.2 billion. Considerable progress had been made toward a safeguards agreement before Iran's political troubles intruded.[36] Even without uranium, a varied annual export trade of A$180 million had been achieved. Again, the Australian posture toward Iran was designed to minimize a loss of markets with any succeeding regime, whatever its social and developmental priorities.[37] As Iran's political situation remained confused, Trade and Resources Minister J. D. Anthony toured Saudi Arabia, Kuwait, and Bahrain. He reported enthusiastically about prospects for the sale of Australian goods and technology to those Gulf states. But he had an eye on the distorted developmental priorities that had contributed to the shah's fall, and he remarked how impressed he had been in the states he had visited by "the balance that has been maintained between social and commercial goals."[38]

Still another reason why the Fraser government did not pursue assertive policies was its judgment that Washington had more than enough advice being thrust upon it from U.S. circles alone. Moreover, there was sympathy with a State Department official's description that "This was an enormously difficult situation that simply defies any attempt at clear-cut response. There was just no major action that we could have taken that would have yielded positive results."[39]

Australia had had a diplomatic mission in Tehran for several years but felt that despite having developed an independent evaluation of Iranian political conditions, it could not pressure or lecture the United States because the U.S. diplomatic and intelligence presence in Iran was far greater, as indeed were its direct interests. Australia had just engaged in a lengthy and largely successful effort with respect to the Indian Ocean force limitation negotiations, and with respect to Washington's investment in ANZUS. As a middle power, Australia's influence with the United States was circumscribed, and to be effective, that influence had to be applied selectively. In a crisis as jumbled and seemingly as intractable as the

Iranian crisis, there was even less incentive to expend Australia's diplomatic credit. The apparent loss of U.S. strategic monitoring facilities in Iran raised the importance of U.S. installations in central Australia. Ironically, the setback in the Gulf may have served to enhance Australia's importance for Washington.

Australia and Southern Africa

Southern Africa offers a further opportunity to assess Australia's approach toward developments in and around the Indian Ocean littoral. From its earliest months in office, the Fraser government has been conciliatory toward black nationalist regimes and aspirations. In early 1976 it accorded diplomatic recognition to the Neto regime in Angola, whose Cuban-dependent government the United States had earlier attempted to undermine. In 1978 Australia refused to endorse the Franco-Belgian-American effort to bail out Zaire, whose resource-rich Shaba province had been invaded by insurgents operating out of Angola. Australia continued to contribute civil aid to Mozambique, a sanctuary for forces operating against Rhodesia (Zimbabwe).

As for Rhodesia itself, Australia repudiated the Smith government's bid for an internal political settlement and threw its weight behind Anglo-American efforts to secure an all-party settlement designed to include insurrectionist movements operating from outside. Australia honored the UN's economic embargo against Rhodesia, as well as its strict guidelines on the issuance of visas to Rhodesians.

Australia agreed that South Africa had been holding South-West Africa (Namibia) illegally and that the territory should be allowed self-determination. Australia participated on the UN Council for Namibia and argued that the South-West Africa People's Organization (SWAPO), a radical organization that had been fighting a low-level guerrilla war in northern Namibia for some years, was a major and an authentic representative of political opinion in Namibia. Australia refused to acknowledge the validity of the Namibian elections sponsored by South Africa in late 1978, which SWAPO boycotted. Australia pledged a troop contribution to a UN peacekeeping force that would supervise political transition in Namibia.

Australia has not supported draconic UN resolutions aimed at

South Africa, but it has vociferously denounced apartheid. It supported cutoffs of arms transfers to South Africa, and it has actively discouraged sporting contacts with South Africa, as well as Australian airline publicity for travel to South Africa. Under the Fraser government, the remaining Australian trade commission in Johannesburg has had its work restricted to responding to inquiries, and official trade incentives have been avoided. The voluntary code of employment conduct for Australian companies functioning in South Africa has been retained and is believed to be generally honored. Diplomatic contacts with South Africa have been kept proper, but cool. The Fraser government has discouraged visits in either direction by senior political or official persons.[40]

It is necessary to explain Australia's southern African policies and to suggest how they might be reconciled with the government's approach to Indian Ocean security questions and problems in the Gulf. The analysis will be divided into the strategic, economic, and diplomatic rationales that appear to have guided Australian policies in southern Africa.

The thinking of the Fraser government has coincided with official advice that Australian security interests in southern Africa are remote and that despite the presence of Soviet and Cuban advisers and technicians, the region is not likely to become a cockpit of open, superpower confrontation.[41] All the same, government spokesmen have maintained that southern Africa could become combustible, fall into disorder and compromise moderate indigenous elements as well as Western interests, and introduce truly radical regimes as well as Soviet or Soviet-proxy influence. A reliance by any side on military solutions to problems in the area seriously enlarges the risk that such conditions will come about, and their reverberations would extend beyond Africa; for instance, they might harm efforts to contain Soviet influence over much of the Indian Ocean littoral.

Australia's reticence to support the Western rescue effort in Zaire was in substantial part dictated by feelings that external intervention of that kind make it more difficult for the West to keep out undesirable outsiders, such as people from Communist countries.[42] In much the same vein, an orderly Namibian settlement would lessen Angola's rationale for hosting large numbers of Cubans, advance rapprochement between Angola and Zaire, and decrease chances for the fashioning of a Soviet belt of influence across the lower part of the continent. South Africa has presented itself as an anchor of friendship and reliability on behalf of Western interests, but its perceived obstructionism concerning Namibia "plays into the hands of those inimical to the West."[43] The significance of South Africa's claim that it provides exceptionally useful intelligence and naval support to the West in and around the Cape is judged to be inflated. It is not believed that at some distant time, a racially more representative regime in South Africa—especially if such a regime evolved in a reasonably peaceful way—would wish to interfere with Western freedom of navigation.[44]

It is useful to underscore the firmness and consistency of the Australian government's outlook. On justifying aid to Mozambique: "The surest way to push southern Africa into the hands of communists and into increasingly radical tendencies is to refuse Western understanding and sympathy, and some assistance in recognition of the plea of the black majority in Africa."[45] On opposing South African apartheid: Without peaceful change scores of thousands might die in armed conflict, and "if there were external intervention, the implications could be incalculable for Africa and the international community."[46] On Zimbabwe: "The longer you have a white minority regime in Zimbabwe seeking by one means or another to prolong white supremacy, the longer the circumstances exist which will help Communists to establish a firm, permanent foothold in Africa." At any rate, although the United States needs to have military forces "readily available . . . , getting rid of the basic inequalities of southern Africa would do more to diminish Soviet influence there than any single act within British or American capacity."[47]

Australia's strategic rationales are in part transposable to economically related rationales. Australia's own commercial stake in southern Africa is slight, and what there is is concentrated in South Africa. Although in 1976–77 two-way trade with South Africa stood at A$125 million, trade with all the black African countries was only A$103 million. Prospects for meaningful growth in the trade with southern African countries outside South Africa are slight, regardless of the types of regimes. The earlier, substantially favorable Australian trade figures with South Africa have by now been converted to a rough parity of exports and imports. The decline in exports to South Africa has in part been caused by a lack of official Australian encouragement. Purely commercial factors, however, such as a diminished South African need for Australian cars and car parts, have been more influential. Australian investment in southern Africa outside South Africa is virtually absent. In 1977 direct investment in South Africa was only 1.5 percent of Australia's worldwide overseas investments, and that investment has weakened even more since then.[48] Australia is not dependent on raw materials originating in southern Africa.

Although Australia has relatively little to gain or lose economically in southern Africa, it takes a wide view. Australia appreciates the fact that dependency by future black African regimes on Soviet/East European aid and trading connections is the other side of the coin of dependence on the Soviets politically. Moreover, Western diplomacy should not be allowed to endanger future access to quantitatively significant and strategically useful southern African resources, among them chromium, platinum, manganese, and uranium. In addition, misdirected Western political policies in southern Africa could produce adverse economic reactions elsewhere in black Africa. Nigeria, for example, has become a major oil producer and the second most important supplier of the United States. Also, Australia has become involved in the North-South dialogue and in such complex issues as international commodity supply and pricing. Australia reasons that both the less developed countries and the industrial nations must reach working, long-term relationships. The Fraser government believes that Australia's political performance on delicate, southern African questions, scrutinized as they are by Third World nations worldwide, can contribute to a climate of international economic harmony and therefore to Australia's and the West's security and commercial interests.[49]

This leads to the third rationale that underpins Australia's southern African policies. This can broadly be described as the search for diplomatic respectability and influence. In the first place, Australia's southern African expressions have for the most part closely paralleled those of the Carter administration. A considerable strain would have been imposed on Australia had the United States followed quite different orientations. As matters have stood, congruent U.S.-Australian southern African policies have been presented by Canberra as consistent with the advocacy of policies designed to check the Soviets in the Indian Ocean. Conciliatory, pro-black-Africa Australian policies are believed to add weight and credibility in Washington to Australia's intervention in Indian Ocean force limitation arrangements with the Soviets and in committing the United States to ANZUS.

More complex has been Australia's need to maintain smooth relations with Third World countries, especially but not exclusively in neighboring Southeast Asia and Oceania. This is a significant objective not only because Australia feels its principal security interests lie in the region, but also because as a middle power Australia cannot in any event expect to exert really conclusive influence. It is not itself an Asian country, and well into the postwar period it practiced a "white Australia" migration policy. The handling of its aboriginal population has become more noticed and controversial, both at home and overseas. Papua New Guinea, Australia's former colonial ward, has been especially vocal on southern African racial questions; hence the logic of a submission from the Australian Department of Foreign Affairs, subscribed to by the government, that support for a white minority government in Rhodesia would seriously damage Australia's relations with numerous African and Asian states. "We would be isolated in international forums, would receive no support from Western European countries and would be increasingly identified with South Africa and susceptible to the same international pressure."[50]

In addition, because of some special, mainly domestic considerations, Australia's southern African policies have needed to be presented to Third World nations in an especially consistent and credible manner. For example, the Fraser government openly disapproved of the up to 200 Australians who enlisted to fight on the side of the Smith government in Rhodesia. But although Australian legislation prohibits recruitment for mercenary service abroad, being a mercenary is not in itself an offense. The Fraser government also disapproved of the viewpoint disseminated by the Rhodesian Information Center in Sydney, but for both internal political and internal administrative reasons, it did not move to close it. Moreover, should the Rhodesian situation become desperate, Australia may find itself overwhelmed by entry applications from many thousands of Rhodesian refugees, mainly white. This in itself could cause strains within Australian society and arouse Third World suspicions that Australia was becoming the haven for supporters of a discredited, racist regime.[51]

The Fraser government's decision to contribute 250 engineering and 50 support troops to a UN supervisory and peace-keeping force in Namibia encapsulated many of the considerations aimed at cultivating Australia's image and influence among others. It should be understood that the decision involved a material, not just a rhetorical, Australian investment and that it had been under serious consideration in Canberra for over half a year. The idea met with extensive and trenchant opposition, within the Department of Defence and other official circles and among ministers and government back-benchers. Some of the objections dwelt on expense, on danger to the troops committed to the task, and on problems of becoming embroiled in an ugly, potentially long-term responsibility. One of the key objections was that Australia should concentrate its scarce military resources in its neighborhood, rather than dissipating them in a distant region of marginal security importance.[52]

The prime minister announced the peace-keeping commitment in February 1979,[53] and several aspects of his statement are of particular relevance to our analysis. He said that Australia's contribution had been solicited not just by the United Nations as such, but that representations had been made by the Commonwealth Secretariat, Britain, and the United States. In other words, Australia could be seen responding to Western and in particular to U.S. requirements and wishes. Fraser pointed out that Australian participation was acceptable both to the South African government and to SWAPO. In other words, Australia could be seen as having succeeded in projecting a responsible image for itself in southern African affairs. Fraser emphasized that the decision had been taken at a time of serious conflict in other, closer parts of the world, such as in Southeast Asia. But Australia could not dissociate itself from problems outside its region—it is part of the wider world. In other words, Australia recognized the importance of linkages as an animating factor in its own world affairs role. Fraser also said that Australia had to be prepared to participate if it expected others to behave constructively and cooperatively on behalf of stability and conflict management. By showing itself to be cooperative, Australia hoped to signal others, among them traditional friends and allies, that they should accept their share of responsibilities, presumably including in circumstances within regions of special concern to Australia.

Conclusion

A dominant concern of this chapter has been to determine, on the basis of reactions to Indian Ocean-related problems, whether Australia under the Fraser government has performed according to some set of reasonably ordered, operational principles. These are principles that would enable informed assessments of Australian interests to be made to serve as the groundwork for undertaking or withholding policy initiatives, and in the light of available sources of influence recommend particular styles of international comportment and particular policy instruments.

Australia has ascribed high priorities to an effective U.S. strategic presence in the Indian Ocean and to the application of ANZUS to Australia's western approaches. Australia has expended considerable diplomatic energy toward these objectives and has offered various inducements to the United States to support and carry out the objectives. The turmoil in Iran, although very worrisome to the Australian government, was less fundamental, or at least far less amenable to Australian influence. Australia understood the limits of its capacity to order events and to affect U.S. policy. Regarding the Gulf, the result was a relatively passive but by no means disinterested approach. As the matter was expressed by Alan Renouf, Australian ambassador to the United States, "While defence matters are of fundamental importance in our relationship, we are no longer in a position to emphasize them too much, for fear that the U.S. Government will say: 'You seem to be haunted by fear which is not warranted.'"[54]

Like the Gulf, southern Africa has been a secondary or derivative interest for Australia. The southern African context did, however, provide room for Australian policy maneuvering. Eventually, through its Namibian peace-keeping-force decision, there was occasion for a concrete and visible gesture. In southern Africa, Australia has been able to practice a form of enlightened self-interest. It did not strike out on its own, nor did it become a protagonist of extreme causes. But what it did do aligned it with popular and in fact ethically impeccable objectives and, at the same time, was believed by Australia to foster its self-defined interests. Moreover, what Australia did in southern Africa was generally in tandem with most Western and especially U.S. policies. This laid up credit for Australia in other spheres, such as input on Indian Ocean force limitation negotiations. Without incurring any significant diplomatic or economic costs, Australia was also able to extend its efforts to win friends and to influence people in the Third World, especially in its own neighborhood.

Questions of whether Australia's assumptions have been intrinsically valid or whether its policies are in the longer run likely to prove cost effective are important, but they have been excluded from this study. Our analysis of Indian Ocean issues under the Fraser government suggests both rationality and congruous policy outputs in the conduct of Australian diplomacy.

Notes

1. For representative syntheses of Australia's position and interests in the Indian Ocean, see Coral Bell, "The Indian Ocean: An Australian Evaluation," in Alvin J. Cottrell and R. M. Burrell, eds., *The Indian Ocean: Its Political, Economic, and Military Importance* (New York: Praeger, 1972); Robert O'Neill, "Australia and the Indian Ocean," in Patrick Wall, ed., *The Southern Oceans and the Security of the Free World: New Studies in Global Strategy* (London: Stacey International, 1977); and Kim C. Beazley and Ian Clark, *The Politics of Intrusion: The Super Powers in the Indian Ocean* (Sydney: Alternatives Publishing Cooperative, Ltd., 1979), esp. Chapter 9, "Australia, the Superpowers and the Indian Ocean." For an excellent nonacademic overview, see Parliament of Australia, *Australia and the Indian Ocean Region,* Report from the Senate Standing Committee on Foreign Affairs and Defence (Canberra: Government Printer, 1976), esp. Chapter 8, "Australia's Involvement with the Indian Ocean and the Region," and the companion volume *Official Hansard Transcript of Evidence,* passim.

2. Andrew Peacock, Minister for Foreign Affairs "News Release," no. M 55, September 13, 1976, p. 6. Also see Peacock, *Commonwealth Parliamentary Debates* (hereafter referred to as *CPD*), House of Representatives (hereafter referred to as HR), February 27, 1979, p. 361.

3. For a representative summary of these views, see Malcolm Fraser's

electorate talk, Office of the Prime Minister, "Press Release," July 16, 1978.

4. See Malcolm Fraser, *CPD,* HR, June 1, 1976, p. 2741; Fraser's UPI interview in *Canberra Times,* January 14, 1976; and J. D. Killen, minister for defence, press conference remarks reported by Brian Toohey in *Australian Financial Review,* July 1, 1976.

5. For the committee's conclusions and recommendations, see Australia, Parliament, *Australia and the Indian Ocean Region,* pp. 195-206. For Senator Sim's views, see his 1976 Australian Institute of International Affairs lecture, "The Soviet Naval Presence in the Indian Ocean," produced in article form in *Australian Outlook* 31 (April 1977). Also see his "Defence and the Indian Ocean," *Pacific Defence Reporter* (October 1978). For an analysis of Sim's 1976 remarks on the tone of government spokesmanship on the Indian Ocean, see Martin Indyk, "Influence Without Power: The Role of the Backbench in Australian Foreign Policy, 1976-1977," Australasian Political Studies Association Conference paper, Adelaide, August 1978, section on "Senator Sim and the Soviet Navy."

6. Consider the observation of the American ambassador to Australia, James Hargrove, that the United States and Australia did *not* "share exactly the same degree of uneasiness" about the Indian Ocean, but that he "understood" Australian concerns, since Australia faced on the Indian Ocean while the United States did not (see transcript of the interview with Alan Reid and Gerald Stone on "Face the Nation," July 4, 1976).

7. For a brief, reasoned statement of the government's assumptions about the importance of the Indian Ocean that reflects a lowering of earlier rhetoric, see J. D. Killen's report to parliament, *Australian Defence* (Canberra, November 1976), pp. 4-5. Also see the updated review and analysis by Gary Brown, *The Strategic Position in the Indian Ocean,* Basic Paper, Defence, Science, and Technology Group, Legislative Research Service (Canberra: Parliament of Australia, Department of the Parliamentary Library, March 14, 1978), esp. pp. 25-28.

8. Malcolm Fraser, *CPD,* HR, June 1, 1976, p. 2738. In a similar vein, see Fraser, ibid., May 9, 1978, p. 2027, and his White House dinner remarks in Office of the Prime Minister, "Press Release," July 27, 1976. Also see Andrew Peacock, *CPD,* HR, May 9, 1978, pp. 20-27.

9. See Andrew Peacock, "Defence and Diplomacy in the Indian Ocean," *Australian Foreign Affairs Review* 47 (November 1976) and *Australian Journal of Defence Studies* 1 (October 1977); Peacock, "Dr. Camilleri and Australian Foreign Policy," *Current Affairs Bulletin* 53 (March 1977):8.

10. See Stephen Barber, *Far Eastern Economic Review,* April 8, 1977; transcript of Malcolm Fraser's London press conference, May 31, 1977; and transcript of Fraser's Washington press conference, June 22, 1977.

11. Rear Adm. Robert J. Hanks, "The Indian Ocean Negotiations: Rocks and Shoals," *Strategic Review* 6 (Winter 1978):25.

12. Michael Richardson in *Age* (Melbourne), August 3, 1976.

13. For representative analyses of the security importance of such passages, see Michael MccGwire, "The Geopolitical Importance of Strategic Waterways in the Asia-Pacific Region," *Orbis* 19 (Fall 1975), and Robert E. Osgood, "US Security Interests in Ocean Law," *Survival* 17 (May/June 1976). For a summary from official Australian sources, see Parliament of Australia, Third United Nations Conference on the Law of the Sea, Seventh Session, Geneva, March 28–May 19, 1978, *Report of the Australian Delegation*, Parliamentary Paper no. 269/1978 (Canberra: Government Printer, 1978), esp. pp. 50–62.

14. See, for instance, the account of the December 1978 Mexico City conventional-arms limitation talks in *New York Times*, December 20, 1978.

15. For example, see the testimony of Leslie H. Gelb, director, Politico-Military Affairs, U.S. Department of State, October 3, 1978, before a panel of the House Armed Services Committee, in *Department of State Bulletin* 78 (December 1978):54–56. Also see transcripts of the October 10, 1978, testimony before the same panel by Brig. Gen. Irwin P. Graham (USAF), representing the Joint Chiefs of Staff, and by Brig. Gen. James M. Thompson (USA), representing the Department of Defense. For commentary, see John Edwards in *National Times*, October 21, 1978.

16. On the U.S. appreciation of ANZUS, see Henry S. Albinski, "American Perspectives on the ANZUS Alliance," *Australian Outlook* 32 (August 1978). Relatedly, see F. A. Mediansky, "United States Interests in Australia," *Australian Outlook* 30 (April 1976), and M. G. Smith, "The Australian-American Alliance: Some Possible Restrictions on US Response," *Defence Force Journal*, no. 3 (March/April 1977).

17. Security Treaty Between Australia, New Zealand, and the United States of America, Article V (*Australian Treaty Series*, 1952, no. 2).

18. Parliament of Australia, Senate, Standing Committee on Foreign Affairs and Defence, *Transcript of Evidence*, Annexure A, pp. 10 and 30, respectively. For an exegetical commentary on the coverage of ANZUS, see J. G. Starke, *The ANZUS Treaty Alliance* (Melbourne, 1965), passim. On recent aspects of the issue, see William T. Tow, "ANZUS: A Strategic Role in the Indian Ocean?" *World Today* 34 (October 1978).

19. ANZUS Council communiqué, in Department of Foreign Affairs "News Release," no. D9, July 28, 1977. The 1978 ANZUS Council communiqué also reflected this sentiment.

20. See John Hamilton in Melbourne *Herald*, June 9, 1978, and Mike Steketee in *Sydney Morning Herald*, June 10, 1978. Peacock disclosed the letter's contents during a June 1978 press conference following ANZUS

Council meetings in Washington.

21. See Malcolm Fraser, *CPD*, HR, May 9, 1978, p. 2028. The author disagrees with the previously published view that the U.S. decision to proceed with Sandgroper was "only remotely linked to immediate Australian/New Zealand security concerns," or that Killen was "disillusioned" that Mondale's announcement had somehow imparted a U.S. "tendency to project predominantly American rather than Australian security interests into ANZUS decision-making" (taken from Tow, "ANZUS: A Strategic Role," p. 404).

22. U.S. Congress, Senate, Committee on Foreign Relations, *The Southwest Pacific 1976, Report of a Special Delegation of Members*, 94th Congress, 2d sess., February 1976, p. 2.

23. For an inventory of the character, staffing, and costs of defense-related facilities in and outside Australia jointly operated by Australia and others, see J. D. Killen, *CPD*, HR, October 10, 1978, pp. 1658–1663.

24. *North West Cape: U.S. Naval Communication Station and the Support Township of Exmouth* (Canberra: Government Printer, 1968), p. 6.

25. For the agreement, see "Defence News Release," no. 71/78, May 17, 1978. For background, see Michael Richardson, *Far Eastern Economic Review*, May 19, 1978.

26. See Frank Cranston, *Canberra Times*, July 1, 1976.

27. Parliament of Australia, Senate, Standing Committee on Foreign Affairs and Defence, *Reference: The Role and Involvement of Australia and the United Nations in the Affairs of Sovereign Australian Territories, 1974–75* (Canberra: Government Printer, 1975), Record of Testimony, March 20, 1975, p. 359.

28. For a technical analysis of Diego Garcia's functions and capabilities, see Lenny Siegel, "Diego Garcia," *Pacific Research* 8 (March/April 1977).

29. On coastal surveillance problems, see (Parliamentary) Government Members Foreign Affairs and Defence Committee, *Report on Surveillance and Reaction*, May 1978.

30. For the order of battle of Australian forces, see *Defence Report 1978* (Canberra, 1978), Appendix 1.

31. On ANZUS member contributions to Sandgroper, see "Defence Press Release," no. 162/78, October 9, 1978.

32. Cited by Drew Middleton in *New York Times*, June 24, 1978.

33. See Andrew Peacock, *CPD*, HR, November 7, 1978, p. 2440; and February 27, 1979, pp. 361, 364; Peacock, statements cited in Minister for Foreign Affairs, "News Release," no. M 12, February 11, 1979, and no. M 14, February 16, 1979; and Malcolm Fraser, *CPD*, HR, February 22, 1979, p. 259.

34. Malcolm Fraser, *CPD*, HR, February 22, 1979, p. 259. For a survey

of Australian policies toward Middle East and Gulf problems, see Margaret E. McVey, "Australia's Middle East Foreign Policy," *World Review* 17 (August 1978).

35. On Australia's petroleum position, see the transcript of an address of January 24, 1979, by Kevin Newman, minister for national development, "Oil–Australasian Response to Dwindling Resources," and Newman's "Press Statement" of February 13, 1979. Also see commentary by Bob Mills in *National Times,* February 24, 1979.

36. See Scott Milson in *Sydney Morning Herald,* January 3, 1979.

37. On problems of Australian trade with Iran, see David Haselhurst in *Bulletin,* February 13, 1979.

38. J. D. Anthony, Minister for Trade and Resources, "Media Release," February 18, 1979.

39. Cited by Richard Burt in *New York Times,* January 12, 1979.

40. For an overview of Fraser government policies, see David Goldsworthy, "Australia's Southern African Policy," *World Review* 17 (June 1978). For the approach of the preceding Whitlam government, see Henry S. Albinski, *Australian External Policy Under Labor: Content, Process, and the National Debate* (St. Lucia: University of Queensland Press, 1977), esp. pp. 112–119.

41. For official assessments, see submissions to the Parliamentary Joint Committee on Foreign Affairs and Defence, Sub-Committee on Southern Africa, by Australia, Department of Foreign Affairs, *Aspects of Southern Africa and Namibia,* and submission, Australia, Department of Foreign Affairs, *Rhodesia*; and by Australia, Department of Defence, *Some Strategic Implications of the Situation in Southern Africa,* all presented in 1978.

42. In support of this conclusion, see the commentary of Brian Toohey, *Australian Financial Review,* June 13, 1978.

43. Andrew Peacock, CPD, HR, September 26, 1978, p. 1349.

44. For a systematic analysis emphasizing the South African aspects of Australia's southern African interests and policies, see F. R. Dalrymple, "Southern Africa," *World Review* 17 (June 1978).

45. Andrew Peacock, memorandum entitled "Notes on Southern African Issues," distributed to Liberal government parliamentarians, August 1977.

46. Andrew Peacock, address to the World Conference for Action Against Apartheid, Lagos, August 23, 1977.

47. Malcolm Fraser, interview in *U.S. News and World Report,* January 15, 1979.

48. See Australia, Parliament, Joint Committee on Foreign Affairs and Defence, Sub-Committee on Southern Africa, *Submission by the Depart-*

ment of Trade and Resources (1978).

49. For the government's North-South dialogue emphasis, see Andrew Peacock's foreign policy review before parliament (*CPD*, HR, May 9, 1978, pp. 2029-2043); his address "Australia and the International Economic Order," Minister for Foreign Affairs, "News Release," no. M 82, July 20, 1978; his Roy Milne Memorial Lecture, "Australia and the Third World," September 15, 1978, (Australia, Department of Foreign Affairs, *Backgrounder*, no. 156, September 20, 1978).

50. Australia, Department of Foreign Affairs submission, *Rhodesia*, p. 53. Also see press appraisals, based especially on Malcolm Fraser's 1977 performance at the Commonwealth heads of government meeting in London, by Michelle Grattan, *Age*, June 17, 1977, and Brian Toohey, *Australian Financial Review*, June 17, 1977.

51. See Australia, Parliament, Joint Committee on Foreign Affairs and Defence, Sub-Committee on Southern Africa, *Submission by the Minister for Immigration and Ethnic Affairs*, 1978; Stuart Simon in *National Times*, December 16, 1978, and *Age*, January 12, 1979.

52. A number of the pros and cons were examined by Andrew Peacock (see *CPD*, HR, August 23, 1978, pp. 618-621). For the critical Defence Department brief, see Laurie Oakes in *Age*, August 14, 1978. Also see commentaries by Chris Ashton, *Bulletin*, November 14, 1978, and January 30, 1979; and by Frank Cranston, *Canberra Times*, January 16, 1979.

53. See Malcolm Fraser, *CPD*, HR, February 20, 1979, pp. 20-21.

54. Alan Renouf, interview with Mike Steketee in *Sydney Morning Herald*, October 23, 1978.

5
African Conflict and Superpower Involvement in the Western Indian Ocean

Larry W. Bowman

Several events of the past decade have sharply focused competing strategic interests on the Indian Ocean and in the African littoral states of the western Indian Ocean. The most important of these are the altered character of the world political economy with respect to the supply and distribution of petroleum, the endemic unrest in the Horn of Africa and the persisting conflicts in the Ogaden Desert and Eritrea, and the steady escalation of African liberation movement pressure against the white-minority regimes of the southern part of the African continent. Each problem has grown substantially as a matter of international concern, both to the affected territories on or adjoining the Indian Ocean and to the superpowers whose interests and desires have increasingly drawn them toward the western Indian Ocean.

In this chapter I will focus on points of conjunction and intersection of developments in the Horn, in southern Africa, and on the sea-lanes of the western Indian Ocean. In doing so, I will assess the dynamics of regional rivalries and suggest how and why these regional developments have increasingly drawn the attention and involvement of the superpowers. Strategic competition in the triangle between the Cape, the Horn, and Diego Garcia will be my purview.

Anyone who undertakes to provide an overview of such a complex set of conflicts and rivalries must find a way of shaping the data. This task is not easy. The regional conflicts themselves are multifaceted, even without the further burden of superpower attentiveness. Nonetheless I will suggest three concerns that broadly shape the parameters of strategic rivalry in the western Indian Ocean.

The first of these is the competition for littoral influence—political, economic, strategic. The forces of nationalism, racism, and liberation threaten to overwhelm the regions of the Horn and southern Africa, and much of the violence would no doubt occur regardless of superpower involvement. But the fact that the regional actors are so sharply divided provides opportunities for access and influence that the superpowers—engaged in their larger global competition—find difficult to resist.

A second issue is that of the strategic stakes on the Indian Ocean itself. Here our concern is with the control of strategic points and with the larger issue of sea lines of communication across the Indian Ocean. These matters involve the interplay among naval strategies, land-based policies, the quest for bases (or "facilities"), and general questions of armaments on and under the Indian Ocean.

Finally there is the broader question of how littoral influence and on-the-sea competition in the western Indian Ocean will be perceived and understood internationally. It could be argued, for instance, that the rivalries there could and would be muted if they were not cast in the larger framework of the global superpower competition. The fact is, however, that both the superpowers and the other actors often see the issues in the context of the global rivalries. Because they do, both superpowers often find themselves drawn into the conundrum of countering one another, if only not to appear weak. This fact does not necessarily lead to wise policy, but it is a matter of considerable importance—particularly in the context of U.S. domestic policy. This question of the perception of political-military trends in the Indian Ocean region must be seen as a fundamental underpinning of strategic rivalries in that area of the world, so obviously distant from the heartland of either of the superpowers.

The Competition for Littoral Influence

In the western Indian Ocean, the focus of strategic rivalry in recent years has been the Horn and southern Africa. In each region local rivalries have provided the base upon which the superpower competition has been pyramided. In the Horn, a long period of Western domination has been eroded by the Ethiopian revolution and the postindependence turmoil of Somalian politics. Still, the picture is not one-sided. Ethiopia has not closed off all ties to the West, Somalia is increasingly being courted by the United States, and the French retain a substantial presence in Djibouti.[1]

In southern Africa, Western interests have been shaken by the success of liberation movements in Angola, Mozambique, and Zimbabwe. These new regimes have understandable sympathies toward the Soviet Union and China who did much to assist their struggles. Yet at the same time Western-oriented multinationals continue to play a prominent role in economic life throughout the region. The pressure for future change in Namibia and South Africa will provide the ultimate test of the West's ability to alter past commitments to minority rule so as to support Africa's demand for majority rule and freedom.[2] How that test is met will likely shape the long-term orientation of the entire southern Africa region.

In both regions the superpowers jockey for preferred positions. For the United States this means either support for old allies and/or clients or the gradual shifting of allegiance to the new social groups and classes that are emerging—a shift complicated by clashing domestic perceptions. For the Soviet Union, the striving for preferred positions has meant the casting of its lot with the Ethiopian revolutionaries and with the various liberation movements of southern Africa. In each case, the Soviet Union and the United States seek through treaties, arms supplies and sales, diplomatic support and protection, economic investment and trade, and more clandestine means of involvement to shape the direction of change in the littoral countries of the western Indian Ocean. Some specific dimensions of this situation require further analysis.

From the Horn to southern Africa, the stakes for the superpowers are substantial.[3] Prestige accrues through the development of close political ties, and moreover, there are strategic and economic considerations of great importance. The Horn has a considerable geopolitical importance in the context of the politics of the Middle East and the Persian Gulf. Any actor dominating one side of the Red Sea would have the potential to exercise influence over the usage of the Suez Canal, which is part of the larger issue of entrance to and egress from the northwest Indian Ocean. Also in the context of oceanic shipping, some observers argue that control of the southern tip of the African continent (the Cape route) is another point of geopolitical importance, because much of the oil shipped to Western Europe and America goes around the Cape.[4]

There is an obvious linkage between control of those areas and the broader perception of who has regional influence. As Western domination has been loosened in the past decade, many Western nations—the United States in particular—have reacted with some alarm. Military planners and conservative groups decry the loss of influence and fear the future loss of access to strategic minerals and resources.[5] The latter is of special concern to those people who wish to assure continued Western access to southern Africa, although views differ widely on how that access can be assured.

It is crucial to note, however, that regional conflicts are not entirely amenable to superpower manipulation. Long-standing local rivalries would no doubt go on, irrespective of superpower concern. Developments in the Horn area since the fall of Haile Selassie illustrate some of the difficulties that the superpowers have in manipulating the situation. The fall of Selassie was seen as a loss to the United States, which had propped up his feudal regime. Yet it was by no means obvious in the immediate aftermath of the Ethiopian revolution just what ideological direction Ethiopia would take.

At the time of the revolution, the Soviet Union had far closer ties with neighboring Somalia.[6] For the Soviet Union, however, the Ethiopian revolution was seen as progressive, and the Kremlin sought to develop good relations with Ethiopia as well. Indeed it is likely that for a time in late 1976 and early 1977 the Soviet Union hoped to forge a federation of Marxist states in the Horn and its environs.[7] Instead, the Somalian government attempted to take advantage of Ethiopian instability by launching their July 1977 invasion of the Ogaden in a classic example of nationalist irredentism.

Unlike the United States, the Soviet Union was able to turn this unexpected series of regional events to its apparent advantage.[8] From the end of 1976, the Soviet Union was making extensive security commitments to the Ethiopian government, although Soviet ties to the Somalian government would not be severed until November 1977. Thereafter the Soviet (and Cuban) commitment to Ethiopia was greatly augmented and eventually led to a twenty-year friendship treaty between the Soviet Union and the government of Haile Mariam Mengistu. This switch in regional allies, however, was not without its costs. The Soviet Union lost its access to the naval facility at Berbera in Somalia—a port more developed and geographically desirable than anything Ethiopia can offer. In supporting Ethiopia, however, the Soviet Union was on the "right" side in the Ogaden War and successfully prevented the United States from having any positive regional role.[9]

The United States has had a difficult time compensating for its loss of privileges in Ethiopia. Somalia's invasion of Ethiopia made an alliance with Somalia difficult, even as the U.S. identification with the old regime in Ethiopia made close ties with the new government in Addis Ababa problematic. Even in early 1980 as the United States sought to augment its military ties in the Horn, fears about how Somalia would use any military assistance complicated joint U.S.-Somalian negotiations.[10]

In the context of western Indian Ocean politics, the United States has compensated for the loss of privileges in Ethiopia primarily by improving its relations with Kenya. A modest military sales program for F-5 jet aircraft, helicopters, and other equipment has begun, and further sales are certainly likely because of the Iranian and Afghanistan crises.[11] More generally, U.S. concern about the Horn has led to increased naval activity throughout the western Indian Ocean and the rapid upgrading of the Diego Garcia base, which will be more fully discussed in the next section.

In southern Africa, Western involvements are long-standing and complex, and they embrace social, economic, racial, and political ties. As in the Horn, the convulsive political developments of the 1970s have upset many of the old patterns and have led to the emergence of the Soviet Union (and others) as contenders for regional influence. For many people this is a matter of grave concern, whether they merely regret the passing of the old settler/colonial order or are more seriously concerned with long-term trends in the political and economic orientations of southern African states.

Speaking generally, the problems for the United States and other Western countries in southern Africa rest on their long-standing ties to white-minority regimes. In the context of the western Indian Ocean, ties to the South African government are the most crucial, but it is not easy to disentangle these concerns from the ongoing problems of neighboring states.

The military coup in Portugal in 1974 was the first major breakthrough for the African people against the power of white domination in southern Africa. Mozambique on the Indian Ocean (and Angola) both eventually signed friendship treaties with the Soviet Union, though each clearly sought to limit the degree of Soviet penetration. The Soviet Union has made further diplomatic gains in southern Africa through its constant support of the now-successful liberation movement in Zimbabwe, and it has emerged also as a major arms supplier to neighboring Zambia.[12] None of these developments, of course, precludes the possibility of friendly diplomatic and commercial relations among the United States, its Western allies, and the newly freed African states. But our general indifference to their previous situation is not easily forgotten.

The ultimate problem in southern Africa is, of course, the Republic of South Africa. This rich and troubled country finds itself under a wide variety of internal and external pressures directed toward its apartheid practices. The white elite is generally very hostile to these pressures, and its members rightly point out how long most Western governments have been closely linked with South Africa. Since President Carter and former UN Ambassador Andrew Young endeavored to shift the focus of U.S. policy somewhat, they have come under increasing attack from the South African government and from "cold warriors" at home.[13]

South Africa remains a difficult problem for the United States. The Botha government is intractable in its resistance to any substantive devolution of political influence to nonwhites. But the country's many minerals are exported to and needed by the major industrial powers.[14] Regionally, if not continentally, South Africa is the dominant military power. The republic may even have detonated a nuclear bomb in a mysterious and as yet not fully explained "flash" above Indian Ocean–South Atlantic waters in September 1979.[15] South Africa also holds the key to the possibility of a peaceful transfer of power in Namibia.

Unlike the Horn, where the U.S. presence in Ethiopia was (with the French in Djibouti) the major external influence until 1974, the situation in South Africa is crowded with other actors—Britain, France, West Germany, and Japan—all of whom have a stake in the direction of any change. South Africa and its friends abroad cleverly argue for the strategic importance of South Africa in world strategy.[16] What is fuzzy in all this is just why an acceptance of apartheid can alone guarantee friendly Western relations with South Africa and the maintenance of "stability" in the region. One could argue quite the contrary point, that it is Western complicity with apartheid that is most likely to fuel the racial antagonisms in South Africa and set the stage for violent change. A policy of economic disengagement and far more intense political pressure might well be much more conducive to Western interests in the long run.[17]

In both the Horn and southern Africa, the superpowers compete with each other and with others for access and influence. The Soviet Union, and China and Cuba, have certain advantages in that they are not tainted by a history of African colonialism. Western advantages attributable to the colonial past are being eroded by an inability to cope with the dynamics of nationalism and liberation felt by the African peoples in both regions. There is little reason to expect that this drive for freedom will diminish. As long as Western countries are unwilling or unable to separate their economic interests from their political ties, they will be compromised in the eyes of Africans. Unless this situation can be rectified, I would expect developments in the littoral states of the western Indian Ocean to run counter to Western policy, regardless of what is done on the ocean itself.

Naval Competition and Littoral Influence

Concern with littoral influence is in part related to the ability that each superpower has to operate effectively on and around the Indian Ocean. Traditionally for both superpowers, the Indian Ocean has been an ocean remote from most of their strategic attention. Since the late 1960s, however, developments in the littoral states and concern about each other's intentions in the Indian Ocean have led to increased naval activity there.

There is a remarkable similarity in what the superpowers desire. Both want open sea lines of communication and opportunities to show the flag, and each hopes to exercise some coastal influence. Each seeks to prevent the other superpower from getting privileged access to key chokepoints or other strategic terrain. In the past there has been little evidence to suggest that either superpower seriously contemplated stationing sufficient forces in the region so that military power could be asserted over any sustained period of time. This orientation may be changing, however, in the aftermath of President Carter's January 1980 assertion, in his State of the Union address, that the United States would use any means, including military force, to repel an attack in the Persian Gulf area.[18]

At the end of the 1960s, the Soviet Union introduced a squadron of ships into the Indian Ocean, which soon numbered about twenty—a number that has remained stabilized since that time.[19] In 1968–69, the Soviet Union made twenty-nine diplomatic port visits in the Indian Ocean region, but that number fell off to two in 1975 and four in 1976.[20] The same pattern was true for the number of Soviet operational ship visits, which grew gradually through the early 1970s and then tailed off in 1975–76.[21] The Indian Ocean is important to the Soviet Union because it provides a sea route to the Far Eastern portion of the country, and such a capability could be important in the context of a Sino-Soviet conflict. The Soviet Union obviously also seeks to monitor Western shipping in and out of the Red Sea and the Persian Gulf. Since the loss of Berbera, however, the Soviet Union has no base in the western Indian Ocean that provides the services now available to the United States at Diego Garcia; the Soviet Union does, however, have some access to facilities in Ethiopia and at Aden in the People's Democratic Republic of Yemen (P.D.R.Y.).

The U.S. response to western Indian Ocean developments has grown in light of littoral developments, the Soviet Union's presence, and increased fears about the safety of sea passage in and out of the Persian Gulf oil fields.[22] Given the high level of the Western world's dependence on Gulf oil, sea-lane security serves as a powerful rationale for the expansion of U.S. naval activities, and the United States did increase its naval activity in the western Indian Ocean in 1978–79. Task forces are regularly sent to the Indian Ocean, occasionally including a nuclear powered carrier.

Perhaps the most important development of the past decade in the Indian Ocean has been the construction of the U.S. base at Diego Garcia. From its initial, modest beginnings as a communications station, Diego Garcia has been steadily upgraded to the point where it is now a permanent multipurpose base.[23] The mission claimed for Diego Garcia is substantial. It is supposed to be able to supply a carrier task force in the region for thirty days without additional backup. A deep-water lagoon has been dredged that can accommodate twelve ships, including nuclear aircraft carriers. Diego Garcia provides a base for P-3 Orion ASW patrol planes, and it has become a major center for carrying out reconnaissance flights over the Persian Gulf, the Red Sea, and East Africa. This air surveillance provides support for U.S. ships operating in the Indian Ocean and monitors Soviet activity as well. Diego Garcia is also a central link in the U.S. worldwide defense satellite communication system. Given the range of activities now being carried out on Diego Garcia, there can be little doubt that it was meant as a signal to the Soviet Union and other powers that the United States intends to remain active in the Indian Ocean.

Shortly after the Carter administration took over in 1977, the Soviet Union reiterated long-standing proposals of its own that the two countries join in negotiations on the demilitarization of the Indian Ocean. The Carter administration quickly responded and for a moment surprised nearly everyone by proposing complete demilitarization of the ocean. This drastic proposal was soon shelved, but both sides seemed interested in limiting their competition, and negotiations were held periodically in 1977 and 1978.[24]

The negotiations focused on stabilizing naval activity. The United States proposed stabilization at current levels rather than engaging in complex negotiations concerning levels of armament, tonnages, and personnel or types of planes or missiles aboard ships. Toward the end of 1977 there was hope that some formulation might be found that would limit the size of fleets and forbid the construction of new bases. Though vague, it was thought that there was enough desire on both sides to guarantee progress.

Developments in the Horn, however, directly led to the breakdown of the negotiations. The events of late 1977 caused the Soviet Union to lose its access to Berbera in Somalia. At the same time, the massive Soviet airlift of supplies to Ethiopia was seen in Washington as an unwarranted expansion of Soviet power that threatened to upset the balance in the western Indian Ocean. The United States was further concerned that the Soviet presence in Ethiopia could pose a serious threat to the security of the oil supply lines out of the Red Sea and the Persian Gulf.

Thus as a consequence of the turmoil in the Horn, both of the superpowers found their interest in an Indian Ocean pact waning. For the United States there was a renewed concern about any limitations on ship deployment in the Indian Ocean. The Soviet airlift had given conservative and military opponents of any Indian Ocean agreement additional ammunition in the context of U.S. infighting over its strategic posture. Any proposals that would limit the potential fleet size or structure were now suspect. Moreover, the Carter administration felt it necessary to downgrade the talks as an indication of U.S. displeasure over the Soviet Union's Ethiopian policy.

For the Soviet Union as well, the events of 1977–78 cast the negotiations into a different light. One key element of the talks had been the idea of freezing deployments at current levels. But after the loss of Berbera, the Soviet Union was no longer interested in a "freeze" that guaranteed the United States continued operational capabilities because of Diego Garcia when the Soviet Union had no comparable base for itself. Thus for both domestic and regional reasons, the impetus for arms limitations in the Indian Ocean slipped away; neither side was any longer interested in a bilateral arms limitation agreement. The "talks" have been moribund since early 1978.

What must be finally considered is the manner in which sea-related issues (such as open sea-lanes and the ability to show the flag) become linked to littoral political issues (such as political, economic, and strategic access to key areas). In the United States, for instance, an alleged threat to sea-lanes is often used as the rationale to justify political ties that might otherwise be difficult to defend. Certainly concern with the Cape route has had a bearing on Western ties to South Africa and the Simonstown/Silvermine facilities at the Cape. Similar arguments are now being used in the United States to justify new military arrangements with Somalia and other countries.

It seems useful to point out, however, that there is actually considerably more accord between the superpowers on sea-related behavior than there is on land-based issues. If either superpower interfered with shipping anywhere in the western Indian Ocean, there could be little doubt that a major global crisis would ensue.

Although naval strategists sometimes argue that conventional naval warfare in a region is possible, they act that way primarily for domestic, political reasons. In this respect the bureaucratic infighting faced by a Sergei Gorshkov probably differs very little from that faced by an Elmo Zumwalt.[25] In reality, it is difficult to imagine that a crisis triggered in the western Indian Ocean could actually be contained there. The region is far from where the superpowers could effectively counter one another, and in all likelihood, any conflict there would quickly escalate to another theater.

It thus seems important to clearly separate ideological and political conflicts on land from the more international issues related to the sea. There really is more superpower competition with respect to the former. But how both kinds of issues are related is in the realm of attitude and perception, and it is to this dimension of competition in the western Indian Ocean that we must finally turn.

Perception and Reality in the Western Indian Ocean

In our consideration of the competition for littoral influence and of the striving for security on the Indian Ocean, it is obvious that each superpower is concerned with the actions of the other. Although the intensity of the competition does not match that undertaken in other strategic areas, it is apparent that both superpowers feel they have an important stake in western Indian Ocean matters.

It is necessary to recognize, therefore, that each superpower views western Indian Ocean developments in both a regional and a global setting. As issues such as access to raw materials, safe sea passage for petroleum, and control of strategic terrain grow in importance, it is inevitable that each superpower will follow more closely and be involved more deeply in regional developments. As an obvious corollary, the deeper the superpower commitment, the more certain it becomes that the issue will assume international strategic importance.

For the Soviet Union, the western Indian Ocean is but one of several areas in which it is newly making its presence felt. The political realities of the area make it a region of considerable opportunity, despite the fact that it is some distance from the traditional spheres of Soviet influence. Through its activities in the western Indian Ocean, the Soviet Union appears to have gained considerable prestige. The USSR was instrumental in helping Ethiopia regain the Ogaden, and Soviet support has been crucial to liberation movements in southern Africa. The Soviet Union will certainly wish to sustain close relations with its new friends in Africa, particularly because there is little doubt that the future of the Horn, southern Africa, and adjoining regions such as the Gulf area will be marked by instability. The Soviet Union's naval capability and its new relationship with local governments together guarantee that the Soviet Union will have a voice in whatever unfolds. From the Cape to Cairo there is concern about the Soviet presence.

Leaders in the United States have a great deal of difficulty deciding how to evaluate and counter Soviet activity in an area like the western Indian Ocean. There is constant tension in U.S. policy circles between those who see all Soviet activity through the mirror of East-West competition and those who evaluate it with a greater sensitivity to the regional settings in which the Soviet-U.S. competition is acted out.

During the first year of the Carter administration, there was a substantial effort to insulate African questions from the dynamics of East-West relations. Led by UN Ambassador Andrew Young, the new administration sought to focus U.S. attention on African questions in their own right and not simply as an adjunct of global rivalries. Within a year, however, this effort was beginning to fail. Developments on the African continent, especially as they came to be perceived in the context of U.S. domestic politics, made it increasingly impossible for the administration to seal Africa off from superpower competition. The impact of Soviet and Cuban assistance to Ethiopia, the intractability of southern African issues, and the political vulnerability of the Carter administration in the wake of events such as the revolutions in Afghanistan and Iran, troubles in Zaire, etc., made it seem politically imperative for the United States to react.

By the end of 1978 National Security Adviser Zbigniew Brzezinski was following the line of a predecessor, Henry Kissinger, and calling the western Indian Ocean region an "area of crisis" and an "arc of instability" where U.S. geopolitical interests were being eroded by a combination of expanding Soviet power and the disintegration of the social-political fabric of some of the traditional allies of the United States. In his most sustained exposition of this thesis, Brzezinski responded to the question, "What are the principal threats to the United States in the future?" as follows.

> Beyond Soviet power, I would say regional conflict, the fragmentation of wobbly social and political structures in societies incapable of absorbing the political awakening of so many more people. . . . And the worst problem of all is the possibility that these two trends would intersect. The increase in Soviet power and the disintegration of political fabric in some regions of the world that are of importance to us. And here I come back to the arc of instability—Persian Gulf, Iran all the way down to southern Africa.[26]

Subsequent events in 1979 and the beginning of 1980 have led to an intensification of superpower rivalry throughout the western Indian Ocean. This can be seen in the collapse of the Indian Ocean demilitarization talks, in the continual upgrading of Diego Garcia, and in the heavy U.S. supply of military equipment to Yemen in early 1979. For its part, the Soviet Union has broadened its naval and air activities throughout the region; a great deal of Soviet activity emanates from Aden in South Yemen (P.D.R.Y.). The Iranian hostage situation and the Soviet invasion of Afghanistan have simply provided further impetus to trends that were already quite apparent.

The reality is that despite their mutual desire for nuclear stability, SALT II, détente, and other key components of their bilateral relations, the Soviet Union and the United States compete almost everywhere else for economic and strategic advantage. They must often show "strength," both to keep themselves in the game and to placate domestic constituencies that favor a hard-line stance toward the other superpower. Yet in the context of the western Indian Ocean and elsewhere, the dynamics of the superpower rivalry may serve to transform local and regional conflicts into something much larger.

That possibility has grave implications for both of the superpowers and for the regional actors. Either for groups who wish to change regional realities or for elites who wish to preserve their privileged positions, access to superpower support can be very tempting. This is true on both sides of the racial confrontation in southern Africa; it is no less evident in the Ethiopia of Selassie or Mengistu. The problem lies both in the way in which superpower support is used and in the way it is viewed. It is difficult for the United States to acknowledge that Soviet assistance might be both sought and welcomed; politically it is impossible to admit that something good might come of it. One can imagine that the Soviet elite views U.S. access and assistance with much the same skepticism.

In the western Indian Ocean, the United States has partly painted itself into a corner. The United States certainly recognizes that an end to feudalism, underdevelopment, and racism is in the interest of the people of the region, and in the interest of the United States as well. But U.S. concern about procedures, its distaste for the violence of others, and its obsessions about Soviet assistance to the forces of change often lead the United States to support the status quo. In so doing, the United States runs the risk of transforming necessary regional changes into unnecessary superpower confrontations. The competition may be tougher, and the United States will have to adjust to the fact that another superpower can project a global presence, but these factors do not mean that the United States should oppose changes in the Horn and in southern Africa. Without a careful reading of regional realities, there is only the prospect of escalating western Indian Ocean issues into global ones. That is something both superpowers should seek to avoid.

Notes

1. There is obviously a vast literature on these diverse subjects. Among the most valuable are Tom J. Farer, *War Clouds on the Horn of Africa: The Widening Storm*, 2nd ed. rev. (New York and Washington, D.C.: Carnegie Endowment for International Peace, 1979); Gérard Chaliand, "The Horn of Africa's Dilemma," *Foreign Policy* 30 (Spring 1978):116–131; Steven David, "Realignment in the Horn: the Soviet Advantage," *International Security* 4, no. 2 (Fall 1979):69–90; and Fred Halliday, "U.S. Policy in the Horn of Africa: *Aboulia* or Proxy Intervention?" *Review of African Political Economy* 10 (September-December 1978):8–32. A special word of praise should also go to the new journal *Horn of Africa* for its commendable efforts to cover this distant region.

2. Again among much literature, see Kenneth Adelman and Gerald J. Bender, "Conflict in Southern Africa: A Debate," *International Security* 3, no. 2 (Fall 1978):67–122; Clyde Ferguson and William R. Cotter, "South

Africa—What Is to Be Done," *Foreign Affairs* 56, no. 2 (January 1978):253–274; John A. Marcum, "Lessons of Angola," *Foreign Affairs* 54, no. 3 (April 1976):407–425; and Michael Samuels et al., *Implications of Soviet and Cuban Activities in Africa for U.S. Policy* (Washington, D.C.: Georgetown University Center for Strategic and International Studies, 1979).

3. See Nimrod Novik, *On the Shores of Bab Al-Mandab: Soviet Diplomacy and Regional Dynamics* (Philadelphia: Foreign Policy Research Institute, 1979); Albert L. Weeks, "Soviet Geopolitical Momentum," *Horn of Africa* 2, no. 1 (January-March 1979):42–53; Gen. George S. Brown, "Current JCS Theater Appraisals: The Strategic Importance of 7 Vital International Areas," *Commanders Digest* 20 (March 17, 1977); Geoffrey Kemp, "The New Strategic Map," *Survival* 19, no. 2 (March-April 1977):50–59; "Russia and Africa: The Mineral Connection," *Economist* 264 (July 9, 1977):82–83; and *War in the Horn of Africa: A Firsthand Report on the Challenges for U.S. Policy*, Committee on International Relations, House of Representatives (Washington, D.C.: Government Printing Office, 1978).

4. For two stark presentations of this view see Patrick Wall, ed., *The Southern Oceans and the Security of the Free World* (London: Stacey International, 1977), and W.C.J. Van Rensburg, "Africa and Western Lifelines," *Strategic Review* 6, no. 2 (Spring 1978):41–50. For a broader perspective on this issue see Larry W. Bowman, "Southern Africa and the Indian Ocean," in Alvin J. Cottrell and R. M. Burrell, eds., *The Indian Ocean: Its Political, Economic, and Military Importance* (New York: Praeger, 1972), pp. 293–306; and Bowman, "Comment" on "U.S. Policy and Southern Africa," by George Houser in Frederick S. Arkhurst, ed., *U.S. Policy Toward Africa* (New York: Praeger, 1975), pp. 141–152. Also see Geoffrey Kemp, "U.S. Strategic Interests and Military Options in Sub-Saharan Africa," in Jennifer Seymour Whitaker, ed., *Africa and the United States: Vital Interests* (New York: New York University Press, 1978), pp. 120–152.

5. See George Ball, "Asking for Trouble in South Africa," *Atlantic Monthly* (October 1977):43–51, and *U.S. Corporate Interests in South Africa*, Report to the Committee on Foreign Relations, U.S. Senate (Washington, D.C.: Government Printing Office, 1978). A fine review of the resource issue is Gordon Bertolin, "U.S. Economic Interests in Africa: Investment, Trade, and Raw Materials," in Whitaker, ed., *Africa and the United States: Vital Interests*, pp. 21–59.

6. J. Bowyer Bell, "Strategic Implications of the Soviet Presence in Somalia," *Orbis* 19, no. 2 (Summer 1975):402–411.

7. Colin Legum and Bill Lee, *Conflict in the Horn of Africa* (New York:

Africana Publishing Company, 1977), p. 13, and Dimitri K. Simes, "Imperial Globalism in the Making: Soviet Involvement in the Horn of Africa," *Washington Review,* special supplement on the Horn of Africa (May 1978):33.

8. Farer, *War Clouds on the Horn of Africa,* pp. 131-142.

9. U.S. dilemmas in the Horn are well surveyed by Raymond L. Thurston, U.S. ambassador in Somalia from 1965-68, in his article "The United States, Somalia, and the Crisis in the Horn," *Horn of Africa* 1, no. 2 (April-June 1978):11-20.

10. Drew Middleton, "U.S. Sending Experts to Seek Persian Gulf Military Sites," *New York Times,* January 11, 1980, and Richard Halloran, "U.S. Looking to Leasing of Bases for Easier Access to Crisis Areas," *New York Times,* January 20, 1980.

11. "U.S. Can Use Kenya's Ports to Get Forces to Persian Gulf," *Washington Post,* February 22, 1980.

12. See Daniel I. Fine, "The Soviets' New Foothold in Central Africa," *Business Week,* March 10, 1980, and John Borrell, "Zambia's Surprising Soviet Arms Deal," *Christian Science Monitor,* February 5, 1980.

13. The diplomatic spy imbroglio of April 1979 is a case in point (see John F. Burns, "South Africa Ousts 3 U.S. Embassy Aides, Charging Air Spying," *New York Times,* April 13, 1979).

14. See Philip L. Christenson, "Some Economic Facts of Life," in Helen Kitchen, ed., "Options for U.S. Policy Toward Africa," *AEI Foreign Policy and Defense Review* 1, no. 1 (1979):38-41, and "Anglo American's Golden Windfall," *Business Week,* March 17, 1980, pp. 134-138, 140.

15. See Thomas O'Toole, "'A-Blast' Was No Lightning Bolt, Panel Decides," *Washington Post,* January 1, 1980; Thomas O'Toole and Milton Benjamin, "Officials Hotly Debate Whether African Event Was Atom Blast," *Washington Post,* January 17, 1980; and Thomas O'Toole, "New Light Cast on Sky-Flash Mystery," *Washington Post,* January 30, 1980.

16. See Carel Birkby, "Cape Sea Route," *Africa Institute Bulletin* 16, no. 2 (1978): 49-53, and Robert Poos, "South Africa: Profile on Defense Policies and Armed Forces," *Armed Forces Journal International* 110 (June 1973):21-35.

17. This position is strongly argued in Randall Robinson, "TransAfrica's Vision," in Kitchen, ed., "Options for U.S. Policy Toward Africa," pp. 20-22.

18. Drew Middleton, "The President Draws the Line: In Persian Gulf," *New York Times,* January 25, 1980.

19. There is a vast literature on the Soviet navy. The classic early statement is Geoffrey Jukes, *The Indian Ocean in Soviet Naval Policy* (London:

International Institute for Strategic Studies, 1972). An invaluable current volume is Bradford Dismukes and James McConnell, eds., *Soviet Naval Diplomacy* (New York: Pergamon, 1979).

20. Charles C. Petersen, "Showing the Flag," in Dismukes and McConnell, eds., *Soviet Naval Diplomacy*, p. 92.

21. Charles C. Petersen, "Trends in Soviet Naval Operations," in Dismukes and McConnell, eds., *Soviet Naval Diplomacy*, pp. 68–69.

22. Among much literature on U.S. naval strategy see Paul H. Nitze et al., *Securing the Seas: The Soviet Naval Challenge and Western Alliance Options* (Boulder, Colo.: Westview Press, 1979), and Capt. John E. Lacouture, "Seapower in the Indian Ocean: A Requirement for Western Security," *U.S. Naval Institute Proceedings* 105 (August 1979):30–41.

23. A solid review of the early buildup of Diego Garcia is provided in Rex Wingerter, "The United States, the Soviet Union, and the Indian Ocean: The Competition for the Third World," *Bulletin of Concerned Asian Scholars* 9, no. 3 (July-September 1977):52–64. There was considerable congressional opposition to the development of Diego Garcia in the early 1970s. This opposition is revealed in several sets of congressional hearings, especially U.S., Congress, House, Committee on International Relations, *Diego Garcia, 1975: The Debate over the Base and the Island's Former Inhabitants* (94th Congress, 1st Session, 1975).

24. For a skeptical view of the entire idea see Rear Adm. Robert J. Hanks. "The Indian Ocean Negotiations: Rocks and Shoals," *Strategic Review* 6, no. 1 (Winter 1978):18–27.

25. See S. G. Gorshkov, "The Sea Power of the State," *Survival* 19, no. 1 (January-February 1977):24–29, and Elmo R. Zumwalt, Jr., *On Watch* (New York: Quadrangle, 1976). A solid analysis of Gorshkov's work is E. T. Wooldridge, Jr., "The Gorshkov Papers: Soviet Naval Doctrine for the Nuclear Age," *Orbis* 18, no. 4 (Winter 1975):1153–1175.

26. "James Reston Interviews the President's National Security Adviser, Zbigniew Brzezinski," *New York Times Magazine*, December 31, 1978.

Part 2

External Powers in the Indian Ocean

6
The October War, the 1973–1974 Arab Oil Embargo, and U.S. Policy on the Indian Ocean

Kim C. Beazley

The intrusion into the Indian Ocean of small contingents of the navies of the Soviet Union and the United States over the last decade has produced the superficial comment among analysts of Indian Ocean affairs that there is a symbiotic relationship between the two naval presences. The notion that one superpower reacts to the other is attractive in its simplicity. Given the significance of their global competition, it is inevitable that each superpower's rationale for its presence in the Indian Ocean includes an element of response to the other's actions, real or anticipated.

A detailed examination of the Indian Ocean policy of each superpower, however, suggests that policy development has been more complicated than the simple action/reaction thesis would suggest. Since both the Soviet Union and the United States have sought to define their interests in the region, bilateral relations with the littoral states have involved issues and concerns that are only indirectly related to superpower competition.

No better illustration of this point can be found than through an examination of the Indian Ocean policy of the United States prior to, during, and immediately after the October 1973 Middle East War and the accompanying Arab oil embargo. During the crisis, the threat to U.S. interests in the Indian Ocean was posed not by the Soviet Union but by the policies of the local states, some of whom were fiercely anti-Soviet in their foreign outlook. The rationale for upgrading U.S. military facilities in the Indian Ocean rested substantially on their value to U.S. diplomatic initiatives to overcome the problems.

The argument about the need to deny the Soviet Union any political advantage that might accrue from a monopoly of the naval presence in the area was not insignificant. It was, however, secondary to a concern that it is necessary to be able to influence the West's principal oil suppliers.

In analyses of U.S. Indian Ocean policy, too much attention has been focused on what is a rather small military presence. It is not intended here to examine in detail the development of U.S. facilities and the deployment of warships, since such information can be readily found elsewhere.[1] It is intended to look more broadly at U.S. diplomacy in the Indian Ocean area and, where necessary, relate it to more-global U.S. policy preoccupations. It is maintained that a more accurate picture of the significance of military activity can thus be obtained.

Evolution of U.S. Indian Ocean Policy 1968-73

From the time of the announcement in 1968 by the British government of its intention to withdraw from the Indian Ocean region, U.S. policy has been characterized by hesitant attempts to define, in an unfamiliar area, the nature and significance of U.S. interests and the appropriate means of defending them. Several local events and trends in U.S. policy have been important, and they may be enumerated as follows: the implications of the Nixon doctrine for U.S. involvement in areas of lesser importance such as the Indian Ocean; concern about the prospect of a world energy crisis; the Indo-Pakistani war in 1971 and its aftermath; and increasing U.S. interest in the Middle East. By 1973 the northwest littoral of the Indian Ocean was firmly established as the focal point of U.S. interest.

The Nixon Doctrine

Several aspects of the Nixon doctrine outlined in Pres. Richard Nixon's speech at Guam in 1969, and elaborated later, were significant in the development of U.S. Indian Ocean policy. In rejecting the strategy of "containing" Soviet and Chinese expansion and influence, Nixon announced that in the future the United States would "balance" the influence of the Communist powers. In Southeast Asia and the eastern littoral of the Indian Ocean, U.S. influence had been much greater than that of the Soviet Union or China. Even with the withdrawal of U.S. ground forces from Indochina, the United States retained substantial forces in Southeast Asia for some time after the doctrine's enunciation. "Balance" was, accordingly, consistent with the retreat of U.S. power.

The situation on the western littoral of the Indian Ocean and on the Indian subcontinent was more complicated. The United States neglected the area while it was preoccupied with Vietnam. Presidents John Kennedy and Lyndon Johnson had offered no objection to the Soviet Union's increasing influence on the Indian subcontinent and its closer ties with Iran. If U.S. policy reflected the view that an increase in Soviet influence in an area of little importance did not automatically entail a U.S. loss, the development could be borne with equanimity. If, however, Nixon's concept of balance required that Soviet influence be matched by a roughly equivalent U.S. interest, then the logic of the doctrine called for increasing, not diminishing, U.S. involvement in the Indian Ocean area.

On the whole, from 1969 to 1973, Nixon presented Congress and the public with a relatively relaxed view of Soviet foreign policy. Nixon told Congress in 1971 that the Soviet Union had a "tactical desire to limit American influence and increase her own among the non-communist states of Asia." Still there was "no irreconcilable conflict between Soviet interests in Asia and our own."[2] Even after the Indo-Pakistani war, Nixon expressed the view that as Soviet influence expanded in the Middle East and Asia, the Soviet Union would be likely to acquire an interest in regional stability. To the extent that the Soviet Union was "an influence for restraint in these areas its policies were acceptable to the United States."[3]

In creating a climate of opinion in which Soviet-U.S. détente could develop, the administration was unwilling to concede that continuing competition could lead to serious disagreement, or that a response to Soviet initiatives would always be essential to protect U.S. interests. Again after the Indo-Pakistani war, the secretary for the navy, John Chafee, stated, "we ought to go slowly in the Indian Ocean and not escalate the thing and see what happens."[4]

A further aspect of the Nixon doctrine was the search for allies in regions of lesser importance to defend Western interests and prevent the emergence of crises that might place pressure on the United States to deploy its own military force. Again, this policy posed few problems on the Indian Ocean's eastern littoral. However implausible powers such as Australia, Japan, and Indonesia might appear to Southeast Asian nations as states capable of defending pro-Western regimes and Western interests, little redefinition of relationships was required for the United States to be able to assign those powers prominent local security roles. In circumstances in which no real threats were likely to emerge, psychological reassurance was what appeared necessary to cover the U.S. retreat. Thus Vice-President Spiro Agnew, on a visit to Singapore, promised to "lean on the Australians" to ensure that they supported local security arrangements.[5] The Five-Power Defense arrangement between Britain, Australia, Malaysia, Singapore, and New Zealand was discussed in glowing terms. Nixon described it as "an impressive example of Asians looking to their own security needs and their own measures. It also demonstrates dramatically how important a vigorous Australian and New Zealand role will be to the future stability of the region."[6]

The United States already enjoyed extensive relations with the above nations—relations that included security arrangements, arms transfers, exchanges of military information, and a limited amount of joint military planning—the type of relations with strong regional powers that the doctrine envisaged. However, the situation was not the same in the case of the states on the northern and northwestern littorals of the Indian Ocean. The United States had washed its hands of disputes on the Indian subcontinent since the mid-1960s, and U.S. involvement in the Central Treaty Organization (CENTO) was largely pro forma. The United States was reluctant to involve itself in local disputes, and relations with the major states in the Persian Gulf—Saudi Arabia, Iran, and Iraq—had not been under active review by senior policymakers for a number of years.

Philip Darby argues that it was the British withdrawal from the Gulf that most concerned the U.S. policymakers when they considered the British position in the Indian Ocean.[7] The administration was aware of considerable local tensions in the region. In the early 1960s the United States had attempted to incorporate the

British Indian Ocean presence in a grand strategy of containing communism in the developing world. By 1969 the United States had come to value the British presence for what it really was—a series of highly localized commitments in areas of potential instability and, in the case of the oil-producing Gulf states, of some significance. Even if the United States was not to assume the British mantle in the Gulf (and U.S. policymakers were determined that it should not), significant diplomatic initiatives would be required simply to put forward U.S. perspectives on the region's security requirements.

Finally the Nixon doctrine raised the question of how to commit U.S. forces in areas such as the Indian Ocean. The argument that in military terms, the Nixon doctrine was a "blue-water doctrine" has become a cliché. Nevertheless, it was accompanied by a distinct shift in defense-spending priorities from ground forces to sea and air forces.[8] Naval arguments about the geopolitical significance of sea-lanes gained new respectability among senior policymakers.

In a period in which the navy's role in projecting power on shore conflicted with the prevailing sentiment of restraint, a shift in the navy's priorities to the sea-lanes provided a valuable rationale for maintaining appropriations. This aspect of the navy's task began to appear in assessments on the Indian Ocean by sections of the national security bureaucracy. For example, Ronald Spiers, then director of the State Department's Bureau of Political-Military Affairs, warned a congressional committee against "the growing Soviet naval capability in reference to the so-called 'choke points' which control ingress and egress to and from the Indian Ocean."[9]

That concern should not be exaggerated. Spiers, in the speech cited above, expressed the view that Soviet action was highly unlikely, given the opportunities to retaliate against Soviet shipping elsewhere. However, the encouragement the Nixon doctrine gave the navalists did enhance support for a new naval role in the Indian Ocean.

Energy Questions and Middle East Issues

British withdrawal from the Gulf coincided with a growing alarm in the Nixon administration over the rapid depletion of the world's reserves of fossil fuels. A presidential task force on energy issues in 1971 highlighted the dependence of West European and Japanese allies on oil from the Gulf. James E. Akins, then director of the State

Department's Office of Fuel and Energy, related the problems to more-direct U.S. interests. He informed a congressional committee in 1972 that what the task force considered the "peril point" for U.S. dependence on imported oil (10 percent of total needs) would be reached in 1973, almost a decade in advance of the time predicted by the task force.[10] The political implications of this for the Western alliance and the United States were severe. Akins warned against the prevailing confidence that the Arabs were not capable of organizing an oil embargo in support of political objectives in the Middle East, and he cited as evidence the increasing unity on price questions in OPEC, successful Arab moves to nationalize oil production within their territories, and the accumulation in the Arab world of large financial surpluses. Akins did not think that Iran would be prepared to increase its oil production to overcome the effects of an oil boycott. He also suggested that competition over access to oil supplies would cause rifts between the United States and its European and Japanese allies.

It is clear from the above that Gulf oil was emerging as an item of significance in the U.S. calculation of options in the Arab-Israeli dispute. As with a variety of other international questions, Middle East issues attained a new significance when the Indo-Chinese war began to receive less attention. An alignment of the conservative Arab Gulf states with the radical front-line states was not considered likely by the Nixon administration,[11] but policymakers were concerned with the possibility. In 1971 the United States increased its diplomatic representation in the Gulf and negotiated with the government of Bahrain for the retention of facilities there for the small U.S. Middle East naval force. These facilities had been leased from the British.[12]

It is important to note that questions of Soviet-U.S. competition were of only indirect importance in U.S. calculations. Clearly, the economic stability of the West and the unity of the Western alliance were important to the central balance. However, the Soviet threat to the West's access to Gulf oil, via either assaults on sea-lanes or local subversion, was not as significant as decisions that the local powers might themselves make. Indeed the chairman of the Senate Foreign Relations Committee, Sen. J. W. Fulbright, could speculate in May 1973 that "our present policy-makers . . . may come to the conclusion that military action is required to secure the oil resources of the Middle East, to secure our exposed 'jugular'."[13]

The Indo-Pakistani War

A response to Soviet actions and policies was of considerable importance in the crisis that for the first time since the Sino-Indian border war a decade earlier focused the systematic attention of senior U.S. policymakers on the Indian Ocean region. The Indo-Pakistani war of 1971 and the associated superpower policies and naval deployments have been dealt with adequately elsewhere.[14] It is the effect of the war on U.S. policy that concerns us here.

For the first time the administration confronted the problem of defining what constituted "balance" in an area of lesser importance. The crisis was also interesting as a dramatic demonstration of the possibility of a Sino-U.S. alignment in the region. Chinese support for U.S. Indian Ocean policy became a minor, if not an insignificant, aspect of U.S. calculations in the area.[15] During the crisis, the administration argued that Soviet actions were inconsistent with the spirit of détente. On reflection, however, administration spokesmen recognized that the Soviet policy had been an extension of a long-standing relationship with India. Nixon, commenting after the event, recognized that Soviet influence with India would continue, and he did not seek to criticize that outcome.[16]

With the conclusion of hostilities, the administration found itself with a Congress that had been highly critical of the U.S. role in the crisis and with some responsibility for the security of what was left of Pakistan. The manifest lack of success of the naval deployment in altering any preferred course of action by a local power, or by the Soviet Union, was no basis on which to argue the need for a U.S. military presence in the Indian Ocean. The deployment of Task Force 74 did reflect a willingness to introduce a naval component into U.S. Indian Ocean diplomacy. However, after the withdrawal of Task Force 74, no other U.S. task force appeared in the Indian Ocean until May 1973 when the Diego Garcia communications facility began functioning.[17]

The events confirmed a decision taken in 1970 to revise requests for appropriations for Diego Garcia from an amount sufficient for a small logistic base to just enough for the establishment of a communications facility to fill a "communications gap" – a less controversial purpose.[18] Although the Defense Department continued to want a more substantial facility, requests for the necessary appropriations were not placed before Congress until after the October War.

The Nixon administration sought to regain lost ground in Congress and in India by a more placatory attitude toward that country. The problem of what to do about Pakistan remained. The preferred course of action was to incorporate Pakistan in a pro-Western regional arrangement. In this case the situation produced by the war's outcome, and the already clear orientation of U.S. Indian Ocean policy toward the northwestern littoral, were joined. The shah of Iran was prepared to interest himself in Pakistan's security problems. Demonstrating this alignment of Iranian, U.S., and Pakistani interests, Pakistan participated in the annual CENTO exercises in November 1972 for the first time in a decade.[19] A U.S. official James H. Noyes stated that

> The three countries [Iran, Turkey and Pakistan] do have a common concern with the Soviet Union. It is differently defined than it was before. There is extensive co-operation and even military training and supply of hardware between Iran and the Soviet Union. But this does not mean that the Iranians . . . are relaxed about having them as neighbours and I think as long as they believe there is a validity to CENTO in a political sense, in a quasi-military sense, in an economic sense, I think we should welcome this.[20]

One aspect of Noyes's statement is worth comment. It was clearly not a call for a strong military alliance against the Soviet Union; rather, it represented a recognition on the part of the United States that a number of local powers that were the object of U.S. interest displayed a vague and ill-defined concern about possible Soviet threats. A relationship that the United States wanted constructed for other reasons was rendered possible by local concerns about the Soviet Union.

A statement made at the same time by a more senior official, Joseph Sisco, encapsulated the changing U.S. perspectives on the Indian Ocean. He told the congressional committee that

> Measured in terms of power alone South Asia may not bulk large in relation to some parts of the globe. Nevertheless it is important to the US. The subcontinent bridges the area between the Persian

Gulf, source of much of the world's energy, and South East Asia, a region which is only just beginning to emerge from a generation of conflict and where hopes for stability remain as yet fragile. Thus the direction taken by the primary actors on the South Asian stage . . . has important implications for our interest in the two neighboring areas and for the sea lanes which link them and Europe and East Asia across the Indian Ocean basin.[21]

Sisco's statement, in focusing on maritime links, demonstrates that U.S. Indian Ocean policy was beginning to assume a genuinely regional character. U.S. perspectives on the area had largely been continental and fragmented in the 1950s and 1960s, concentrating on Southeast Asia, South Asia, and the Middle East's "northern tier" for a land containment of the Soviet Union and China. The new interest, linking the sections of the littoral, was access to the Gulf.

Persian Gulf Diplomacy 1971-73

A more significant factor for future U.S. policy than developments associated with naval activity was the changing U.S. relationship with Iran and, to a lesser extent, with Saudi Arabia. From 1971 the two powers were referred to as the "twin pillars" of Western security interests in the Gulf. Between 1971 and 1973 the United States firmly assigned Iran the type of regional role the Nixon doctrine envisaged for pro-Western, middle-sized powers.

There were several differences between U.S. relations with Iran and U.S. relations with Japan or Australia. In the first place, the relationship with Iran had declined in the 1960s so that a U.S. initiative was required to consolidate it, and neither side was fully familiar with the other's perspective on regional security requirements. Second, the Iranians relished the role thrust upon them. This may be contrasted with Australia's reluctance to enter the Five-Power Defense arrangement and Japan's insistence that its links with Southeast Asia were economic and not military. Third, unlike Southeast Asia in the post-Vietnam War era, the Gulf could not readily be classified as an area of "lesser importance." The administration, nevertheless, pursued a strategy appropriate to the assumption that it was and thus risked assigning the control of a relationship that might become vital to the United States to another power—a power with marked imperial ambitions in an unstable area.

In November 1972 the shah announced the extension of Iran's "security perimeters" from the Persian Gulf and the Gulf of Oman to the western Indian Ocean. The Iranian government commenced construction of a naval and air base at Chah Bahar on the Arabian Sea,[22] and expenditure for the shah's navy increased from $5.5 million for 1963–68 to $55 million for the 1968–73 period. Under the fifth plan, covering the years 1973–78, the expenditure was estimated to be $1,200 million.[23] Aside from the imperial aspects of the shah's policy, Iran was influenced by a concern to protect the sea-lanes from threats posed by local radical groups. Although these groups might receive some Soviet support the problem was largely an indigenous one. Although the shah was confident that his bridge building with the Soviet Union in the 1960s had lessened the Soviet threat, the uncertainty likely to accompany his new policy meant that the shah appreciated the protection offered by a closer U.S. relationship.

The problem for the United States was that the shah's policies were viewed with concern by the conservative Arab Gulf states. In 1970 the shah had seized several Gulf islands that had been regarded as the territory of powers on the other side of the Gulf. The shah sought to reassure them, and he stopped objecting to the U.S. presence at Bahrain, which appeared to lend weight to his guarantee that territorial claims on Bahrain had been dropped. In early 1973 the shah began to provide assistance to the sultan of Oman for the suppression of a rebellion in Oman's Dhofar province. This action provided a demonstration of the shah's willingness to cooperate with another Gulf state and of his determination to prevent a radical group attaining power at one of the Gulf's chokepoints.[24]

In response to these developments, the United States began a most uncritical relationship with the shah. In May 1972, during a visit to Iran, Nixon informed the shah that the United States was prepared to sell Iran F-14 and F-15 aircraft. In a memorandum issued from Nixon's office in July, the Departments of State and Defense were informed that the government of Iran would, in effect, determine what weapons systems it could purchase. A staff report for the Senate Foreign Relations Committee commented, "The President's decision to sell Iran virtually any weapons system it wanted was unprecedented for a non-industrial country; . . . The decision not only opened the door to large increases in sales to Iran but also effectively exempted Iran from normal arms sales decision-making processes in the State and Defense Departments."[25]

The president's decision meant that legislative provisions relating to arms sales, which required a review of the impact arms sales to one country might have on a neighbor's security concerns, did not apply to Iran. Indeed, at the same time the United States gave some clandestine assistance to the shah's own "destabilizing" initiative. With the knowledge of Henry Kissinger, the president's principal national security adviser, the Central Intelligence Agency (CIA) aided a Kurdish insurrection against Iran's hostile neighbor Iraq.[26]

By 1973 the Gulf had emerged as the focus of U.S. Indian Ocean policy. Administration attitudes to the deployment of U.S. forces in the area were, on the whole, governed by the restraint implicit in the Nixon doctrine. Steps had been taken that improved the capacity of the United States to intrude forces, and in 1972 most of the Indian Ocean was made the responsibility of the Commander in Chief, Pacific (CINCPAC) – a new role for a command diminished in significance by the retreat in Indochina. In the same year, the small Middle East Force at Bahrain was improved qualitatively by stationing more modern ships there. Diego Garcia enhanced naval communications in the area. The administration, however, emphasized the ability of the United States to move forces into the Indian Ocean rather than the value of a permanent force or even regular visits there. Defense Secretary Melvin Laird was identified with efforts to expand the role of Diego Garcia, but nevertheless he argued in early 1972 that "our strength in the Indian Ocean lies not so much in maintaining a large standing force . . . but rather in our ability to move freely in and out of the ocean as the occasion and our interests dictate."[27]

Immediate Impact of the October War and the Oil Embargo

The October War accentuated trends already evident in U.S. Indian Ocean policy. It also added a new dimension to them. More attention was given to the question of the capacity of the United

States to unilaterally defend its interests in the area. The need for such a military capability came to the fore immediately after war. As relations with the littoral states were reconstructed, this aspect of the Nixon and Ford administrations' policies tended to be set aside in favor of arguments on the value of naval presence for building relations with allies and counteracting the Soviet presence. But the need remained implicit in the administrations' requests for an expanded military presence in the Indian Ocean.

The immediate impact of the October War on the Nixon administration was to produce a deep disenchantment with allies within and without the region. The policies of the Europeans and Japanese during the oil embargo seemed to confirm Akins's earlier assessment that the interests of the United States and those of its allies could diverge. Concerning allies within the region, Rodger P. Davies, the deputy assistant for Near East and South Asian affairs, stated in December 1973 that the oil embargo and price rise were going to "require considerable attention and hard work to keep them from affecting our overall relationship with countries in the Gulf."[28] The coincidence of the Arab oil embargo and the price rise meant that Iranian policy caused the United States almost as much concern as the policy of the Gulf Arab states.

In the confused atmosphere, in which the United States perceived itself to be alone or at least without enthusiastic allies, Kissinger and the new Defense Secretary James Schlesinger decided there should be a carrier task force in the Indian Ocean. On December 1, 1973, Schlesinger announced that a force had been dispatched and that henceforth regular carrier visits to the Indian Ocean would take place.[29] The presence of the force in the Arabian Sea after the Arab-Israeli ceasefire, but while the oil embargo continued, suggested that it was intended to influence the policy of the Gulf states.

The task force was deployed in the Indian Ocean until April 1974, leaving shortly after the oil embargo was lifted in March, and officials agreed that the presence had served a useful diplomatic purpose. Seymour Weiss, the director of the Bureau of Political-Military Affairs, concluded that the task force "was a reinforcement for the . . . successful efforts of Kissinger to bring the partners in the conflict to the peace table. . . . It played the traditional role which military power should play, that of supporting diplomatic initiatives."[30] It did not represent coercion but a demonstration of the importance the United States attached to bringing the parties together.

It would be difficult to argue that the presence of the carrier task force altered any Gulf state's policy. When the oil embargo was lifted, U.S. officials attributed the decision to Kissinger's efforts to gain conservative Arab confidence in his Middle East peace negotiations.[31] The only obvious effect of the military presence was that it engendered local hostility, and Saudi Arabia pressed the government of Bahrain to withdraw the use of facilities from the Middle East Force.[32] As in the case of the Indo-Pakistani war, the U.S. military presence provided an opportunity for the Soviet navy to portray its activities in the Indian Ocean as guaranteeing the autonomy of the littoral states.

Whatever the efficacy of the military presence, in February 1974 in Department of Defense put forward proposals for additions to Diego Garcia. The alterations were to make the site a support facility rather than simply a communications station. The airfield was to be extended to permit the handling of large transport planes and the basing of P-3 maritime patrol aircraft, and additional fuel storage capacity would hold as much fuel as the oilers attached to a normal visiting carrier task force. These limited repair and replenishment facilities considerably improved the capacity of the United States to deploy naval units in the important sectors of the Indian Ocean. In addition, the facilities could service an airlift of material to the Middle East should the difficulties experienced with the Mediterranean route during the October War recur.[33]

From 1974 to 1976 the appropriations proposals pursued a tortuous route through Congress. They were vigorously opposed in the Senate by Senators Edward Kennedy, John Culver, Mike Mansfield, Claiborne Pell, Thomas McIntyre, and Stuart Symington in particular. The opposition argued that the extensions would provoke a Soviet response and an unnecessary arms race, tarnish the reputation of the United States among the littoral states that were committed to the exclusion of great power rivalry, and end the restraint implicit in the Nixon doctrine. Indeed it was the passage of the appropriations bill through Congress that provided the focus for much of the public discussion of Indian Ocean issues.

Changing Rationale of Indian Ocean Policy

Roughly two broad lines of argument were adopted by Nixon and Ford administrations in support of their Indian Ocean policy. One was to stress the diplomatic value of the naval presence in relations with the littoral states. As memories of the embargo receded and the U.S. policy toward the northwestern littoral began to be dominated by economic and arms sales issues, a second line assumed more prominence—the importance of balancing Soviet initiatives in the region.

A most sweeping claim for the value of a naval presence was made by Seymour Weiss. He argued that military forces made the United States a regional power, able to participate in and influence local politics. "We have to be able to play a vital intermediary role precisely because we are a regional power with forces of our own in both the Mediterranean and the Indian Ocean and maintain a continuing political and security dialogue with many of the parties involved."[34] A presence, officials argued, would serve a number of tasks. It would give credibility to a threat to uphold U.S. interests by force. It would encourage local allies of the United States by signaling a U.S. interest in the region's affairs. In placid times, the U.S. military presence was a gesture of goodwill; in times of crisis, a reinforcement of naval forces would compel local powers to consider U.S. views.

It was thus inevitable that the U.S. naval position in the Indian Ocean should be connected with threats made from time to time by Schlesinger and Kissinger to use force to secure oil supplies should the West be threatened with "economic strangulation."[35] Seizing oil fields meant an attack in the Gulf. A congressional committee staff report surveying options concluded that the option that involved a seizure of Saudi oil fields, those of the smaller Gulf states, and Iranian production on the coast would be the plan most likely to be adopted. Production in that area alone could supply the needs of the United States and its allies. Soviet naval counteraction would be more circumscribed than would be the case in the Mediterranean where the Soviet Union found it relatively easy to surge naval forces.[36] A report on Pentagon contingency planning also suggested that an unhindered and sedate "promenade" by U.S. forces across the Indian Ocean would demonstrate the seriousness of U.S. intentions and also give local governments time to alter their policies.[37]

Despite Schlesinger's confidence that it was "indeed possible to conduct military operations" against the Gulf states,[38] there remained serious military and political objections to such action. Kissinger acknowledged that a Soviet response would have to be considered.[39] Retreating Arab forces would be likely to sabotage the oil fields, and the time needed for repairs could well be greater than the time needed to negotiate a solution to the crisis. Having taken the fields, U.S. forces would confront the problem of almost permanent occupation in the face of a nationalist Arab attack. The European response to past oil boycotts indicated that the United States would fight alone and possibly with the overt hostility of erstwhile friends—a bad basis on which to commence action that might lead to general war.[40]

With these substantial objections to a unilateral military intervention, the repetition of the threat requires some explanation. In part it was an aspect of the confusion among U.S. policymakers immediately after the war. In 1976 Akins, who was ambassador to Saudi Arabia in 1974, referred to this state of mind in a discussion on energy conservation. "If it [the embargo] had lasted another six months I suspect the energy problem would be viewed here more seriously than it is. But my instructions from Washington bordered on hysteria and had I replied that a continuation of the embargo would have been good for the American body and soul, my tour as Ambassador would have been even more abbreviated than it was."[41]

The U.S. sense of isolation during the crisis enhanced the attractiveness of unilateral action. Indeed, military intervention to secure vital interests, irrespective of the attitudes of ertswhile allies and friends, appealed to an isolationist trend in the U.S. foreign policy community, a trend that reemerged in the post-Vietnam period. Some U.S. officials argued that only the United States could be relied on to protect general Western interests in the Indian Ocean. Admiral Thomas Moorer rejected suggestions that NATO ought to consider a multilateral military presence in the Indian Ocean by noting that "the NATO nations have viewed the alliance in terms of certain geographical constraints which do not extend to the Indian Ocean. . . . The interests in the Indian Ocean area that individual nations such as France, the UK, or Japan might have, as well as the US of course, are closely associated with their individual national interests."[42]

The policy undoubtedly also involved an element of calculation. Threats of military action indicated to the states on the northwestern littoral that the United States had been deeply disturbed by their actions. It informed them that during future embargoes they too could expect massive damage and dislocation. It was probably also an indirect warning to Western allies of the dangers of catastrophe if they failed to prepare themselves to withstand future oil embargoes or again permitted their policies to diverge too greatly from those of the United States in similar crises. At the time when the threats were openly discussed by Kissinger and Schlesinger, the United States was bickering with its allies over conservation measures, oil credits, and bargaining tactics with the oil producers.[43]

The threats were curiously out of step with the general tenor of U.S. diplomacy in the Gulf. At the same time that the threats were being made, Kissinger was negotiating with the Saudi Arabians and the Iranians a series of joint commissions that would deepen U.S. economic and military cooperation with the Gulf states. The threats raised local suspicions as to U.S. intentions and made the Gulf states notably less enthusiastic about U.S. initiatives. The Gulf states put on record their intention to resist U.S. blandishments, and the heads of state of OPEC countries supported them, declaring in March 1975 their readiness "to counteract [U.S./allied] threats with a unified response whenever the need arises, notably in the case of aggression."[44]

Needless to say, the administration's argument on this question did not prove popular in a Congress interested in restricting presidential war-making powers and in encouraging restraint in U.S. foreign policy. Sen. Stuart Symington suggested that "if we make it easy for the Navy to go places and do things we will find ourselves always going places and doing things."[45]

The administration was therefore inclined to add to its rationale the seemingly contradictory assertion that the U.S. naval presence enhanced good relations with the relevant littoral states. Deputy Secretary for Defense William Clements argued, "Countries such as Pakistan, Iran, Saudi Arabia, Kuwait and Ethiopia all feel a sense of security by our additional presence in the area."[46] In November 1974 the U.S. carrier task force in the Indian Ocean participated in

Midlink 74, the largest CENTO exercises conducted to that point in the Arabian Sea.[47]

Participation in Midlink 74 served several purposes. The future of the Middle East Force at Bahrain was in doubt, and the use of ships deployed elsewhere in the Indian Ocean demonstrated that part of the latter's function could still be performed and was acceptable to local powers. It served notice on U.S. allies and the Soviet Union that U.S. links with major regional powers remained intact, despite disagreement over energy policy. Locally, associating forces that had at one stage been deployed as a hostile gesture to Arab Gulf states with an acceptable regional organization might lessen the objections to their continuing presence.

The significance of the military presence as an aspect of U.S. diplomacy on the Indian Ocean's northwestern littoral declined after 1974. It nevertheless remained an adjunct to the massive U.S. involvement in the defense programs of Iran and Saudi Arabia and to the general programs of economic and technical cooperation in the Gulf. The scale of these latter activities dwarfed any other aspect of U.S. diplomacy in the Indian Ocean area. The figures for U.S. arms sales to the Gulf countries adequately indicate the massively increased level of U.S. involvement after the October War. In 1970 the orders were worth $128 million; in 1971, $492 million; 1972, $870 million; 1973, $2,193 million; 1974, $4,400 million; and in 1975, $4,492 million.[48]

Early in 1974 the United States was critical of the European "arms for oil" deals in the Gulf, but by the end of the year it was clear that the United States had abandoned this cautious attitude. It was pointed out to Schlesinger at a press conference that there appeared to be some inconsistency between a policy that advocated a U.S. capability to intervene in the Gulf and one that armed the Gulf states to resist an attack. Schlesinger acknowledged the argument but assigned a higher priority to the arms sales since they, in his view, bettered relations.[49] By selling arms, the United States inevitably became involved in decisions of major importance for the region's security and stability.

The relationship of the United States with Saudi Arabia required a substantial reorientation of Saudi defense perspectives. A national guard, adequate to maintain order among dissident tribal elements, had been considered sufficient for Saudi purposes until the 1970s.

However from 1974, the United States presided over the establishment of a Saudi navy and air force. Officials such as Joseph Sisco were quick to point out that the Saudi navy would not be effective outside confined waters.[50] Nevertheless, the fact that in the future Saudi Arabia would assume a role in protecting sea-lanes in the Gulf and the Red Sea was a considerable addition to what the Saudis had hitherto considered their security tasks.

Iran remained the focus of U.S. policy on the northwestern littoral. The policy of furnishing the shah with any requested weapons system continued, and included among Iranian purchases between 1974 and 1976 were six Spruance-class destroyers (later reduced to four) and three diesel submarines. All the ships and submarines were not deployed until the early 1980s,[51] and the purchases were designed to improve Iranian capabilities in the northern Indian Ocean. The naval sales were only one small aspect of the intense cooperation between the two powers on defense matters. The United States provided, and made use of for its own purposes, highly sophisticated electronic intelligence-gathering facilities in Iran. The United States also continued to promote and assist in the installation of sophisticated land and air weapons systems.

The point of the preceding detail has been to illustrate that following the October War, arms sales to the Gulf area and the associated U.S. involvement in regional security planning must be regarded as the significant features of U.S. Indian Ocean policy. That policy was not substantially influenced by any fear of Soviet threats to sea-lanes or by any substantial fear of increased Soviet diplomatic activity. They were a response to a local threat to "choke off" oil supplies and to the emerging significance of the region in the international economy. The value of the U.S. presence in the Indian Ocean lay in any support it might give in stressing to local countries the usefulness of a U.S. defense relationship. Administration spokesmen also saw value in having the force in the background as a more menacing aspect of U.S. diplomacy in case U.S. policy and policies of the local states should diverge again in the future.

It would be wrong to argue that considerations of Soviet naval deployments and Soviet diplomatic activity played no part in U.S. Indian Ocean policy. As memories of the war receded, countering Soviet activity came more to the fore in the Nixon and Ford administrations' rationales for expanding Diego Garcia. Schlesinger used reports of extensive additions to the Soviet facilities in Berbera, Somalia, to argue that

> although we would strongly prefer to see no Soviet build up of military presence in this region it appears the USSR intends to undertake such a build up. Since an effective military balance is essential to the preservation of regional security and stability in this area of great importance to the economic well-being of the industrialized world, we feel we should have logistical facilities which will permit us to maintain a credible presence. In a period of transition to a new set of power relations only the United States among the Western nations has the stature to ensure that the balance is maintained.[52]

Administration officials made no sustained effort to prove the case that the small Soviet presence threatened sea-lanes, even though Schlesinger did argue that 85 percent of Soviet naval activity in the Indian Ocean took place in the Gulf of Aden close to the lanes plied by oil tankers coming from the Persian Gulf. He also pointed out that in the 1975 OKEAN exercises, the Soviet navy's activity in the Arabian Sea appeared to be directed toward the interdiction of shipping.[53] However, given the size of the Soviet Indian Ocean squadron, its shore facilities, and the difficulties involved in reinforcing it, sustained interdiction operations appeared to be out of the question. Schlesinger in fact suggested that in a general war the Soviet Union might consider withdrawal from the Indian Ocean desirable.[54]

As indicated in Schlesinger's statement above, the administration was interested in depriving the Soviet Union of any political value that might accrue from having the only superpower naval presence. Denying the Soviet Union this advantage could be as readily achieved by a mutual withdrawal from the Indian Ocean as by a balanced presence. The other objectives of the U.S. naval presence could not.

Conclusion

Since 1975 there has been greater emphasis by analysts of Indian Ocean affairs on Soviet-U.S. competition. Soviet activities in Africa were used by the Ford administration as an argument against proceeding with naval arms limitation talks. Having proposed such talks, President Carter suspended them in early 1978 in response to Soviet activities in the Horn of Africa.

With all the fears that have been expressed about Soviet intentions in Africa, the Red Sea, and Afghanistan the composition of the U.S. naval force in the Indian Ocean and its logistic support have not altered from what was proposed in the immediate aftermath of the October War. The first serious proposals for expanding that force—those for the creation of an Indian Ocean fleet—did not come in the wake of a Soviet initiative but followed the collapse of the position established by the United States in the Gulf. The main interest of the United States in the Indian Ocean remains access to oil. The principal threat to that access remains local developments in which the hand played by the Soviet Union is a minor one.

Notes

1. See, for example, K. C. Beazley and I. Clark, *Politics of Intrusion: The Super Powers and the Indian Ocean* (Sydney: Alternatives Publishing Cooperative, Ltd., 1979), Chapters 1-3.

2. *Department of State Bulletin* (hereafter referred to as *DSB*) 64 (March 22, 1971):384.

3. *DSB* 66 (March 13, 1972):380.

4. Quoted in statement by Sen. Clairborne Pell in U.S. Congress, Senate, Subcommittee on Military Construction of the Committee on Armed Services, *Military Construction Authorization FY 1975, Hearings,* 93rd Cong., 2d sess., July 10, 11, 12, and 18, 1974, p. 493.

5. J. M. McNaughton, "Agnew Hints US Might Fill Void in South Pacific Left by the UK Pullout," *International Herald Tribune,* January 11, 1970.

6. *DSB* 64 (March 22, 1971):380.

7. Philip Darby, *British Defence Policy East of Suez 1947-1968* (London: Oxford University Press, 1973), p. 325.

8. An example can be found in the navy's share of total defense spending. In fiscal year 1968 the navy received 27.5 percent; in FY 1970, 29.6 percent; in FY 1973, 31.6 percent; and in FY 1975, 31.9 percent (Australia, Parliament, Legislative Research Service, *The Strategic Position in the Indian Ocean,* September 23, 1974, p. 1).

9. *DSB* 65 (August 23, 1971):201-202.

10. U.S., Congress, House, Subcommittee on Foreign Policy and

Economic Affairs of the Committee on Foreign Affairs, *Foreign Policy Implications of the Oil Crisis, Hearings*, 93rd Cong., 1st sess., May 1973, pp. 152–154.

11. U.S., Congress, House, Committee on Foreign Affairs, Subcommittee on the Near East and South Asia, *US Interests in and Policy Toward the Persian Gulf, Hearings*, 92nd Cong., 2nd sess., February and August 1972, p. 146.

12. Ibid., p. 23.

13. R. J. Levine, "Armed Force and Scarce Materials," *Wall Street Journal*, July 17, 1974.

14. See, for example, J. M. McConnell and A. M. Kelly, *Superpower Naval Diplomacy in the Indo-Pakistani Crisis*, Professional Paper no. 108 (Arlington, Va.: Center for Naval Analysis, February 1973).

15. Spier's successor as director of the Bureau of Political-Military Affairs, Seymour Weiss, was pleased to suggest some years later that the "People's Republic of China applauded US involvement in the area" (U.S., Congress, House, Subcommittee on the Near East and South Asia of the Committee on Foreign Affairs, *Proposed Expansion of US Military Facilities in the Indian Ocean*, 93rd Cong., 2nd sess., February/March 1974, p. 45).

16. DSB 66 (March 13, 1972):388.

17. *Declaration of the Indian Ocean as a Zone of Peace*, Report of the Secretary-General to Ad Hoc Committee on the Indian Ocean, A/AC 159/1, May 3, 1974, p. 8.

18. M. Bezboruah, *U.S. Strategy in the Indian Ocean: The International Response* (New York: Praeger, 1977), p. 66.

19. *New York Times*, July 26, 1973.

20. U.S., Congress, House, Subcommittee on the Near East and South Asia of the Committee on Foreign Affairs, *U.S. Interests in and Policies Toward South Asia*, 93rd Cong., 1st sess., March 1973, pp. 112–113.

21. Ibid., p. 164.

22. R. K. Ramazani, "Emerging Patterns of Regional Relations in Iranian Foreign Policy," *Orbis* 18, no. 4 (Winter 1975):1061.

23. U.S., Congress, Senate, Subcommittee on Foreign Assistance of the Committee on Foreign Relations, *US Military Sales to Iran*, Staff Report (Washington, D.C.: Government Printing Office, July, 1976), p. 20.

24. A. Taheri, "Politics of Iran in the Persian Gulf Region," in A. Amirie, ed., *The Persian Gulf and Indian Ocean in International Politics* (Teheran: Institute for International Political and Economic Studies, 1975), p. 145.

25. U.S., Congress, Senate, *US Military Sales to Iran*, p. 41.

26. W. Shawcross, "Banned Report Says America Left Kurds in the Lurch," *Sunday Times* (London), February 15, 1976.

27. U.S., Congress, Senate, *Military Construction Authorization FY 75*, p. 493.

28. *DSB* 69 (December 17, 1973):725.

29. U.S., Congress, House, *Proposed Expansion of US Military Facilities in the Indian Ocean*, p. 35.

30. Ibid., p. 24.

31. See statement by Alfred L. Atherton, *DSB* 71 (December 2, 1974).

32. *Christian Science Monitor*, October 3, 1974.

33. Beazley and Clark, *Politics of Intrusion*, pp. 31–33.

34. U.S., Congress, House, *Proposed Expansion of US Military Facilities in the Indian Ocean*, p. 24.

35. See, for example, *DSB* 72 (January 27, 1975):101, and *Time*, February 10, 1975.

36. *Oil Fields as Military Objectives*, Feasibility study prepared for the Committee on International Relations by the Congressional Research Service (Washington, D.C.: Government Printing Office, August 21, 1975), pp. 41–85.

37. *Time*, February 10, 1975.

38. News conference with Schlesinger at the Pentagon, January 14, 1975.

39. *DSB* 72 (January 27, 1975):101.

40. *Strategic Survey 1974* (London: International Institute for Strategic Studies, 1975), pp. 30–32.

41. Hearings before a Subcommittee of the Senate Commerce Committee, May 1976, p. 439.

42. U.S., Congress, Senate, Committee on Armed Services, *Military Procurement Supplemental—Fiscal Year 1974, Hearings on S-2999*, 93rd Cong., 2nd sess., March 1974, p. 55.

43. These views were expressed to the writer in an interview with a senior British Ministry of Defence official in London in October 1975. For further discussion see Beazley and Clark, *Politics of Intrusion*, pp. 34, 39.

44. U.S., Congress, *Oil Fields as Military Objectives*, p. 16.

45. U.S., Congress, Senate, Committee on Armed Services, *Disapprove Construction Projects on the Island of Diego Garcia, Hearing*, 94th Cong., 1st sess., June 1975, p. 38.

46. U.S., Congress, Senate, *Military Procurement Supplemental—Fiscal Year 1974*, p. 47.

47. E. Sagar, "CENTO Naval Exercises," *Hindu*, November 20, 1974.

48. U.S., Congress, House, Special Subcommittee on Investigations of the Committee on International Relations, *The Persian Gulf, 1975: The Continuing Debate on Arms Sales, Hearings*, 94th Cong., 1st sess., June–July 1975, p. 19. The figures also illustrate a point made earlier in the

chapter on the increasing U.S. interest in the Gulf between 1970-73.

49. News conference with Schlesinger at the Pentagon, January 14, 1975, cited in U.S., Congress, House, Special Subcommittee on Investigations of the Committee on International Relations, *Oil Fields as Military Objectives, A Feasibility Study,* Prepared by the Congressional Research Service (Washington, D.C.: Government Printing Office, 1975), p. 81.

50. U.S., Congress, House, *Persian Gulf, 1975,* p. 31.

51. U.S., Congress, Senate, *US Military Sales to Iran,* pp. 22-23.

52. U.S., Congress, Senate, *Disapprove Construction Projects on the Island of Diego Garcia,* p. 11.

53. Ibid., pp. 8, 12.

54. Ibid., p. 59.

7
Carter's Diplomacy and the Indian Ocean Region

Ashok Kapur

Introduction

Writing about President Jimmy Carter's diplomacy is not easy. Although the issues are important, the political mood in Washington and President Carter's thinking and style do not permit serious negotiations between states. There is a long agenda of unsettled international security issues: the future of détente, SALT II and SALT III, economic and military relations between the United States and the People's Republic of China (PRC), Middle East peace, superpower relations in Africa, the management of nuclear and conventional arms proliferation, Indian-U.S. relations, and so on. This agenda is unlikely to be settled before the 1980 presidential elections. At the time of writing (October 1979) the general mood in Washington was to carry on with political and bureaucratic maneuvers, to keep saying that all is well, and to talk rather than to negotiate or listen to others—whether friend or enemy. In this context a study of Carter's Indian Ocean diplomacy, specifically with regard to the Indian Ocean naval limitations or stabilization talks, deals with a topic that is not simply a bit dead but that is completely dead. Today, Indian Ocean arms control issues lack momentum, if momentum is defined as change, or the likelihood of change, in the pattern of security (or insecurity) in the Indian Ocean region.

This is a revised version of a paper presented at the International Conference of Indian Ocean Studies, University of Western Australia, August 16-23, 1979. The author wishes to thank the University of Waterloo and the University of Western Australia for travel support.

According to the conventional wisdom, states behave the way they do because of their position in the international system and not because of internal decision-making attributes or personality variables.[1] State behavior is thus a consequence of the behavior of other states toward it and the distribution and hierarchy of power in the international system. This focus also stresses an action/reaction process between states. The influence of domestic cleavages in foreign-policy decisionmaking is not seen as a major explanatory tool.

This chapter, however, will suggest an alternative perspective. It argues that the position of a state in the international system only partly explains a state's behavior. Instead, actions or reactions in the external arena may be the consequence of domestic cleavages or electoral politics. I will argue that U.S.-USSR behavior and their presence in the Indian Ocean region are based less on action/reaction at the interstate level and are based more on action/reaction in intrastate or intraelite activity in the United States. To reach this conclusion one must understand the nature of the competition between the superpowers.

Since the mid-1950s the superpowers have clashed in the Middle East, in Africa, and in South and Southeast Asia. Whether it be Angola, the Horn of Africa, southern Africa, or the Indian Ocean, U.S. policymakers express concern about Soviet moves.[2] The naval posturing of the superpowers against each other in the Indian Ocean since 1968 represents competitiveness—an extension of their competition in the Mediterranean Sea, the Pacific Ocean, and the littoral regions.

This image of superpower competitiveness in the Indian Ocean region is correct as far as it goes, but it does not go far enough. According to an alternative view, the superpower competition is limited in nature. As George Lichtheim points out, there has been a *basic entente* between the United States and the USSR since Yalta, and public statements of the leaders of the two countries should not be taken literally.[3] The competition is controlled and does not threaten the basic interests of the superpowers; indeed, the two have a vested interest in supporting the proposition that international security depends on the primacy of the two principals in world affairs. Although there is an arms race of global significance between the superpowers it is controlled, and there is no arms race in the Indian Ocean. The periodic upgrading of naval forces and the periodic fleet cruises do not alter the superpowers' relationship in the littoral and the naval environments. Both superpowers have parallel interests, and neither side is in a position to deny them to the other side. Parallelism rather than opposition between the superpowers is the name of the game, and it points to development or maintenance of mutually supportive superpower relations. Informal parallelism is a substitute for formal and negotiated agreements because publicly acceptable agreements require a settlement of controversial definitional issues. This requires bureaucratic coordination, and consequently, formal interstate negotiations produce opportunities for bureaucratic veto. Such coordination is problematic in systems that are ridden with intraelite power struggles and bureaucratic battles. In such a system it is preferable to have an informal, and probably ambiguous, arrangement rather than a publicly negotiated and formal agreement unless there is a strong authority structure that can settle intraelite debates.

On the other hand, the existence of parallel interests and the image of public competition between public rivals are not necessarily antagonistic activities. The combination has its uses. If the quest to formalize an agreement between states gives an opportunity for latent intraelite competition to become radicalized and publicized (to the point that bureaucracies become overcommitted to their respective positions), keeping interstate relations competitive keeps the intraelite competition latent. This is an important goal that political leaders must consider to manage their bureaucracies.

The description of superpower policy and perceptions suggests that the Indian Ocean naval presence of the superpowers may be a method to foster the image of superpower competition so that the domestic and international constituents of each superpower can be managed. A president who is seen to be tough with the Russians—as President Carter tried to be in his actions against Soviet combat troops in Cuba—appeals to a conservative domestic audience. As Tom Wicker pointed out "Mr. Carter's get-tough-with-Castro policy won't help anything except his re-election prospects."[4] This approach could also appeal to foreign clients who must worry about being tough with the Russians and who worry about the reliability of U.S. support.

The alternative view makes sense because a number of common

interests bring together the superpowers in the Indian Ocean region. Both seek to control regional conflicts through superpower intervention. Both seek nonproliferation when there are at least four potential nuclear powers—India, South Africa, Pakistan, and Israel—in the region. Both have similar concerns with respect to the law of the sea, such as their desire to secure the freedom of navigation in the straits. Both seek to control revolutionary movements that could affect their interests. This is particularly true for the USSR because Middle East revolutions could have a spillover effect in the Muslim central Asian portion of the Soviet Union. Both worry about the emergence of third parties in world politics.

These examples indicate that beneath the picture of overt naval rivalry in the Indian Ocean and competition in the littoral regions, there is the phenomenon of parallel if not commonly shared system-maintenance interests. As such it is not excessive to argue that it seems that the superpower competition is mostly geared to image building to satisfy domestic and international constituencies and that the competition is manageable and predictable.

U.S. Interests in the Indian Ocean

The United States has a long list of declared interests in the Indian Ocean region.[5] One of them is to ensure that the sea-lanes, particularly the chokepoints in the straits that convey half the world's seaborne oil through the Indian Ocean, remain open for the United States and its allies. Broadly speaking, it is necessary to possess a capacity for "sea control" or "sea denial" in the entire ocean to satisfy that interest. But today an ocean-wide capacity for sea control or sea denial seems unnecessary if the goal is to ensure oil security. For the United States and its allies, the real place to interdict or to defend against enemy interdiction is the source of supply, and this means the Persian Gulf and not the entire Indian Ocean.

Three methods exist to ensure oil security. The first method is to have reliable political relations with the oil suppliers. If ideological differences do not divide the United States and the suppliers and if the political relationship is free of conflict, then the role of military force becomes unnecessary. Unfortunately this approach is problematic for the United States because of its commitment to Israel and because of the U.S. style of thinking in which "political trust" is not a sound basis for interstate relations. The second method is to find a regional partner—such as the shah of Iran—that will receive U.S. military equipment and U.S. advice and police the region on behalf of the United States. This method is also problematic. Although it is possible to establish a patron-client relationship in contemporary international affairs, regional clients like the shah of Iran preside over unstable elite structures, and their weakness at home interferes with their capacity to project power abroad. As early as 1976, if not earlier, U.S. experts voiced doubts about the shah's capacity to police the Persian Gulf, let alone the Indian Ocean. Iran's weakness, therefore, accounted for a U.S. commitment to continue its naval presence in the Persian Gulf. The generalized significance of the point is that collaboration with a domestically vulnerable regional partner increased the U.S. commitment. Not only does the United States have to maintain its own forces to protect the oil security interests of the West, but it also has to ensure the stability of the military environment of its regional client. Therefore, another method is required.

The third method is the "go it alone" method. In 1948 the United States established a Middle East naval presence, and that small presence continues to exist. The United States has maintained, at different times, communications facilities in Ethiopia, Iran, and Australia as a part of a worldwide communication chain. This chain now includes Diego Garcia and possible cooperation with South Africa. After the 1962 war between India and China the U.S. Pacific Fleet began to make periodic visits to Indian Ocean ports. Today the U.S. Pacific and South Atlantic fleets have their respective spheres of operation in the Indian Ocean. Insofar as Diego Garcia is not negotiable in the superpowers' Indian Ocean naval talks, that facility represents a gradual upgrading of the U.S. naval presence in the Indian Ocean. The decision to establish Diego Garcia means that the floating presence of the Pacific and the South Atlantic fleets now has been supplemented with a permanent presence on an island that is about a thousand miles or so away from potential crisis points along the Indian Ocean littoral. The continuation of the go-it-alone approach by the United States implies that diplomacy and political trust are not seen as the bases on which to organize the distribution of influence and power in the Indian Ocean region. However, the upgrading of the U.S. naval presence in a slow and gradual fashion implies that the balance between the perceived threats to U.S. interests and the existing force structure is adequate at present.

In a historical perspective it should be noted, however, that the slow development of the U.S. naval presence in the Indian Ocean has not been guided by only a single concern. Different concerns at different times explain the intrusion of U.S. naval power into the Indian Ocean. In the late 1940s Soviet behavior in Iran was used to explain a U.S. naval presence in the Middle East. This rationale was strengthened after the Soviet navy established a presence in the Mediterranean in the early 1960s and in the Indian Ocean in the late 1960s. But the initial entry of the U.S. Pacific Fleet into the Indian Ocean occurred after the India-China war in 1962, and the anti-China rationale was repeatedly emphasized in U.S. diplomatic communications at that time. In Middle East and South Asia military crises (1967, 1971, and 1973, for example) the deployment of U.S. naval forces was explained as a response to the Soviet threat and as U.S. support for its allies. The development of U.S. naval power in the 1971 South Asian crisis was seen as an effort to limit the Soviet commitment to India, to curb the Indian threat to West Pakistan, and above all, to codify the "rules of the game" of superpower competition. In that instance, superpower competition in the Indian Ocean was meant to strengthen the superpowers' détente internationally—to ensure that crisis management represented rule making and communication between the superpowers. Since the oil embargo in 1973, however, statements of Secretaries Kissinger, Schlesinger, and Brown have, from time to time, included veiled threats against the Arab oil producers. These threats have nothing to do with the danger of Soviet communism.

The functions of a U.S. naval presence in the Indian Ocean today may be summarized as follows. First, there is a concern to have oil traffic security. Second, there is a concern to secure oil price security. Third, a visible naval presence can be used as a sign of the availability of U.S. support for pro-U.S. constituencies in the littoral states. Fourth, the availability of naval power could be used in a crisis. A final function is to be able to deploy submarine-launched ballistic missiles in the Indian Ocean. The purpose of this deployment is strategic in the sense that the Arabian Sea and the Bay of Bengal serve as stations so missiles can be positioned against Soviet and Chinese targets.

These goals indicate that U.S. behavior in the Indian Ocean is not meant only as a response to Soviet activities. Some of the goals relate to regional adversaries who are not necessarily Soviet proxies. Conceptually, U.S. external behavior in the Indian Ocean region may be divided into at least four categories. The first represents the dominant image of superpowers competition, of action/reaction beween the superpowers. The second is less public and, as suggested earlier, is more significant. It reflects the development over time of a parallelism in U.S.-USSR interests and relations in the Indian Ocean region. The third category refers to the superpowers' quest to formalize their relationship through a naval agreement. The Indian Ocean naval talks initiated by the Carter administration in 1977 was a step in that direction. Finally there is a growing confrontation between the superpowers and the regional powers. This is marked by a widening gap between the attitudes and policies of the regional powers and those of the superpowers on a variety of issues, such as the North-South dialogue, the law of the sea, nuclear proliferation, Indian Ocean peace zone, Middle East peace, and so on. These four categories constitute the parameters of Indian Ocean international relations at present and in the foreseeable future.

If U.S. external behavior is seen as basically motivated by a desire to respond to external threats, a growth in the number of threats and of U.S. threat perception in relation to the Indian Ocean region should logically increase U.S. involvement in littoral politics and on the Indian Ocean. Instead, comparing the Nixon/Ford/Kissinger administrations and the Carter/Vance/Brzezinski administration, we find a growing gap between the official U.S. pronouncements about the growing dangers of Soviet and Cuban military involvement and the policy outcomes. That is, the "noise" level of U.S. public diplomacy is growing, and the "action" level is declining.

Two different assessments can be made about the gap between "more U.S. talk" and "less U.S. action" on the one hand and the growth of independent power centers in the region (whether these are seen as Soviet proxies or as independent regional power centers) on the other. The first assessment is that more U.S. talk of the Kissinger and Carter variety is a cover for a policy of noninvolvement in issues that do not affect U.S. interests. The United States mostly has important but not vital interests in the region. (The exception is oil.) The Carter policy is a continuation of the Nixon doctrine.

Beginning in the 1970s the emphasis was to let regional rivalries dissipate regional power centers, and on this point the superpowers agree. A low-level U.S. naval and diplomatic presence is therefore adequate for U.S. needs to secure resources, to build bridges with the pro-U.S. constituencies in the regional power centers, and to project military power *if* that becomes necessary in the future. As such the current level of the U.S. naval presence is meant primarily to serve diplomatic, intelligence-acquisition, and communication roles. In this perspective talk and veiled threats are intended to be for cosmetic purposes. The primary aim of U.S. diplomacy is to engage in resource diplomacy, not regional peace making.

The second assessment is different from the first. It argues that the U.S. noninvolvement posture at present is not a policy but the result of an inconclusive debate within the United States and weak U.S. leadership. The weakness is magnified by Carter's personality, the debate between Vance and Brzezinski, and the quest by the Congress to have a voice in foreign policy. The congressional aspect points to a structural change in the U.S. policymaking process, which is reinforced by the absence of a consensus in the Carter administration. This aspect, however, did not begin with Carter. It began after Nixon's downfall, and it was revealed by the Ford/Kissinger administration's African policy.

Implications of Differing Viewpoints

There is a significant variance between U.S. speechmaking and action and between action and effect, particularly during the Carter presidency. The U.S. debate is only in part about how best to respond to the changing international environment, including that of the Indian Ocean. The debate is also a power struggle between members of the U.S. elites, and it relates to general U.S. foreign policy. This struggle became apparent during the Kissinger era (1969–76). As Coral Bell points out

> Between Mr. Dulles' death in early 1959 and Dr. Kissinger's promotion in September 1973, there was really no strong figure as secretary, and this succession of weak monarchies allowed a great strengthening of the competitors for the policy-making role. The presidents themselves and their "courtiers," especially in Mr.

Nixon's time; the enormous bureaucracy of the Pentagon, especially when Mr. McNamara was Secretary of Defense; the vastly ramified "intelligence community," especially the C.I.A.; the Chiefs of Staff jointly and severally; the congressional leadership, and through it assorted lobbies and pressure groups; all these represented competitors, and rather often successful ones, in the formulation of policy. Most of them had views on detente, and *prima facie* not many of them seemed likely to be favorably oriented to it.[6]

Kissinger's problems (Cambodian bombing, the implementation of Vietnamization from 1969 onward, Turkey and Cyprus, Angola issues during 1974–76) became apparent when the Nixon presidency failed as a result of Watergate.[7] In evaluating U.S. policymaking during those years, and thereafter in the Carter presidency, it is worth applying a hypothesis from Soviet studies. J. L. Nogee argues that if a minority viewpoint is likely to lose the argument in the top level of the decision structure, the dispute will be communicated to a wider group, so that "broadening the scope of the conflict may change the outcome."[8] This hypothesis should be refined. If the decision unit has a strong leader (Lenin, Joseph Stalin before 1927, Harry Truman, John Kennedy) and there is a debate between different factions, then the disputes will flow upward for decision by a strong leader. However, if the top leader is weak and there are competing viewpoints, or if there is a struggle for power in the high echelons of the decision unit, then there will be a downward broadening of the dispute. In this second hypothesis the broadening of the scope of the policy dispute or of the power struggle is likely to lead to continuous debate and bureaucratic battles rather than to decisionmaking or conflict resolution. The latter process is dramatized in the Carter administration, but as noted earlier, it originated during the Nixon/Kissinger/Ford era. In part this development can be explained as a consequence of the competition between the executive and the congressional branches of the United States in the foreign policy domain. However, horizontal tension between the two branches does not explain the vertical debates in the executive branch of the U.S. government. Within the executive branch, the presence or absence of a strong leader is an important variable.

In assessing the adequacy of current U.S. policies to respond to changes in the Indian Ocean regional environment, it is necessary to identify briefly the types of changes that are taking place in the region. Saul B. Cohen has correctly identified the area as the potential third geostrategic region in the world, following the trade dependent maritime world and the Eurasian continental world.[9] Today the Indian Ocean region is the crux of the Third World, and the littoral states are the major seekers of a new international economic order. Furthermore, four probable nuclear powers have emerged in the region (India, Pakistan, Israel, and South Africa). Along with Brazil and Argentina those powers make up an impressive list of states that are nuclearizing the southern half of the globe and thereby impinge on the international security debate. The nuclearization is happening in the context of militarization of the Indian Ocean environment by several states. These developments reveal the emergence of secondary powers in the region. Of those, India, Australia, and South Africa are noteworthy in the political-military sphere.

India's capacity to project its naval power beyond the Indian subcontinent is limited at present. In the past a prominent Indian thinker, K. M. Panikkar, emphasized the importance of Indian Ocean defense in Indian strategy.[10] Until recently India's naval establishment had limited budgetary and high-level political support. The Indian government followed a military policy centered on China and Pakistan. Lately, however, India's navy is beginning to emerge as the third or the fourth or the fifth most important naval force in the Indian Ocean (depending on evaluations of the French and the British naval presence). Depending on the status of Indo-U.S. relations, the Indian navy may or may not support U.S. aims in the region.

Australia's orientation has been mostly toward the Pacific Ocean, but gradually Western Australia is expanding its economic and cultural interests in the Indian Ocean region. Even Canberra is slowly beginning to develop a Third World orientation in its foreign policy for the Indian Ocean region. This development is reflected in Canberra's strong interest in Indian Ocean naval developments and in its involvement in the discussions about the Indian Ocean peace zone. South Africa's naval capacity in the Indian Ocean is presently limited to coastal activity. Nevertheless South African defense experts try hard to impress U.S. defense officials with the importance of the Cape route for Western security. In view of South African racial issues, U.S.-South African naval cooperation is likely to remain inhibited. Still, the National Aeronautics and Space Administration has been critically dependent on South Africa for the U.S. space program,[11] and furthermore, South Africa's Silvermine communications network probably extends to the Bay of Bengal.[12] So, South Africa's interest in the Indian Ocean environment is obvious.

The trends in Indian Ocean regional relations point to a troubled future for the United States in that area. With the growing local nationalism, the U.S. plea for order in the world is half-lost because of the cultural and ethnic forces that actively generate controlled disorder. In other words, President Carter is presiding over a country that faces serious challenges to its authority in regional international relations in the Indian Ocean area.

This trend did not start with events in the 1970s; indeed, its origins can be traced historically. Since the mid-1800s the size of the international system has been expanding, and the number of actors and the number of transactions have grown. The real threat to U.S. global interests did not come with the wave of anticolonialism in the 1950s. At that time the United States was highly regarded as the engine of Third World development and as the source of high and intermediate technology in a seller's market. The United States did not have to worry about Third World independence because U.S. aid and trade policies enabled it to penetrate Third World industrial and political infrastructures. Today, the regional infrastructures are stronger. The Third World nations have more experience in dealing with foreigners, and as third parties they have the capacity to deny their voluntary participation to the superpowers. Undoubtedly the superpowers continue to have a greater capacity to mobilize military and economic power, but their capacity to establish viable regimes is not firm.

Most beneficiaries of U.S. largess outside the North Atlantic industrial orbit (Japan, India, Iran, and Pakistan, for example) have accepted U.S. technology but have rejected U.S. political culture. Indeed, as technology flowed into those countries, cultural nationalism also grew. Today there is a major interface between the technology flow from the West to the non-Western world and the transfer of raw materials from the latter to the former. (However, the reverse may be true with regard to Japan.) There is also an interface between the growth of technology transfers and cultural nationalism. Resource diplomacy and cultural nationalism are driving forces in Indian Ocean international relations.

The People's Republic of China (PRC) usually gets credit for encouraging the growth of Third World and third party cultural nationalism, but China's contribution is actually limited. China has implied that the world needed a third force. It was never clear, however, if China was staking its own claim to be the third force or whether it was making the claim on behalf of the Third World. China's critics argue that its aspirations are muddled and that the country is unprincipled. On the one hand China aspires to gain a seat at the big-power table, and on the other hand it aspires to lead the Third World. According to the superpowers, détente has come about because both powers are traditional, not revolutionary, powers and they are not interested in a major change in the present world order. Détente implies that the superpowers would prefer that Third World revolutions and the quest for an altered world order be curbed. Since 1972 China has behaved like a traditional state, and now it is not credible as a Third World leader. Furthermore, China has failed to establish a dominant political, military, or economic position in South and Southeast Asia, and it is therefore doubtful whether it can be a principal force in Indian Ocean international relations. It appears to be winning tactically as an honorary NATO member, but it may be facing strategic defeat in the international arena. If China gets too close to the United States and if the U.S. image of a "loser" grows, there could be a loss in the PRC's international status.

If a capacity to act is the true measure, then OPEC rather than China struck the first real blow against the superpowers' view that there were only two principals in the international arena. The oil crisis of 1973 hurt all developed countries economically and psychologically, and it brought into the open the probability of Third World collaboration. The central lesson of OPEC diplomacy is not simply that the oil weapon works; that conclusion is the consequence of oil being a unique strategic resource. Rather the real lesson of OPEC diplomacy is that collective action made public the possibility and the advantage of collective self-reliance by third parties in international diplomacy. This is a new element with global significance for Third World international relations and for international relations generally. The OPEC blow is the most significant, but other blows—such as actions by Third World states in Southeast Asia, South Asia, the Middle East, and Africa during various crises—point to the rise of a growing pattern of third party activity that cannot be explained as proxy actions.

The challenge by the Indian Ocean states is directed against both superpowers. Neither superpower has much use for nonalignment as a third force, and both assert that international security is the responsibility of the two principals. The superpower theory works in bilateral superpower military relations, in Europe and in Northeast Asia, but the superpowers are not perceived as the primary determinants today by many local and regional elites in the Indian Ocean region.

This trend has several implications. The number of actors who impinge on regional and local power balances has grown in the 1970s, as has their self-confidence to act contrary to superpower interests if regional power balancing so requires. Vietnam, India, and Iran have acted at different times without respecting superpower admonitions. Even a tiny state like Afghanistan is not responsive to Soviet supervision. The number of international transactions and interactions has increased in political, military, and economic areas. There is a growing consciousness in the world that the superpowers have become dependent on and possibly vulnerable to Third World conduct. Of course, this does not mean the end of the superpowers' influence. It means that the size of the decision units in international and regional military and economic security issues has grown and that the superpowers must now accommodate third party views and interests.

Overall, the strategic picture in the Indian Ocean with respect to superpowers conduct is not as gloomy as some commentators suggest. *Peking Review* has alleged that "the two superpowers have beefed up their military strength in the Indian Ocean" and that "the scramble for the area between the United States and the Soviet Union will become even fiercer in the days to come."[13] The 1976 Stockholm International Peace Research Institute (SIPRI) *Yearbook* makes the judgment that

> the conversion of Diego Garcia into a fully fledged US naval and air base would considerably complicate the delicate situation in the In-

dian Ocean. If the proposal is carried through, then one great power will have established a major strategic naval base from which it could deploy its strategic nuclear submarines in the Indian Ocean conveniently and economically. The other great power will then almost certainly search for a similar base in the area, and a new strategic arms race will have begun.[14]

Each assertion is plausible but is imprecise. The PRC view makes sense if the premise is that contention between the superpowers is permanent and another war is likely. The SIPRI view makes sense if the premise is that a single new base (Diego Garcia) is enough to produce another arms race. These premises are questionable.

There is no logical link between "beefing up" and "even fiercer superpower competition." The image of fiercer competition is devoid of meaning; superpower talk is usually fierce in the Indian Ocean region. Undoubtedly, developing Diego Garcia into a permanent facility beefs up the U.S. presence. However, Soviet leader Leonid Brezhnev emphasized publicly the need to have a "fair and square" bargain between the superpowers.[15] In 1977 President Carter initiated talks to stabilize, and to eventually demilitarize, the Indian Ocean. The willingness to negotiate is a sign that "beefing up" does not mean a growing competition as the Chinese allege.

President Carter's decision to open naval talks with the USSR was a bold one. The 1977 Carter diplomatic posture had a number of motives. First, since Soviet diplomacy constantly plays the disarmament theme before Third World audiences, President Carter's move diluted the Soviet propaganda advantage. Talk is cheap, and there was nothing to be lost by speaking about Indian Ocean demilitarization. Second, by making the issue a bilateral one, the superpowers could buy time against UN demands to make the Indian Ocean into a peace zone. Third, the talks strengthened détente because they pointed to the existence of a common interest to avoid a naval race in the region. Fourth, formal negotiations enabled the United States to get a better feel for Soviet policies and intentions in the region. According to a U.S. journalist the superpowers agreed in June 1977 that the negotiations should be bilateral and confidential, that both had significant strategic interests in the Indian Ocean, that stabilization came before reductions, and that there was agreement about the types of arms to be discussed. There was no agreement about the definition of a base. The Soviet Union showed greatest concern about U.S. strategic forces in the Indian Ocean—missiles, submarines, and B-52 bombers. The USSR sought a "narrow view of each side's legitimate interests" and "strict limitations" beyond that.[16] According to *Strategic Survey,* the USSR demand in January 1978 was to renounce construction of new bases or to expand existing ones.[17] Fifth, bilateral Indian Ocean talks were a double-edged sword. To avoid prejudicing the outcome, UN peace zone diplomacy could not be effectively pressed by the Third World, and at the same time Third World naval advocates could not press their case for modernization when the superpowers appeared to be moving toward demilitarization.[18] Finally, in 1977 détente was in trouble, and the initiation of new arms control talks signaled to Moscow the U.S. interest in continuing to discuss international security in regions that were marginal to the central balance.

The negotiations were seriously undertaken up to February 1978. In the last round of the meetings the two sides were six months away from agreement. A status quo agreement was intended, and by the last round of talks the area of negotiability had been established. Diego Garcia was not negotiable. The factor motivating an agreement on the Soviet Union's side was its desire to limit the deployment of U.S. strategic ballistic missile carrying submarines (SSBNs) in the Indian Ocean. The U.S. interest was based on the fear that if the Soviet navy succeeded in securing bases or facilities in Vietnam, that change would increase the operational efficiency of the Soviet naval forces in the Indian Ocean. It would increase the on-station and resupply capacities of the Soviet navy in the region, and it would require a stretching out of the U.S. Pacific naval presence into the Indian Ocean. The premise behind this concern was that prospects did not exist for the establishment of a Fifth Fleet in the Indian Ocean.

The factors that pushed the United States and the USSR toward negotiations, therefore, were diverse and not common. Moreover, they were limited in importance. For the Soviet Union the concern about the U.S. deployment of SSBNs in the Indian Ocean was bound by time. The deployment of the *Trident* in the 1980s was likely to lessen the importance of the Indian Ocean as an arena for U.S. strategic deployment. For the United States the concern about Soviet acquisition of facilities in Vietnam declined in importance in

1978. Vietnam was in no mood to create a permanent dependency on the USSR. The suspension of the Indian Ocean talks in February 1978 meant that the superpowers did not share a common interest in freezing their naval presence at the 1977 level. That is, neither side was willing to negotiate on the basis of the status quo, although both sought stability through parallelism. Furthermore, both sides had interests in the region, and these interests did not require competitive action/reaction between the superpowers. Even if one superpower were to withdraw from the region, the other would probably stay. So formal agreement was unnecessary and problematic because the Indian Ocean regional environment was fluid. The regional power structures were changing. Ambiguity in the environment, therefore, required ambiguity in the response of each superpower to the situation.

In the current Indian Ocean environment, ambiguity has its uses. The direction of future challenges—for instance, in Africa—is unclear. One view is that a racial war in southern Africa is unavoidable; therefore the United States should take the side of goodness and the likely winner—the blacks—and abandon the whites. But there is another viewpoint that argues that the blacks in South Africa and on the African continent have yet to make up their minds about the whites. Accommodation between blacks and whites is possible, starting with the dismantling of apartheid, moving toward real economic reform that gives the blacks a stake in the system, and eventually leading to meaningful social and political change. The new South African prime minister, Pieter Botha, seems to want a change if his countrymen will allow it. The Soviet Union will not liberate the blacks, but instead seeks a seat at the big-power table if and when the time comes to settle South Africa's fate. The likely pattern of Soviet involvement in Africa is similar to its involvement in the Middle East, that is, to stay involved even if that means shifting regional partners or clients. The African blacks know this, and therefore they have not made up their minds about the role of an armed struggle with Soviet help. They are willing to negotiate a deal between South African and black moderates.

A second view suggests that the Soviet presence in Africa creates an opportunity for the United States to encourage the Russians to "stew in their own juice." Therefore noninvolvement or limited involvement is the policy. The prescription is that the United States should not react to Soviet penetration into Africa (and into the Middle East) because the penetration carries with it the causes of its own failure. To win the military battle is not necessarily to win the peace.

However appealing this view is, some elites find it dangerous. The image of U.S. inertia in the perceptions of the decision makers in the littoral states could result in a belief that the United States is weak. According to a recent statement by Ayatollah Khomeini, the president of the United States is "impotent."[19] This statement is heavy stuff for the U.S. ego. It clashes with the widely held U.S. belief that without U.S. participation and leadership there can be no stable world order. For this reason the "cold warriors" assert the need for moral leadership and military intervention in response to the extension of the Soviet and the Cuban military presence into the Indian Ocean region.

If the first approach advocates inertia as policy and the second one advocates intervention as an alternative to weakness, yet a third approach should be considered. Neither superpower is in a position to assert its leadership position in the Indian Ocean littoral today. Today, superpower concert is not possible, and superpower détente is of limited significance in shaping the parameters of Indian Ocean international relations. The need for the future is substantially different: a quiet, political, bilateral, resource and development diplomacy rather than the public military diplomacy of a superpower-led world order. However, the U.S. decision structure is slow and bureaucratic, the present political leadership is weak, and the domestic debates are unsettled. The addition of the third approach is unlikely to produce a speedy resolution of domestic U.S. debates unless moderates in the United States link up with moderates abroad and pursue extensive negotiations rather than the politics of intensive talk and warmongering with domestic and international enemies.

Notes

1. Michael P. Sullivan, *International Relations: Theories and Evidence* (Englewood Cliffs, N.J.: Prentice-Hall, 1976), p. 153.
2. Recently Marshall D. Shulman, a high-ranking U.S. expert on the

Soviet Union, told the House of Representatives Subcommittee on Foreign Affairs that "the most serious potential problem" between the superpowers is the possibility of an escalating war in southern Africa. Cited in Tom Wicker, "Bad News for Zimbabwe," New York Times service, *Globe and Mail* (Toronto), October 23, 1979, p. 7.

3. George Lichtheim, *Imperialism* (New York: Praeger, 1972), pp. 146-147.

4. Tom Wicker, "Bad News for Zimbabwe."

5. See Library of Congress, Congressional Research Service, *The United States, India, and South Asia: Interests, Trends, and Issues for Congressional Concern*, Prepared at request of the Subcommittee on Asian and Pacific Affairs, House Committee on International Relations (Washington, D.C.: Government Printing Office, 1978), pp. 11-14. For the historical background about U.S. Indian Ocean policy see Kim C. Beazley and Ian Clark, *Politics of Intrusion: The Super Powers and the Indian Ocean* (Sydney: Alternatives Publishing Cooperative, Ltd., 1979), particularly Chapter 1.

6. Coral Bell, *The Diplomacy of Detente* (New York: St. Martin's Press, 1977), p. 38.

7. Ibid., pp. 46-50.

8. J. L. Nogee, ed., *Man, State, and Society in the Soviet Union* (New York: Praeger, 1972), p. 229.

9. Saul B. Cohen, *Geography and Politics in a Divided World*, 2nd ed. (Oxford: Oxford University Press, 1975), p. 66.

10. K. M. Panikkar, *India and the Indian Ocean: An Essay on the Influence of Sea Power on Indian History* (London: George Allen and Unwin Ltd., 1945), pp. 82, 93.

11. Mohd. A. El-Khawas and Barry Cohen, eds., *The Kissinger Study of Southern Africa*, National Security Study Memorandum, 39 (Westport, Conn.: Lawrence Hill and Co., 1976), Annex 8.

12. Republic of South Africa, *South Africa 1977 Official Yearbook*, 4th ed., p. 946.

13. *Peking Review*, January 12, 1972.

14. Stockholm International Peace Research Institute (SIPRI), *1975 Yearbook*, (Stockholm: Almqvist and Wiksell Förlag, 1976) pp. 81-82.

15. *Pravda*, June 12, 1971.

16. Jack Fuller, "Dateline Diego Garcia: Paved-Over Paradise," *Foreign Policy*, no. 28 (Fall 1977):175-186.

17. *Strategic Survey* (London: International Institute for Strategic Studies, 1977), p. 102.

18. For a discussion of the Indian Ocean peace zone concept, see SIPRI, *1975 Yearbook*, pp. 436-438.

19. *Globe and Mail* (Toronto), November 8, 1979, p. 1.

8
Soviet Arms Supplies and Indian Ocean Diplomacy

Ian Clark

This chapter is intended as a contribution to the ongoing debate on the issues of dependency and political leverage in relation to conventional arms supplies, and it will explore these questions in the specific context of Soviet supplies to selected Indian Ocean littoral states.[1] It is not my intention to argue that the sole, or even the dominant, Soviet motivation in supplying arms is to secure a degree of political or diplomatic influence over the recipient states; indeed, it is now clear that economic considerations are far from negligible in determining Soviet supply policy.[2] Nevertheless, recent events around the Indian Ocean littoral provide us with interesting insights into the performance of the Soviet military supply program and allow us to arrive at a revised assessment of the politico-diplomatic impact of those supplies, a process of review and reassessment that, we may assume, is likewise being conducted in Soviet leadership circles.

Military supplies have traditionally been the foremost instrument of Soviet diplomacy in the Third World, and the Indian Ocean littoral states are no exception in this regard. The limited dimensions of Soviet economic aid disbursements, the small scale of Soviet trading relationships, and the infertile ground for Soviet cultural penetration in those countries have all served to underwrite the primacy of military supplies and military instruction in Soviet-Indian Ocean diplomacy. Accordingly, even if it is conceded that the notion of political leverage makes sense only in the context of a totality of a multifaceted relationship, the military supply nexus must be regarded as highly significant in the Soviet case.

There is, perhaps, a need for some justification of the adoption of an Indian Ocean focus in order to analyze this aspect of Soviet policy. Such justification is provided by the fact that certain key recipients of Soviet military equipment are Indian Ocean littoral states and by the fact that Indian Ocean states, collectively, now account for a substantial proportion of total Soviet supplies to Third World countries. The importance of the Indian Ocean dimension of the Soviet supply program has been concealed by the manner in which statistics are presented; the breakdown of the Soviet arms trade is commonly given either on a country by country basis or on a regional basis, and of course, the Indian Ocean itself is not listed as one of the regions. From these country and regional lists we can, however, piece together some measure of the prominence of the Indian Ocean littoral states as a destination for Soviet conventional arms supplies. For instance, over the period 1955–74, if deliveries to Egypt and Syria are excluded (which alone accounted for 45 percent of the total Soviet supplies to the Third World), then some 90 percent of Soviet military supplies were directed to the Indian Ocean or immediate hinterland states.[3] A similar calculation for the period 1964–73 gives a figure on the order of 80 percent, by value, of Soviet weapons exports directed toward the Indian Ocean states.[4] Recent deliveries to countries such as Ethiopia, the People's Democratic Republic of Yemen, and Afghanistan continue this overall trend.

It should also be recalled that some of the Third World countries that have the closest links with the USSR, and especially those that have been the recipients of large quantities of Soviet military equipment, have formalized their links with the Soviet Union during the 1970s by means of treaties of peace and friendship. Again, it is highly significant that many of the countries that have signed the treaties are Indian Ocean or immediate hinterland states. They include Mozambique, Somalia (formerly), Ethiopia, Iraq, Afghanistan, and India. Accordingly, this chapter will survey the recent development of the Soviet Union's military relationships with India, Iraq, and the Horn of Africa to provide illustrations of the current status of Soviet military supply diplomacy in each of the main Indian Ocean regions covered in this book.

Soviet-Indian Military Relations

The emergence of cordial Soviet-Indian ties in the mid-1950s was not immediately followed by the supply of Soviet military equipment to India, unlike the USSR's simultaneous courting of Egypt. The small quantity of equipment that was transferred prior to 1962 – mostly transport aircraft and helicopters – was ostensibly of a noncombatant nature. It was in 1962 that the Soviet-Indian military relationship solidified, and that development was expressed in the signing of the accords for the MiG project, whereby India was licensed to produce supersonic MiG-21 fighter aircraft. Despite the many problems with the MiG project, it has remained the backbone of the Soviet military link with India since 1962.

The MiG project has passed through several stages of development. In the early years, Hindustan Aeronautics, Ltd. (HAL), simply assembled entire kits imported from the Soviet Union.[5] It was 1970 before the Indian air force (IAF) took delivery of the first MiG constructed from "indigenous" components. In 1972 an agreement was finalized for HAL to manufacture an improved version, the MiG-21M, which became operational in 1974.[6] The new version, like its predecessor, was produced at three HAL facilities located at Hyderabad, Koraput, and Nasik.[7] Finally, in 1978, a protocol was concluded for yet another refinement of the MiG, this time designated the MiG-21 BIS, which was reported to have a superior engine and superior avionics.[8]

In terms of the general supply of Soviet military equipment to India, it does not appear that the signing of the treaty of peace and friendship in August 1971 represented any significant change of policy. All three branches of the Indian armed services were using Soviet equipment by 1971, and their holdings included some 450 T-54/55 and 150 PT-76 tanks, 8 MiG-21 squadrons, and 5 SU-7 squadrons, as well as an assortment of naval craft such as Foxtrot-class submarines, Petya-class frigates, Poluchat-class patrol boats, and Osa-class torpedo boats.[9]

Since 1971, there does not appear to have been any marked change, either in the tempo or the range, in Indian acquisitions from the Soviet Union. In fact, from a variety of sources, it is possible to illustrate the nature and extent of major Indian arms purchases from the USSR since 1971.

Table 8.1

SOVIET SUPPLIES TO INDIA, 1971-1978

Armored vehicles	T-54/-55 tanks[a]	450
Aircraft	SU-7B	50 (in 1971)
	MiG-21M	(licensed production from program of 150)
	MiG-21 PFMA/MF	Small numbers imported from USSR to compensate for shortfalls in domestic production
	IL-38[b]	7 delivered or on order
	Helicopters	Various
Naval Craft	Foxtrot-class submarine	4
	Petya-class frigate	7
	Kashin-class destroyer	2
	Nanuchka-class corvette	5 from 8 ordered
	Osa-class torpedo boat	total 16 of which 8-10 received since 1971
	Polnocny-class landing craft	6

[a] The Military Balance 1977-1978 includes T-62 tanks but the subsequent issue, 1978-1979 does not. The International Defense Review no. 4 (1976), page 535 also reports Indian acquisition of T-62s but this was not confirmed.

[b] These are not listed in The Military Balance 1978-1979.

Sources: Annual issues of The Military Balance, World Armaments and Disarmaments: The SIPRI Yearbook; and Jane's Fighting Ships.

As is the case for other recipients of Soviet military supplies, the story of Soviet-Indian military cooperation is not without its periods of friction and rumors of Indian dissatisfaction. The complaints have never been expressed as vociferously as they were by Egypt, since there has been no open rupture in Soviet-Indian relations, and yet there have been persistent indications of discontent below the surface. The main sources of Indian complaint appear to have been in relation to retransfers of spares and equipment by India, the availability of spares from the Soviet Union, and the terms and conditions of some of India's agreements with the USSR. The evidence pertaining to these issues will be briefly reviewed as India's response to them constitutes a significant dimension of our assessment of the degree of India's dependence upon the USSR as a result of the armaments nexus.

Although it has been generally recognized that the United States has had some difficulties with third party retransfers of its military equipment, similar Soviet problems have attracted far less scrutiny. It is now clear, however, that the USSR, no less than the United States, has been anxious to see its "end-use" clauses observed and to maintain final authorization over the retransfer of spares and parts for its own equipment. The potential retransfer problem first became public when Egypt requested spares for its MiG aircraft from India after the termination of direct Soviet supplies to Egypt. An Indian mission apparently visited Cairo during 1975, and HAL, interested in developing its own export potential, seemed likely to gain a contract for the supply of spares to Egypt.[10] However, the deal was blocked by Soviet intervention. The Indian government later released a statement that claimed that the Egyptian deal had been prevented because of "contractual commitments,"[11] and the fact that it was Soviet intervention that prevented the deal was confirmed by Pres. Anwar Sadat, who cited the incident as a main reason for the termination of the Soviet-Egyptian friendship treaty.[12] Moreover, it does not appear that the incident was an isolated one. According to one report, an Indian attempt to supply aircraft spares to Indonesia was similarly subject to a Soviet veto.[13]

The issue of supplies to third parties has not been the only cause of Indian uneasiness, although the evidence pertaining to other areas is more tenuous. There appears to have been some Indian dissatisfaction with the availability from the Soviet Union of necessary spares for equipment, although whether the unavailability has occurred as a form of political leverage, as was the case with Egypt, or whether it has simply reflected constraints in Soviet defense production remains unclear. In any case, one account, which is unfortunately undocumented, makes the following claim:

> The trouble began when the Soviets started holding up spare parts shipment after the December war, and later began refusing to deliver

advanced equipment.

Spares for the Mi-4 helicopters, replacement gun barrels for the T-54/55 tanks, torpedoes for the Foxtrot-class submarines and ammunition for the 130mm guns became increasingly difficult to obtain. Military missions going to Moscow in 1972, 1973 and 1974 found themselves coming back empty-handed or with only a fraction of their requirements.[14]

The matter of nonsupply of advanced equipment is less clear-cut. The fact that only India, among the many close recipients of Soviet equipment, has not acquired the MiG-23 Flogger has occasionally been cited in this context, with the implication that the USSR has turned down Indian requests to supply this aircraft. Indeed, SIPRI reported that India had placed an order for fifty such aircraft in 1974, but the aircraft have never materialized in the IAF.[15] It may, therefore, be the case that the Soviet authorities refused to sanction the sale. Alternatively, it may be that the order was never placed for the reason that Indian air force personnel did not want that particular aircraft. When it came to selection of the new deep-penetration strike aircraft for the IAF in 1978, it appears that the air force had strong reservations about the MiG-23, mainly on account of its limited range.

Finally, India has had some differences of opinion with the USSR on the question of payment. It is generally argued that a major reason for the attractiveness of Soviet supplies is financial. They are comparatively cheap, and the Soviets are willing to accept payment in rupees. However, these factors have not prevented some financial bickering between the two parties. On the one hand, as is true for almost every aspect of Soviet-Indian trade, there has been throughout the 1970s the running sore of the ruble-rupee exchange rate and the persistent Indian charge that the ruble has been inflated. This unhappiness has served to take some of the edge off the impression of "generous terms" for Soviet equipment. On the other hand, it also appears that India has not been unaffected by the growing Soviet predilection for payment in hard currency for its arms supplies.[16] As early as 1972 it was reported that India was being required by the Soviet authorities to make its MiG license payments in U.S. dollars.[17] It should be noted, however, that the terms and conditions of payment for Indian purchases have created vexing questions for arms sellers other the USSR as well; India has had difficulty in arranging acceptable financial terms with such countries as Britain, Canada, and Sweden to name but a few examples.

It is not being suggested that either India's policy of diversification in sources of arms supply, or its policy of eventual self-reliance for military equipment, has been solely inspired by tensions within the Soviet-Indian military relationship. Such an interpretation would indeed be a gross distortion of the events of the past decade. In fact, many circumstances, including India's industrial potential, its espoused nonalignment, its acute sense of military vulnerability after 1962, and its unhappy experience with other suppliers such as the United Kingdom and the United States, would have dictated a course for India in which reliance upon external suppliers would be reduced and overreliance on a single supplier would be self-consciously avoided. What India's experience with the Soviet Union has caused is a reinforcement of India's faith in the wisdom of those two tenets of arms policy.

Consequently, any study that seeks to explore the degree of buyer dependence upon a military supplier must take into account the degree of diversification in arms purchases as well as the extent of indigenous defense production. It becomes immediately apparent that India has highly developed policies in both these areas, even if all the results hoped for have not been realized.

The impression, which is sometimes fostered, that the USSR is virtually India's sole supplier of military equipment is a totally misleading one. Nor has any radical change in the variety of Indian suppliers come about solely as a result of the "genuine nonalignment" policies of the Janata government; the evidence of diversification was as strong during the period of Mrs. Gandhi's leadership. India has long been involved in a number of licensed production projects with Britain and France. In the case of Britain, the most prominent examples are the arrangements with Hawker-Siddeley for the manufacture of the Gnat, with Vickers for the Vijayanta tank, and the licensed production of the series of Leander-class frigates. With regard to France, India has long been involved in the licensed production of helicopters (in cooperation with Aerospatiale) and of assorted missiles.

More recently, however, there has been compelling evidence that

India is persisting in this policy of diversification. In October 1978, after a delay of some years, it was announced that the new generation of Indian deep-penetration squadrons would be composed of Anglo-French Jaguars. India has placed an initial order for some forty of the aircraft, and after their delivery the plane will be manufactured under license in India. Additionally, in refurbishing the aircraft complement of the aging carrier *Vikrant,* it is now confirmed that India has selected the British Sea Harrier.[18] Likewise, although India's submarine force is entirely ex-Soviet, India has for some time been exploring the possibilities of collaboration in submarine production with a range of countries, including West Germany, Sweden, Holland, and France but excluding the USSR. Finally, the next major purchase that will be made by the Indian armed forces is for a new-generation battle tank. Contrary to widely circulated reports that India had placed an order for T-72 tanks with the Soviet Union,[19] it has recently been made clear that no final decision has, as yet, been made. Under consideration, apart from the T-72, are the Chieftain and the Leopard 11.[20]

Apart from diversifying its sources of foreign supply, India has also sought to expand its own domestic defense production and to increase the proportion of its indigenous license-produced equipment, although it remains far from certain that these policies have produced the desired results. One of the arguments in favor of indigenous production is that it leads to foreign exchange savings, but some analysts have denied that such savings have occurred, especially in connection with the MiG project. Childs and Kidron, in fact, have estimated that the actual cost of a HAL-manufactured MiG could be double that of a fully imported aircraft from the USSR.[21] Similarly, Huisken has noted that

> the ambition to save foreign exchange is difficult to realize in practice. Indian production of the MiG-21 is a case in point. The average unit manufacturing cost of these planes has been calculated at 14.4 million rupees of which 8.3 million rupees were in foreign exchange to cover Soviet-supplied materials and components. The cost of a fully-imported aircraft was 6-7.5 million rupees.[22]

It is implicit in the above argument that a large percentage of the components still has to be imported, even in equipment built under license in India. In 1974 the Indian government stated that the import content of the MiG-21M was some 40 percent,[23] which reflects the hard reality that although Indian defense industries have made large strides, they are still far from self-contained. Similarly, the first of the Leander frigates manufactured by Mazagon in Bombay had an import content of 82 percent, and the sixth and last, launched in 1977, had an import content of 44 percent.[24] Nonetheless, despite these apparent shortcomings and despite the low production rates achieved in both of these projects, India maintains that it makes sound political sense to press ahead with indigenization of defense production wherever possible. Most recently, India has attempted to accelerate the process of indigenization in connection with the new MiG-21 BIS and has, if newspaper reports are accurate, attempted to secure Soviet agreement to the buy-back clause, which is becoming a standard feature of Indian arms agreements.[25] In accordance with the buy-back clause, the holder of the license agrees to purchase parts and components from the Indian manufacturer for the licensee's own equipment. To what extent the Soviet authorities will accede to this request remains to be seen, and it may be regarded as a test case in Soviet arms supply policy and indicative of the delicate balance of influence that seems to be emerging between the arms supplier and the arms recipient as the arms trade becomes an increasingly competitive one.

Soviet-Iraqi Military Relations

Iraq represents something of a hybrid case as far as Soviet Indian Ocean politics are concerned. The reason for this is that Soviet interests in Iraq are only intelligible in terms of a confluence of two perspectives, one of which is more narrowly confined to the core Middle East dispute, and the other of which is related to broader Indian Ocean strategic matters. In other words, in analyzing the pattern of Soviet military deliveries to Iraq, we must be careful to bear in mind Iraq's situation as a quasi-front-line state in relation to Israel and not simply its role in Soviet Indian Ocean littoral diplomacy. It is only in terms of this dual perspective that we can appreciate the large quantities of arms received by Iraq from the USSR. In fact, over the period 1955–74, Iraq ranked third in the list of Third World recipients of Soviet military supplies.[26]

The USSR has been the prime supplier of Iraqi equipment for the past two decades and, according to some estimates, has delivered some $2 billion worth of equipment, divided equally between the pre- and post-1973 periods. Major inflows of weaponry occurred during and after the war in June 1967, making good the Iraqi losses incurred during the war and boosting the amounts of Iraqi equipment beyond prewar totals. According to Lenczowski, by 1971 the Soviet Union had delivered to Iraq some 50 MiG-21s, 50 to 60 SU-7s, 100 to 150 tanks (bringing the total to 600), 300 personnel carriers, and assorted guns and rockets.[27] The following year saw the signing of the Soviet-Iraqi friendship treaty, and that was followed by an intensified period of military collaboration between the two countries in accordance with Article 9 of the treaty, which stated that the parties would "continue to develop co-operation in the strengthening of their defense capabilities." Several months later, in September 1972, a joint communiqué issued at the end of Pres. Ahmad Hassan al-Bakr's visit to the USSR testified that the two parties "had agreed on concrete measures to strengthen further the defensive capacity of the Iraqi Republic with the aim of increasing the combat readiness of its armed forces."[28]

The increased tempo of deliveries to Iraq (and to Syria) at this time coincided with the slowdown in supplies to Egypt, and that trend is highlighted by figures provided by Gur Ofer. Ofer periodizes Soviet deliveries to Iraq, giving average annual deliveries, and then displays the growth rates between the periods (see Table 8.2).[29]

Table 8.2
Soviet Military Aid to Iraq

Millions of rubles per year			Annual growth rates	
(a) 1955–66	(b) 1967–71	(c) 1971–74	b to a	c to b
29	40	195	3	149

Among other factors, the table reflects the impact of the Yom Kippur War.[30] Of interest is the fact that although the USSR had declined to supply its more modern TU-22 Blinder bombers to Egypt during the October War, a squadron of those aircraft was stationed in Iraq. However, according to most accounts, the aircraft were under strict Soviet control and were not used for war-related operations.³¹ Since 1973, the USSR has continued to be a major source of Iraqi equipment, with one report identifying a large new Soviet-Iraqi arms package in August 1976.³² Although the terms of the Soviet sales to Iraq are not made public, there is a widespread consensus among Western analysts that Iraqi purchases have, at least partially, been funded by supplies of oil to the USSR. The principal Soviet arms deliveries to Iraq since 1974 have included several hundred T-62 tanks, Scud SSMs, 4 squadrons of MiG-23 fighters with an order for the large Soviet IL-76 transport, as well as an assortment of small- to medium-sized naval craft.

Despite this well-established habit of military cooperation between the two countries, it is evident that Iraq has not been susceptible to undue Soviet influence and that there have been indications of various sources of tension between the two states in the last few years. As one writer concluded with respect to Iraq, "there is no evidence that the Soviet Union has been able to convert its position into real economic and political influence."³³

There are many reasons why this should have been so. Most generally, Iraq's economic ties with the West have become more visible since 1973, and like the other oil producers, Iraq's increased purchasing power has led it into the market for Western goods and technology. Such a trend is reflected in the fact that since 1973, Iraqi imports from the Soviet bloc have dropped from 25 percent to 9 percent of the Iraqi total.³⁴

More specifically, the course of events in the Horn of Africa during the Ogaden War of 1977–78 imposed some serious strains on Soviet-Iraqi relations. Although the Soviet Union executed an adroit change of alliances, substituting Ethiopia for Somalia as Moscow's principal ally on the Horn, Iraq maintained a consistent support for Somalia and did not follow the Soviet lead. In the Ogaden War therefore, there was the confusing situation of Iraqi (Soviet-supplied) Antonov-12 transports flying military equipment to Mogadishu to assist the Somalian offensive against the Soviet-supported Ethiopians, a situation that becomes doubly confusing when it is recalled that the Ethiopian forces were also being assisted by Israeli military instructors. Moreover, Moscow's support for Mengistu has led it into confrontation with Eritrean movements toward which Iraq has traditionally been very sympathetic. As an Iraqi newspaper, *Al Thawrah*, put it on August 16, 1977, with obvious reference to the apparent Soviet turnabout on Eritrea, "We cannot change our position as long as the Eritrean people are fighting for their just and legitimate rights." The dispute over Eritrea had the additional tangible effect of making Moscow's airlift of supplies to Ethiopia even more complex since the Iraqis blocked Soviet overflight facilities. Saddam Hussein al-Takriti is reported to have told the Soviets bluntly that "if their attitude towards the Eritrean conflict didn't change, we could not allow their transport aircraft to use our facilities."[35] It is not in the least difficult, given this general context, to accept at face value the various reports circulating during 1977 that the Iraqis were seeking to reduce the number of Soviet military advisers stationed in Iraq.

As was the case for India, any survey of recent Soviet-Iraqi military relationships would be incomplete without some recounting of the extent of Iraq's diversification of its sources of military supplies, although precisely what significance we should attribute to such diversification is not self-evident. To make only the most obvious of points, diversification in a client-state's sources of military equipment may be understood as prima facie evidence of that client's autonomy from a major-power supplier, but whether as cause or symptom of that autonomy is unclear. A recipient state may have greater freedom of action because its arms purchases are diversified, or alternatively, it may only be able to diversify its purchases because of some other feature of its relationship with the major power—yet another instance of the old chicken-and-egg relationship.

At any rate, as in the case of India, Iraq has some history of buying equipment from suppliers other than the USSR, although it should be emphasized that the Soviet Union still is the dominant supplier. This process of diversification appears to have accelerated in recent years, and a few illustrative examples may be cited. France has, since 1974, supplied Iraq with some 47 Alouette III helicopters, and Britain has supplied a number of Landrovers and Rangerovers, which, in combat terms, we must concede to be of trifling significance. By 1975, however, reports were circulating that the Iraqi air force was going to make some major new purchases and that it was interested in acquiring the French-made Mirage F-1.[36] The decision to go ahead with that purchase was finally made in 1977,[37] and according to *The Military Balance 1978–79,* an order was placed for 32 Mirage F-1C fighters. Such a major reequipping of the Iraqi fighter force from non-Soviet sources cannot fail to have political overtones and repercussions. Since we can safely assume that the Soviet authorities would have pushed hard to persuade the Iraqis to make a Soviet purchase, the very fact that the Mirage deal has been concluded is in itself evidence of Moscow's circumscribed influence in such matters.

Soviet Military Supplies and the Horn of Africa

Soviet involvement in the Horn of Africa, and its military supply policy in that area, reflect a recurrent pattern that has been demonstrated in various Third World regions of interest to the USSR. What has permitted the USSR to intrude diplomatically and militarily into some areas has been the prior existence of a regional dispute and the fact that one party to the dispute has received assistance from the West. The USSR's blandishments have been persuasive in such a context, with the result that the Soviet Union has usually taken advantage of, and contributed to, the emergency of polarized regional conflicts in which the local parties are supported by the rival superpowers. Furthermore, it has also been a recurrent theme in Soviet-Third World relations that the creation of such polarized conflict situations, and Moscow's military backing of one of the parties, have been obstructive to the fulfillment of the USSR's wider regional ambitions in the long run as circumstances change. For instance, Soviet intrusion into the subcontinent was facilitated by Pakistan's adhesion to the Western alliance system, but the very diplomatic and military support that made the Soviet connection attractive to India came back to haunt Moscow in the latter 1960s when the Soviet Union attempted to cultivate a relationship with Pakistan as well. Likewise, the perennial tensions between Iraq and Iran and Iran's close military ties with the West formed an additional reason for Iraqi interest in Soviet military equipment, but that nexus with Iraq later served as a severe constraint upon Moscow's attempts to generate correct, if cool, relations with the shah and to establish important economic links with Tehran.

The course of Soviet diplomacy on the Horn of Africa and its associated military aid policies there can best be appreciated as instances of that generalized pattern. Moscow's initial entry into the politics of the Horn of Africa was made possible by the regional tensions associated with postcolonial boundaries, and classically, Moscow's intrusion was effected by means of a military assistance package. In the early 1960s the Western powers were reluctant to comply with Somalian requests for military equipment, mainly on account of Western links with Ethiopia and Kenya and Somalia's irredentist claims upon those countries. Accordingly, the USSR gave concrete expression to its coincidence of interests with Somalia by making available to it a $30 million military credit in 1963. Military cooperation between the two countries advanced further after the 1969 coup, which brought Mohammed Siyad Barre to power, and the early 1970s saw significant accretions to the military strength of Somalia.

The year 1974 represented the culmination of Moscow's policy in the area and also the first challenge to its continuance in view of changing circumstances. On one hand, the USSR formalized its relations with Somalia by means of a treaty of peace and friendship in mid-1974. As with most Soviet treaties of its kind, it contained a military cooperation clause in the form of Article 4, which declared that the cooperation "will envisage, in particular, assistance in the training of Somali military personnel and in the mastering of weapons and equipment delivered to the Somali Democratic Republic for the purposes of enhancing its defense potential." Almost simultaneously, the revolution in Ethiopia and the overthrow of Haile Selassie's empire, called into question the future course of Soviet policy in the Horn of Africa as a whole. Eventually the USSR was to discover that the very military supply policy that had allowed it to "win" Somalia and to utilize Somalian naval facilities was to turn back upon itself and to lead to the "loss" of that particular client-state. How this came about, as well as what the circumstances tell us about the political utility of arms supplies, is the main focus of the following analysis of events in the Horn of Africa between 1974 and the termination of the Ogaden War in early 1978.

It soon became evident after the revolution in Ethiopia that the USSR was aspiring to a more ambitious policy in the Horn than that pursued up to that time. Moscow saw, in the ideological leanings of the new Ethiopian leadership, some prospects for an expansion of the Soviet position in the Horn that would finally create a situation of Soviet "hegemony" to counterbalance the U.S. hegemony in the

Middle East core, particularly Israel and Egypt. Typically, *Pravda* observed in mid-1976 that since the coup in Ethiopia, "the country's progressive forces, headed by revolutionary and democratic members of the armed forces, have instituted a number of important reforms."[38]

But was Moscow prepared to cultivate Addis Ababa to the extent of losing the Soviet Union's position in Somalia altogether? Obviously, any attempt to pass judgment on the success, or lack of success, of recent Soviet policy in the Horn area must depend upon an assessment of Moscow's goals or preferred outcomes. From this perspective, there is good reason for believing that the final outcome of the war and diplomacy in the Ogaden—an exclusive tie with Ethiopia at the expense of any significant link with Somalia—was a fall-back position and not the goal the USSR originally sought.

Such a conclusion is speculative, but there is some evidence to support it. From Moscow's point of view, the most preferred outcome would have been one in which the USSR would have been the principal ally of both Somalia and Ethiopia, thus permitting the Russians to maintain their investment in Berbera while using their position to exclude the West and to reach some settlement between the two African states. This interpretation conforms with Moscow's reluctance to alienate Somalia in the first half of 1977. For instance, on May 6, 1977, the Soviet Union and Ethiopia signed a Joint Declaration on Principles of Friendly Relations and Cooperation between the two countries, not, be it noted, a treaty of friendship and cooperation. It is plausible that the wording was selected by Moscow in an attempt to not offend President Barre by giving the same status to this diplomatic document as to the one signed with Somalia in 1974.[39]

Similarly, we may view the reported proposal, put by Fidel Castro in Aden in March 1977, for a "Marxist" confederation embracing Ethiopia, Somalia, Eritrea, and Djibouti as pointing in the same direction. Whether such a proposal was made seriously or suggested tongue-in-cheek cannot be known, but it reveals the logic of Soviet foreign policy. If Moscow genuinely hoped that such a confederation would be considered, that hope is testimony to the naiveté of the Soviet policymakers, but it may also be seen as a desperate attempt to avoid having to choose between Ethiopia and Somalia, a choice that pressed remorselessly and eventually had to be made. In short, the original Soviet hope was for a Soviet foothold in Ethiopia in addition to the one in Somalia, not in exchange for it.

Such an interpretation also finds general support in the evidence provided by Soviet military supply policy during this period, and it is to this evidence that I now turn. Soviet military sales to Ethiopia fall into several distinct phases, and the key dates in the evolution of Soviet arms supply policy appear to have been December 1976, May 1977, and finally November 1977.

The first significant Soviet-Ethiopian arms deal appears to have been concluded in December 1976, although no public statement was made to that effect.[40] The deal was reported to be worth some $100 million, but in fact, little appears to have come of this deal beyond the delivery in April of some thirty-one ancient T-34 tanks. Moreover, the tanks were shipped to Ethiopia from Aden and were not transferred directly from the USSR, even if the Soviet Union was responsible for arranging the deal. Although Somalia's tank force included a considerable number of T-34s, Somalia had also received some 100 of the more modern T-54/55 tanks prior to 1977, and consequently the initial Soviet arms deal with Ethiopia can be understood as a gesture of goodwill toward Ethiopia but one of doubtful military significance. It also was a clear signal that Moscow was not, at that stage, prepared to make the type of sale that would provoke a crisis in its relations with Somalia.

The next phase began in May 1977. Following the final termination of Ethiopian military connections with the United States in April, Mengistu visited Moscow early the next month, and a further military supply agreement is believed to have resulted from that meeting. The agreement was reported to involve equipment to the value of $300 to $400 million, although whether this estimate included the previous amount or was in addition to it is not clear.[41] The *New York Times* of September 2, 1977, quoted diplomatic sources as confirming a Soviet-Ethiopian deal of some $385 million. However, this information appears to refer back to the May agreement, even if it was only in September that the most important deliveries were actually made. There is, therefore, evidence of a gradual escalation in the Soviet shipments as the USSR found itself increasingly sucked into a situation that was not of its initial choosing.

Limited quantities of more sophisticated Soviet equipment, such as the T-54/55 tank, began to arrive from June onwards, but observers noticed that deliveries were stepped-up after mid-September. Certainly the main deliveries of MiG-21 aircraft were not made until the later date, because Ethiopian pilots were training in the USSR and the aircraft would have been useless before the training was complete.[42] The stepped-up deliveries reportedly included crated MiG-21s, T-54/55 tanks, armored personnel carriers (APCs), and "Stalin Organ" missile launchers.[43]

The pattern suggests that the USSR was reluctant throughout to alienate Somalia completely but that the exigencies of the fighting in the Ogaden placed increasing pressure on Moscow to move beyond sending token supplies to Ethiopia. The persistence of the pattern is corroborated in the final denouement toward the latter part of 1977. It is not known precisely when the Soviet Union terminated all arms supplies to Somalia, although it can be doubted whether any significant quantities would have been delivered during 1977. In fact, it is plausible that President Barre's hurried visit to the USSR at the beginning of September was in connection with the drying up of Soviet supplies. Symptomatic of the strain that Soviet-Somalian relations were undergoing at that juncture was the terse communiqué issued after the visit, which stated merely that the sides "exchanged opinions on questions of mutual interest."[44] At any rate, supplies to Somalia had ceased by mid-October, according to the Soviet ambassador in Addis Ababa.[45] In November, the crisis was finally reached, and on the thirteenth of that month, President Barre announced the expulsion of Soviet and Cuban advisers from Somalian territory.

It is significant that the major Soviet airlift and sea lift of equipment to Ethiopia came after the final breach with Somalia and not before it. It is generally accepted that large-scale supply operations to Ethiopia commenced on November 26, some two weeks after the public rift between Somalia and the USSR. Given this chronology, it seems reasonable to conclude that it was only after the relationship with Somalia was deemed to be irretrievable in Moscow's eyes that the USSR shed its final restraints and rendered Ethiopia the kind of military assistance necessary to push the Somali forces out of the Ogaden.

The overall amount of the Soviet military supplies to Ethiopia between May 1977 and early 1978 is difficult to assess. On the one hand, we have been given the fairly hard figures obtained by U.S.

intelligence, and made public by Zbigniew Brzezinski on February 23, that as of February 1978 Ethiopia had received some 400 tanks and 50 MiG aircraft.[46] These figures were published in *The Military Balance 1978–79* as reflecting the situation in mid-1978. In addition, Ethiopia also acquired some MiG-23 Floggers.[47] The total value of Soviet deliveries was widely reported in the Western media as being in the vicinity of $1 billion.[48] The major problem with this assessment of the Soviet supply program is that it coincides with President Barre's own estimate, and in consequence, there is a natural tendency to suspect that the figure was inflated as part of Barre's concerted campaign to pressure the Western powers into making good his own country's losses after the break with Moscow. Barre, for instance, cited the figure in an interview granted to *Newsweek*, which had the evident purpose of evoking Western sympathies for Somalia's plight.[49] Moreover, part of the difficulty in evaluating the amount and value of the supplies sent to Ethiopia derives from the confused and contradictory reports about the scale of the Soviet airlift to Ethiopia during November-December 1977.

To complete this survey of Soviet arms diplomacy on the Horn of Africa, some general observations can be made on the theme of arms supplies as a form of political leverage. First, the point has already been made that in the long run, the salience of arms supplies within Soviet–Third World diplomacy as a whole has tended to be counterproductive. Repeatedly, the very instrument that has facilitated Moscow's involvement in regional conflict situations has subsequently become the major impediment to the development of wider Soviet diplomatic goals. The USSR's relationship with Somalia was born of the sword, and eventually it died by it. If we accept the view that Moscow sought to avoid making a choice between Somalia and Ethiopia, then, unhappily for Moscow, the course of events dictated that the one thing that Addis Ababa must have—i.e., arms—was the one thing Mogadishu could not tolerate. In that sense, the USSR became a prisoner of its own policy.

The second point is a logical extension of the previous one. It was apparent all along to the Soviet authorities that the one development that more than any other would jeopardize Soviet regional ambitions on the Horn, as they gradually came to be formulated and fostered after 1974, would be a direct military clash between the two regional parties. Given the numbers of Soviet military advisers in Somalia (some 1,700), it is most unlikely that Mosow would have been uninformed of Somalian plans for an incursion into the Ogaden, and it follows that the Soviet authorities would have sought to avert such a development. And yet the USSR, which had for many years been almost the sole supplier of Somalia's armed forces, was incapable of preventing this challenge to its regional goals. Barry Blechman has arrived at a similar conclusion.

> The present situation on the Horn dramatically illustrates just how fragile an instrument of political influence arms transfers can be. . . . The Soviet Union was not able to deter Somalia from waging war against Ethiopia, despite the many years of Soviet arms shipments to Somalia. The lesson to be learned from the Horn of Africa is that a supplier often cannot control what the recipient does with its arms. Once the arms are in the client's possession, words and blandishments may not be sufficient to limit their use.[50]

However, this may not be the last word on the issue. The old argument that regional client-states become so tied to a source of military supplies that they cannot defect from their superpower patrons has certainly taken many knocks in recent years, most momentously, of course, in the case of Egypt. But to say that clients can defect from their patrons is not to say that they can defect with impunity. It also has to be borne in mind that Somalia's Ogaden gamble did not pay off and that as far as can be seen, Barre has so far been unsuccessful in generating the alternative sources of military supply that he has long been seeking. Taking this observation in conjunction with the internal strains upon Barre's regime ever since the 1977–78 war, there may yet be some credibility in the recent reports that Somalia would not be averse to a reopening of its connection with the Soviet Union.

The final observation can be made about the Soviet control of Ethiopia. It has been suggested by some analysts, and by some U.S. administration spokesmen, that the USSR did, in fact, exercise its influence in 1978 and that it did so by preventing the Ethiopian leadership from pursuing the war into Somalian territory. Moreover, according to this analysis, the USSR restrained Ethiopia from an invasion of Somalia at Washington's behest and in response to U.S. pressure that further Soviet-Cuban-Ethiopian "provocative" actions on the Horn would have detrimental consequences for Soviet-U.S. relations in general and for the SALT talks in particular.

It need scarcely be pointed out that an acceptance of this version of events requires several acts of great faith. The argument is open to criticism at each of its stages, both that U.S. pressure was successfully exercised against the USSR and that Soviet pressure was successfully exercised against Ethiopia. Above all, the argument is weak in projecting a serious Ethiopian intention to dismember Somalia. It does not seem plausible that Mengistu could have entertained such adventures at a time when he was already facing massive internal problems of regime stability, not least among which was an imminent war against Eritrean secessionists, and when he would have known that to invade Somalia would have lost him his major diplomatic advantage as the defender of the status quo sanctioned by the Organization of African Unity (OAU).

Conclusion

The USSR's most tangible presence in the Indian Ocean region, apart from its naval incursions, has been by way of military deliveries to selected littoral states. Clearly, the scope and magnitude of these supplies warrant close examination by Western policymakers and constitute a major consideration in the conventional military sales policies of the Western powers themselves.

Nonetheless, it can be argued on the basis of this brief review that there is little evidence to support the grosser tales of political dependency upon Moscow, said to be the fate of those Indian Ocean states that have equipped their military arsenals from Soviet sources. This conclusion seems valid for at least two distinct reasons. In the first place, the creation of important and long-lasting military supply networks has not, in any of the cases examined, ensured the political compliance of the recipient state with the USSR's general Indian Ocean policies. Second, and perhaps even more striking, is the fact that in no case has the military supply nexus prevented the recipient from embarking on more or less ambitious policies of weapons diversification or even from undertaking major reorientations in its arms purchase policy.

Finally, although the conflict-ridden nature of the Indian Ocean littoral has made the acquisition of Soviet weaponry an attractive option for various regional states, the USSR has repeatedly discovered that its arms supplies may be an encumbrance to the attainment of regional goals, as well as a means of attaining them. Although it has traditionally been our understanding that political returns have compensated for economic costs in the Soviet military supply policy, this situation now appears to be undergoing a fundamental reversal, and the main point of interest in analyzing the Soviet arms supply diplomacy is whether the economic incentives are now strong enough to compensate for the disappointing political returns.

Notes

1. For recent explorations of this theme, see U. Ra'anan, "Soviet Arms Transfers and the Problem of Political Leverage," in U. Ra'anan, R. L. Pfaltzgraff, Jr., and G. Kemp, eds., *Arms Transfers to the Third World: The Military Buildup in Less Industrial Countries* (Boulder, Colo.: Westview Press, 1978); A. Rubinstein, *Red Star on the Nile* (Princeton, N.J.: Princeton University Press, 1977); I. Clark, "Autonomy and Dependence in Recent Indo-Soviet Relations," *Australian Outlook* (April 1977).

2. This argument is developed in Ian Clark, "Recent Trends in Soviet Conventional Arms Export Policy" (Paper presented to the Twenty-first Australasian Political Studies Association Conference, August 1979).

3. Calculated from State Department figures and reproduced in *The Soviet Union and the Third World: A Watershed in Great Power Policy* (Washington, D.C.: Congressional Research Service, 1977), p. 69.

4. See U.S., Congress, Senate, Subcommittee on Foreign Assistance of the Committee on Foreign Relations, *Foreign Assistance Authorization: Arms Sales Issues, Hearings,* Washington, 1976, pp. 24-27.

5. For a brief history and critical analysis of the MiG project, see D. Childs and M. Kidron, "India, the USSR, and the MiG Project," *Economic and Political Weekly* (Bombay), September 22, 1973.

6. *Flight International,* February 10, 1972.

7. Government of India, *Ministry of Defence Report 1974-5* (New Delhi: Government of India Press, 1975), p. 68.

8. See *Hindu,* October 28, 1978.

9. See *The Military Balance 1970-71* (London: International Institute for Strategic Studies, 1971) and P. R. Chari, "Military Co-operation with Soviet Union," *Hindustan Times,* October 18, 1977.

10. *Flight International*, February 20, 1975, p. 286.

11. See text in *Indian and Foreign Review*, April 15, 1976.

12. A Rubinstein, *Red Star on the Nile*, p. 325.

13. "Foreign Curbs Hinder India's Arms Sales," *Far Eastern Economic Review*, June 3, 1977.

14. "India Unhappy over Soviet Arms," *Armed Forces Journal International* (March 1975):14.

15. See Stockholm International Peace Research Institute, *World Armaments and Disarmament: SIPRI Yearbook 1975* (Stockholm: Almqvist and Wiksell Förlag, 1976), p. 231.

16. For background, see Clark, "Recent Trends in Soviet Conventional Arms Export Policy."

17. Childs and Kidron, "India, the USSR, and the MiG Project," p. 1727.

18. *Overseas Hindustan Times*, June 21, 1979.

19. See *The Military Balance 1978-79*, p. 61.

20. See the statement by Defense Minister Jagjivan Ram in *Overseas Hindustan Times*, June 21, 1979.

21. Childs and Kidron, "India, the USSR, and the MiG Project," p. 1726.

22. R. Huisken, "The Development of the Conventional Arms Trade," in R. J. O'Neill, ed., *Insecurity* (Canberra: ANU Press, 1978), pp. 34-35.

23. *Lok Sabha Debates*, April 18, 1974.

24. See *Report of the Comptroller and Auditor General of India, 1976*, Part 5, "Mazagon Dock Ltd." (New Delhi: Government of India Press, 1976), p. 33; also *Hindu*, November 26, 1977.

25. *Hindu*, October 28, 1978.

26. *Soviet Union and the Third World*, p. 69.

27. G. Lenczowski, *Soviet Advances in the Middle East* (Washington, D.C.: American Enterprise Institute for Public Policy Research, 1971), p. 153.

28. See text in *Soviet News* (USSR embassy, London) September 26, 1972, p. 310.

29. "Soviet Military Aid to the Middle East—An Economic Balance Sheet," in *Soviet Economy in a New Perspective*, Papers submitted to Joint Economic Committee, U.S. Congress (Washington, D.C.: Government Printing Office, 1976).

30. For full details of Soviet deliveries to Iraq during the war, see J. D. Glassman, *Arms for the Arabs* (Baltimore: Johns Hopkins University Press, 1975).

31. Ibid., p. 126.

32. *Soviet Union and the Third World*, p. 135.

33. D. L. Price, "Moscow and the Persian Gulf," *Problems of Communism* (March-April 1979):7.
34. Ibid., p. 7.
35. Quoted in C. Legum, ed., *African Contemporary Record 1977-78* (New York: Africana Publishing Co., 1979), p. A43.
36. See, for instance, *Flight International*, July 31, 1975, p. 149.
37. *Aviation Week and Space Technology*, July 25, 1977.
38. *Pravda*, May 16, 1976.
39. For text, see *Pravda*, May 9, 1977.
40. For references to this deal, see *Africa Research Bulletin* (1977):4396; and D. Albright, "Soviet Policy," *Problems of Communism* (January-February 1978):32.
41. *Africa Research Bulletin* (1977):4464; Legum, *Africa Contemporary Record*, p. A43.
42. *Africa Research Bulletin* (1977):4558.
43. *Africa*, no. 75 (November 1977):33.
44. *Pravda*, September 1, 1977.
45. *Africa Research Bulletin* (1977):4592.
46. Ibid. (1978):4743-4744.
47. These were reported as ordered in February 1978 in *Defense and Foreign Affairs Digest*, no. 3 (1978):24. *The Military Balance 1978-79* puts the number at twenty.
48. See Legum, *Africa Contemporary Record*, p. A43.
49. *Newsweek*, February 13, 1978, p. 16.
50. U.S., Congress, House, Subcommittee on International Security and Scientific Affairs of the Committee on International Relations, *Review of the President's Conventional Arms Transfer Policy*, Washington, 1978, p. 22.

9
Soviet Naval Policy in the Indian Ocean

Geoffrey Jukes

Although Soviet naval units appeared from time to time in the Indian Ocean before 1968, it was only in that year that a permanent presence began to be established. Previous appearances, whether Soviet or Czarist, were essentially only for transit, whether by naval exploration vessels (the Russian counterparts to Captain Cook), by the Russian Baltic Fleet on its way to the disaster of Tsushima in 1904–5, or by units built in European yards proceeding eastward to join the Pacific Fleet or going westward for major refits and overhauls. Since 1968, however, the Soviet navy has undoubtedly taken a permanent interest in the Indian Ocean, which it did not take before. The question is, why?

There are two major pitfalls in attempting to answer that question. One is the relative paucity of information from Soviet sources, and the other is the temptation, in the absence of detailed Soviet information, to view the Soviet navy through Western spectacles. It is easy to forget that the Soviet Union is primarily a land power, that naval strength and policy have been essential outgrowths of that land power, and that the navy has been indulged or starved according to the predilections of a defense establishment dominated by the army. There is therefore a substantial risk that Soviet intentions and capabilities will be derived by analogy from those of the maritime powers, for whom naval policy was vital in the days before aircraft and even now can often be held with justification to be so.

Before considering actual Soviet Indian Ocean activities, it is as well to recall the context in which the Soviet navy emerged from its role as a "handmaiden of the army" into the role of a significant power on the high seas.[1] In the late 1930s, Stalin acquiesced in the building of a surface fleet that would include major units such as battleships. Construction began, but most of the program was terminated abruptly in 1940 when it was decided that steel production would not be adequate for both tanks and battleships, and the requirements of the army were given priority. Naval construction did not begin again in earnest until 1948, and the forces procured comprised large numbers of diesel attack submarines, frigates, destroyers, and cruisers of fairly orthodox designs. In the atmosphere of the time, the program was interpreted in the West as largely offensive in nature, if only because of its sheer size. However, the characteristics of the submarine that was procured in the largest numbers (the W class), the relatively weak anti-aircraft armaments of the surface ships, the lack of aircraft carriers, and the fact that the largest forces containing the new warships were deployed in the enclosed Baltic and Black seas tended to indicate an overall defensive concept. The primary function of the navy was that of protecting Soviet coastlines near the heartland of the Soviet Union against major amphibious or naval assaults, using a combination of submarines, surface warships, and shore-based aircraft.

The dimensions of the program clearly imposed strains on defense production capacity, and as soon as Stalin died the program was reviewed and curtailed. Naval construction came to an almost complete halt from 1957 to 1961. Although small inshore units continued to be produced, only a trickle of units capable of operating on the high seas appeared–the tail end of the large production runs.

During the late 1950s there was clearly a major debate on the future shape of the navy, within the general debate on strategy and defense policy that followed Stalin's death in 1953.[2] Two elements of naval strength–submarines and maritime reconnaissance-strike aircraft–were accepted as necessary and desirable (as were coastal surface forces), but a good deal of doubt was cast on the need for large surface warships. When construction resumed in 1961, the new designs were very different from those of the Stalin years. Ship designs were more innovative, but also ships were built in much smaller numbers. Almost without exception, there was a shift in emphasis from the gun to missiles and various types of antisubmarine armament. In the eighteen years that followed, there was a good

Soviet Naval Policy in the Indian Ocean

deal of chopping and changing over surface-to-surface missile armaments, notably in the replacement of long-range surface-to-surface missiles by weapons of considerably shorter range, but the emphasis on the antisubmarine role remained constant, right up to and including the Kiev class of aircraft carriers. It is the antisubmarine role that, in the eyes of the rest of the defense establishment, serves as the primary justification for the increasingly sophisticated surface ships, and it is this aspect of Soviet naval procurement that is probably most apposite to the Indian Ocean situation.

The basic Soviet naval interest in the Indian Ocean is likely to have derived from a series of reasonable but wrong assumptions about U.S. submarine missile deployment intentions.[3] By 1964, the United States had developed its Polaris missile from the 1,200-nautical-mile range of the A1 version to 1,800 in the A2 and almost 3,000 in the A3. The A1 version could reach Soviet cities only from a position off the Soviet north coast, and it was this fact that led to the agreement with Britain to base a force of U.S. Polaris submarines in Scotland. Once the A2 version became available, in 1962, the eastern Mediterranean became a feasible deployment area for Polaris submarines, and an agreement was concluded with Spain in 1963 for a base there. When the A3 version became available in 1964, it was only necessary to draw a circle of the appropriate range centered on Moscow to show that the northwestern Indian Ocean would be a very attractive deployment area. It would then have been natural for the Soviet naval staff to look for supporting evidence, in the form of negotiations for a base such as those that had preceded the deployments from Scotland and Spain, and such supporting evidence was available in the shape of Anglo-U.S. negotiations, which took place between 1962 and 1966, concerning the British Indian Ocean territorial island of Diego Garcia. Further supporting evidence was available in the Australian-U.S. negotiations for the establishment on the North West Cape of a radio station capable of communicating with submerged submarines. Although it subsequently turned out to be a wrong inference, because the United States did not in fact establish a submarine base at Diego Garcia, it was entirely reasonable to deduce from the evidence and from the history of the two previous deployments that a U.S. missile submarine force was likely to take station in the Indian Ocean sometime in the late 1960s or early 1970s.

The Soviet navy had, as the result of the postwar Stalin programs, become the second largest navy in the world. Its entire justification lay in the perceived need for an ability to counter the forces of the other major powers. From 1961, the submarine-launched ballistic missile (SLBM) program meant that the only navy that was larger, that of the United States, had acquired the capacity to destroy Soviet cities without coming anywhere near Soviet territorial waters. Such a situation presents a navy with the alternatives of either declaring its impotence or enhancing its antisubmarine effort, both in terms of technology and in terms of the areas in which it operates. It was hardly likely that the first alternative would be adopted. The second alternative first involved the sending of existing antisubmarine forces into waters where the new antagonist might be found (e.g., into the Mediterranean in 1964), and second, it involved the development of new ships and methods to improve antisubmarine warfare capabilities. Both of these tendencies were apparent in Soviet policy from 1961 onward.

The situation in the Indian Ocean differed from those in the Norwegian Sea, the Mediterranean, and the Caribbean (where the Soviets showed increased activity from 1969 onward, mainly because of the proximity of the main U.S. submarine base at Charleston, South Carolina) in that the U.S. missile submarine force did not deploy there as anticipated. As a result the Soviet navy, having first entered the Indian Ocean for familiarization in advance of an expected combat mission, has found other functions to fulfill.

Doctrinal justification can be said to have been presented by the commander-in-chief of the navy, Adm. S. G. Gorshkov, first in a series of articles on navies in war and peace, published between February 1972 and February 1973,[4] and subsequently in a reworked and amplified version of those articles published as a book on the sea power of the state in 1976.[5] When the articles appeared, there was a great deal of debate among analysts outside the Soviet Union as to whether they constituted advocacy of an increased peacetime role for the navy or a statement of policy reflecting the achievement of such an increased role.

The years since Admiral Gorshkov's writings appeared have seen a continuation of improvement in the quality of the fleet, but the total number of new units and the annual rates of construction are totally inadequate to provide one-for-one replacements for the ships built between 1948 and 1957 that are now nearing the end of their useful life. Some use has been made of the naval units for "flag showing" (though relative to the time spent in the Indian Ocean, Soviet ships do less port visiting than U.S. ships do, and the visits they do make are usually confined to a small number of countries) and for indicating Soviet support for one of the participants in a crisis (e.g., India in 1971, Iraq in 1973, and Ethiopia in 1977-78). This suggests that Gorshkov's point was taken by the political leadership, but the low replacement rates indicate that it was not taken to the extent he might have hoped. The bilateral numerical comparisons made between the U.S. and Soviet navies are misleading for several reasons. They put the Soviet Union in the lead in the number of major surface combatants only if the large numbers of overage ships are counted as still in service and fully effective, and the comparisons ignore the fact that for the Soviets the antagonist is not the U.S. navy alone, but an entire complex of alliances that includes on the U.S. side every other navy of significance, including the navies of Britain, West Germany, France, and Japan. For submarines, the position is somewhat different, but there also the very high Soviet figure used in Western public debate includes a large number of overage vessels. In any event, the Western navies have no need to match the Soviet totals in all types of submarines, if only because the number of Soviet targets is small by comparison with those provided by the navies and merchant fleets of the Western alliances.

Since its primary function in the Indian Ocean has remained unfulfilled because no U.S. deployment has taken place there, other uses have been found in the area for the Soviet fleet from time to time. Thus Soviet policy failures in respect to Somalia, leading to the expulsion of the Soviet forces from their facilities at Berbera, were followed by some use of the Soviet naval presence to assist Ethiopia in its campaign against the insurgencies in the South and North. In addition to their "permanent" presence, Soviet naval forces were temporarily present in Bangladesh after the war of 1971, where they were used to clear the port of Chittagong of wrecks. Prior to the reopening of the Suez Canal in 1975, a Soviet minesweeping force cleared the mines from the southern approaches to the canal, and U.S. and British salvage forces cleared the northern approaches and the canal itself in collaboration with the Egyptians. Larger task forces have been sent into the Indian Ocean on two occasions – in 1971 and 1973 – in each case to shadow U.S. task forces that had been sent in earlier. Thus the Soviet presence has combined antisubmarine area familiarization, assistance to local powers, shadowing of Western naval forces, and a modicum of flag showing around the area. What has been lacking, and is still lacking, has been any evidence of the maintenance of a task force designed to interfere with mercantile traffic, tanker or other, on the sea-lanes of the Indian Ocean.

The future of the Soviet presence would seem to depend upon developments in submarine missile technology. Up to now, increases in the range of submarine-borne missiles have involved the deployment of the submarines into new sea areas, which became suitable as new missiles brought new targets into range from areas around the Soviet and U.S. peripheries. This process, however, is not infinitely extendable. Missiles already in service in the Soviet navy, and about to come into service in the U.S. navy, make it possible to keep enemy targets under threat without leaving home waters. The missiles also, of course, offer the alternative option of threatening targets from anywhere in the oceans of the world. However, the option of keeping the submarines at home is undoubtedly cheaper, as well as more cost effective in the sense that submarines in home waters can be more extensively protected against enemy attack than if they are in distant areas. It is most likely, therefore, that the 1980s will see a reduction in distant deployments of missile firing submarines (the process has already commenced in the U.S. navy with the withdrawal of submarines from the eastern Mediterranean) and consequently in the need for distant-water antisubmarine forces to counter them. That being so, the combat mission that first brought the Soviet navy into the Indian Ocean on a permanent basis is likely to cease to have even the hypothetical significance that it has had in the past. Its role will then become a more political one, and the question of the presence of any outside superpower's naval force will necessitate a more purely political decision between the U.S. and Soviet leaderships. The possibility of a total withdrawal, leading to conversion of the Indian Ocean into a peace zone, can be ruled out altogether. (Given the antagonisms among the various powers of the Indian Ocean periphery, the concept of a peace zone is dubious even if outside powers are absent.) Western naval presences, though often justified in terms of a hypothetical Soviet threat are really determined by a perceived Western need to maintain a means of bringing pressure on oil producing states, in protection both of Western oil supplies and of Western investments in the area. This perceived need existed long before any Soviet presence came into being and would continue even if that presence were withdrawn, and that very fact makes the total withdrawal of the Soviet presence unlikely. The actual level of the presence however may well already be the subject of tacit bilateral understandings, the determinants of which are not naval technology but political considerations of the Soviet-U.S. relationship.

The recessing of the bilateral U.S.-Soviet discussions on the limitation of Indian Ocean naval deployments has been justified by the United States in terms of Soviet activities in Africa. The Soviet navy in fact played only a very small part in the events in Angola, Mozambique, and Ethiopia, and the increase in naval forces off the Ethiopian coast in early 1978 took place after the talks had been recessed, and after the Soviet expulsion from Somalia. Underlying the differing interpretations of détente outside the area of NATO–Warsaw Pact confrontation is a purely tactical situation. The U.S. facilities at Diego Garcia are on a remote island, with no remaining native population, that is owned by a U.S. ally (Britain), which is extremely unlikely to ever give the United States notice to quit. The Soviet facilities in Somalia, like those formerly held in Egypt, were granted by the grace and favor of a local government that, when its own and Soviet interests diverged, expelled its guests. The Soviet Union now operates from Aden with a similar lack of security of tenure. In short, the situation presents the United States with no urgent necessity to negotiate. It has a naval presence role that is linked to the political situation in the Gulf and support for pro-Western governments there, especially in the aftermath of the revolution in Iran, and it has some facilities on Diego Garcia. The Soviets do not have facilities, but they do have a naval presence whose symbolic value can be invoked to cover a situation for which its true relevance is no more than peripheral.

In view of the Soviet Union's uncommunicativeness about its intentions and capabilities, and the present transitional stage of the Soviet navy's forces capable of operating on the high seas, it is possible only to speculate about future Soviet naval missions in the Indian Ocean region. The mission most feared by the West (including Japan) is an interdiction of oil supplies, whether by physical seizure of the oil installations or the countries in which they are located, by seizure or sinking of tankers, or by blockage of the Strait of Hormuz through which all tanker traffic leaves or enters the Gulf.

An invasion of the territory of Iran is, of course, a physical possibility for the Soviet Union, but it would be a very major undertaking since Iranian oil resources are located in that country's southern provinces, the furthest away from the Soviet border. It would be unnecessary to invade Iran solely in order to deny its oil to the West, because that purpose could be achieved by other means that did not entail occupation. It is sometimes argued that a pending Soviet oil shortage could lead the Soviets to seize an oil-producing country to ensure a continuing supply, and if such a seizure were contemplated, Iran is an obvious candidate because it has a common border with the Soviet Union.

The plausibility of this scenario depends on its underlying political assumptions. There is considerable room for doubt whether an acute Soviet oil shortage is pending, because the problem may be merely one of increased future extraction costs arising from a gradual exhaustion of the more accessible oil resources and the consequent need to utilize oil resources in remoter and climatically more difficult areas, such as the Yakutsk Republic. Even if the problem turns out to be one of absolute shortage, it does not follow that the remedy for it is invasion. Most states have no oil, and their normal recourse is to buy it, not seize it. If the logic of a desperate situation were to dictate recourse to seizure by invasion, Japan, France, and Germany would appear to be impelled by it more inexorably than the Soviet Union, which is less dependent on Middle Eastern oil than any other major power, including the United States. The scenario therefore rests on an implicit predatoriness of the Soviet Union for which there is no evidence in Soviet political or military doctrine, nor very much in historical Soviet behavior with regard either to the Middle Eastern area or to other strategic raw materials (e.g., rubber) in which the Soviet Union is deficient. Even if it is assumed that other powers would not react, that resistance could be completely crushed, and that captured oil installations could be protected from sabotage, a putative future Soviet oil deficiency could be made up more cheaply by purchase than by invasion.

For the more modest objective of denial of oil to the West and Japan, there are several possible methods. All suffer from the limitation that for most oil producers, oil revenues are a major source of funding for development, so that interruption of the oil flow is a tactical device to be used for their own purposes (e.g., to bring pressure on the West to force a favorable outcome to the Arab-Israeli dispute) rather than to further the interests of a third party that many of the oil-producing countries view with hostility. The probability therefore is that any Soviet action to interrupt oil supplies would be undertaken only as an overt act of war. Since the major industrial countries hold oil stocks that could sustain their economies for several months, during which time counteraction would clearly be contemplated and perhaps carried out, it is difficult to see what circumstances would lead the Soviet Union to contemplate such an act. However, even if these considerations are ignored, the question of practicality arises. If the Soviet Union wished to destroy the West's oil supply, how would it go about doing so?

The most obvious way to do so would be to wipe out the fixed installations—wells, pipelines, refineries, tank farms, and tanker-loading terminals—by air and missile attacks from bases in Transcaucasia. Given the relatively short distances involved, the Soviet ability to mount such an operation without need for foreign facilities or assistance, and the weak air and missile defenses of the Middle East, such an operation would not be particularly difficult to mount. It has been possible for the Soviets to do it at virtually any time in the past twenty-five years, and no Soviet Indian Ocean presence is required for it. Quite possibly Soviet naval and air reconnaissance capabilities in the Indian Ocean could contribute to such an operation, but their presence or absence would have only a marginal effect on its success or failure. There is therefore no reason to postulate that the cutting off of Western and Japanese oil supplies would have any direct relevance now or in the near future to Soviet decisions to maintain, increase, reduce, or abolish its Indian Ocean naval presence.

Two other possible ways to interdict the oil supply need to be considered. One is the sinking of tankers, and the other is the imposition of a blockade or physical blockage at some entrance or exit point, the most obvious being the mouth of the Gulf, or the Strait of

Hormuz. In the first case, although the sinking of tankers is certainly feasible, it is difficult to see it taking place outside a general war context in which Soviet warships in all oceans would be targets for naval and air forces of all the other maritime powers of any consequence. In such circumstances the life expectation of the surface-ship component of the Soviet Indian Ocean force would be measured in days rather than in months, and using surface ships to sink tankers, the effects of which would take several months to be felt, does not seem the most logical form of utilization. Submarines pose a more credible threat, but although the nuclear powered submarine has virtually unlimited range, it does not carry unlimited munitions. Any base, tender, or fleet train set up in an area to service submarine operations would itself be a prime target for Western counteraction. Therefore a major Soviet submarine effort against Western sea-lanes is likely to be mounted nearer to the tankers' destinations in Europe and Japan, simply for operating convenience and closeness to bases in Soviet home territory, which are more effectively protected and therefore more likely to continue to function in a war.

In the second case, the problem for a would-be blocker of straits is that none of them, except the Suez Canal, constitutes a real bottleneck. The Strait of Hormuz, for example, is about twenty-one miles wide at its narrowest point, with about nineteen miles of that stretch between 120 and 210 feet deep. To sink a few ships in it would create a navigational hazard, but to block it physically would require an organized operation. Something like 100 supertankers would have to be sunk in a line across the entire nineteen miles, probably with a second line on top in the deepest parts, and the barrier would then have to be defended for several months until Western oil stocks ran out. Such a defense would have to be against attempts by the world's major navies, air forces, and salvage organizations to blow holes in the line. An operation of this sort might well prove beyond the resources of the entire Soviet navy; it is certainly too ambitious for that small part of the navy that can be spared for operations in the relatively distant Indian Ocean.

This is not to say that tanker traffic could not be interfered with at all; obviously it could, though Soviet merchant shipping would be extremely vulnerable to counteraction in the much narrower passages at the entrances to the Baltic and Black seas that are used by traffic to and from all major ports in the European USSR. But there is a considerable difference between interference and total interdiction, and the problems of physical blockage appear extremely formidable. The point should also be made that about 80 percent of the world tanker tonnage belongs either to the United States or to one of its allies. When Soviet and East European tanker tonnage is deducted from the remaining 20 percent, it is clear that even selective harassment could produce no more than marginal inconvenience unless directed at U.S.-, NATO-, or Japanese-owned tankers, with all the consequences that that might entail.

Once the possibilities of seizure, blockage, or harassment are discarded as being of low probability, what is left for Soviet naval forces to do in the Indian Ocean? Not a great deal beyond what they do now. Area familiarization against a possible U.S. missile submarine deployment will continue, if only because the manning system in the Soviet navy, with its heavy reliance on conscripts, leads to an annual turnover in the warships of almost one-third of the nonofficer complement and therefore to a constant need to train new personnel in operating in tropical waters.[6] Thus the Soviet naval presence acquires its own self-sustaining momentum from the exigencies of the Soviet training cycle.[7] Since the loss of the facilities in Somalia in November 1977, the port of Aden has been the principal local center for the Soviet military. If the internal situation in Ethiopia becomes sufficiently stable, however, the Soviets might well prefer to supplement, if not replace, the Aden facilities with use of Ethiopian naval facilities at Massawa.

The location of ground support and airfields is not determined entirely by naval preferences. The Soviet push for influence in Somalia and South Yemen in the 1970s was largely an attempt to compensate in the periphery of the Arab world for the erosion of Soviet influence nearer the center, especially in Egypt, Sudan, and North Yemen. The ability granted to the Soviet navy and air force to make use of Somalia and South Yemeni real estate was a by-product of success that, in the case of Somalia, proved to be evanescent. For the present it suits the Soviet Union to assist Ethiopia in suppressing the Somalian-supported insurgency in the South and the Eritrean revolt, which is supported by Egypt, Sudan, and Saudi Arabia, thus demonstrating to friends and enemies alike that Soviet assistance brings results and opposition brings setbacks. In this assistance the naval and air force presences play no major role, but they do serve as a manifestation of commitment, as do the presences of U.S., British, and French troops in West Berlin, Australian air force elements in Malaysia, and U.S. troops in South Korea.

One further element affecting the Soviet naval presence is China. In one general sense, the maintenance of a Soviet distant-water presence in the Indian Ocean is an assertion of superpower status and hence of insistence on being taken into account on a global scale. Certainly in this general sense, China is one of the powers with which the Soviet Union competes. But more specifically, there is a possible combat role for which Soviet defense planning must provide, namely, war with China. Should such a war eventuate, the Soviets would probably want to confine its scope and keep it nonnuclear, relying on their qualitatively superior conventional forces to win it for them and on their nuclear superiority to deter China from using its relatively limited nuclear arsenal.

In this scenario, the major Soviet weakness is the vulnerability of the land supply routes from the rest of the USSR to the Soviet Far East. There is no all-weather road across Siberia, and in places the Trans-Siberian Railroad runs very close to the border. A new railway, the Baikal-Amur Main Line, is being built parallel to it, several hundred miles further north, but as a further insurance, the Soviets might well rely on sea transport. In peacetime, most traffic between the Soviet Far East and the rest of the Soviet Union is carried by rail or air, and the proportion passing by sea is insignificant, but the considerable amount of trade between Soviet ports and countries in Asia means that relatively large numbers of Soviet merchant ships circulate in Indian and Pacific ocean waters. In a Sino-Soviet war these ships would be a supply resource for the Soviet Far East and an easy target for Chinese submarines operating in the Indian Ocean, from facilities that might be provided by any one of the several Indian Ocean states that have a pro-Chinese orientation. Like the anti-SLBM role, this Soviet naval combat mission is hypothetical because Chinese submarines do not operate in the Indian Ocean. But as a Soviet defense planning contingency it is more credible than some that have been postulated. Since the activity is similar in nature to the practice of antisubmarine warfare against putative U.S. missile submarines, there is no additional training burden involved.

The most important relationship the Soviet Union has in the Indian Ocean region is the one with India. The naval repercussions of this relationship have, however, not been large. Surface ships and submarines of Soviet design have been supplied to the Indian navy since 1965, but the basis of the transactions has been one in which Indian crews are trained to handle the ships, and the ships then become fully Indian in all respects. Soviet warships pay occasional goodwill visits to India, but there have been no joint exercises, and despite numerous rumors, no base facilities have been provided for Soviet ships in Indian ports. In the Gulf region, Soviet assistance to Iraq in building the naval base at Umm Qasr has not apparently been followed by a quid pro quo in terms of Soviet naval access to the base, beyond occasional goodwill visits.[8] The political dividends the Soviets received appear to have been in oil politics, notably in the development of the North Rumayla oil field, with payment for Soviet assistance to be made in oil from the new field. Building the new base at Umm Qasr relieved the Iraqi navy of the pressure it felt from Iran when the navy was based at Basra and therefore vulnerable to interdiction of its passage down the Shatt-al-Arab to the Gulf. It therefore clearly serves an Iraqi strategic interest rather than a Soviet one; the arrangement was mutually profitable, but the rewards to the Soviets were taken in economic not strategic terms.[9]

The levels of Soviet presence in the Indian Ocean during 1979 were temporarily increased during April-June by the presence of the second Soviet aircraft carrier *Minsk*, a Kara-class cruiser, and the *Ivan Rogov*, the first ship of a new class of amphibious assault ship. Although the *Minsk* merely represents an improved capability in antisubmarine warfare, being configured to act as the command and control ship of an ASW task force, and the Kara-class ship only a replacement for an aging Sverdlov-class cruiser,[10] the *Ivan Rogov* represents a qualitative leap in Soviet amphibious warfare capability. There is ample scope for several such ships in the Pacific Fleet's home area, but the *Ivan Rogov* also provides a significant possibility for improvement in the Soviet capacity for distant, limited war. In 1964 a British distant, limited war ship, the commando carrier *Bulwark*, played an important part in quelling army revolts in Kenya and Tanzania by providing quick-reaction forces to support the civilian governments. The ultimate intention of the Soviet Union may be to use the *Ivan Rogov* or subsequent ships of that class to endow its Indian Ocean force with some capacity to project Soviet power ashore in support of a friendly government.

Since the ship only arrived in Vladivostok in 1979, it is too early to say whether it will be used in that role, or whether it will be employed to provide a better in-theater amphibious warfare capacity in the Soviet Far East, for which there is certainly a need. But it should at least be noted that the option exists and that the first ship of the new class has been sent to the Pacific, an unusual step in itself, given that each of the three fleets in the European USSR also has a marine force and that the Northern Fleet's requirement for the sort of capacity that the *Ivan Rogov* provides is also quite strong. It may be that the intention is to provide some form of a counterpart to the proposed U.S. quick-reaction force for the Gulf region, or it may simply be that it is thought that the Pacific Fleet requires an improved amphibious warfare capacity because of the possibility of war with China in the Far East, a theater with long coastlines and many islands. Only passage of time and the development of an operating pattern for the *Ivan Rogov,* the *Minsk,* and the new nuclear-powered strike cruisers (ships of about 30,000 tons, capable of carrying a mixture of VTOL aircraft and helicopters, two of which are being built in Leningrad) will show whether or not the somewhat overdue improvement in amphibious warfare capability is intended to provide an enhanced capability for a distant, limited war. Official Soviet pronouncements throw no light on the question. The much larger U.S. capacity for such operations has been denigrated in the past as imperialist in function, but nuclear weapons and aircraft carriers also were denigrated by the Soviets while they did not have them.[11]

In summary, therefore, the Soviet Pacific Fleet's direct utility in some of the more apocalyptic scenarios that can be envisaged for the Indian Ocean area is not high, but at lower levels of crisis, its range of options will be somewhat increased by the introduction of new types of warships. A constraint will be posed on this theoretically increased intervention capacity by the enforced retirement over the next few years of elderly warships, including over half the destroyers, which at present construction rates will not be replaced on anything like a one-for-one basis. Because the Soviet Union's major responsibility continues to lie in its home waters, where it must be prepared, for defense planning purposes at any rate, to confront the Japanese maritime self-defense force, the Chinese navy, and a substantial part of the U.S. fleets in the Pacific, a prolonged detachment of significant numbers of major units to the Indian Ocean is likely to remain uncommon, especially as the number of available ships declines.

Notes

1. For a detailed account, see R. W. Herrick, *Soviet Naval Strategy* (Annapolis, Md.: U.S. Naval Institute, 1967).

2. This general debate is discussed in Raymond L. Garthoff, *The Soviet Image of Future War* (Washington, D.C.: Public Affairs Press, 1959), and its naval aspects are considered in Herrick, *Soviet Naval Strategy,* Chapter 7. See also Michael MccGwire, "The Evolution of Soviet Naval Policy 1960-74," in M. MccGwire, K. Booth, and J. McDonnell, eds., *Soviet Naval Policy: Objectives and Constraints* (New York: Praeger, 1975).

3. For a more detailed discussion, see G. Jukes, "The Indian Ocean in Soviet Naval Policy," *Adelphi Paper,* no. 87 (London: International Institute for Strategic Studies, 1972).

4. *Morskoy Sbornik* [Naval anthology] (Moscow), all monthly issues between February 1972 and 1973 except July 1972 and January 1973.

5. S. G. Gorshkov, *Morskaya Moshch' Gosudarstva* [Sea power of the state] (Moscow: Voyennoye Izdatel'stvo Ministerstva Oborony SSSR, 1976).

6. The Law on Universal Military Service of October 1967 lays down a term of three years service in the navy or coastal elements of the frontier guards. There are no volunteer ratings and very few volunteer junior petty officers (see J. E. Moore, *The Soviet Navy Today* [London: MacDonald and Jane's, 1975], pp. 45-58).

7. The Soviet military training year begins on December 1, and ships usually rotate to and from the Indian Ocean around that time; some return home to discharge time-expired ratings, and they are replaced by other ships with a one-third complement of raw recruits.

8. The frequency of visits fell off sharply after 1973, from nineteen in the thirty months from July 1971 to December 1973 to seven from January 1974 to June 1976 (Australia, Parliament, Senate, Standing Committee on Foreign Affairs and Defence, *Australia and the Indian Ocean Region* [Canberra: Australian Government Publishing Service, 1976], pp. 211-226).

9. Ibid.; twelve of the twenty-six visits between July 1971 and June

1976 were by auxiliaries, six of them by tankers, suggesting that Iraqi oil was used to fuel Soviet Indian Ocean warships.

10. The Sverdlov-class cruisers were built in the 1950s and will probably be withdrawn in the 1980s. Only a few of them have been modernized; their main asset is their size, which makes space available for command staff and electronics (see G. Jukes, "Das Problem der Uberalterung der Schiffe in der Sowjetischen Marine," *Marine Rundschau* [January 1977]:4-9).

11. In 1962 Admiral Gorshkov said that aircraft carriers "are irrevocably passing into oblivion" (*Pravda,* July 29, 1962), and Admiral Isakov called them "floating mortuaries" (*Nedeliia,* June 9, 1962). In 1967 Gorshkov spoke of their "inevitable decline" (*Morskoy Sbornik* [February 1967]). In the articles on navies in war and peace (*Morskoy Sbornik* [February 1972-February 1973]), he made no derogatory references to them; by then the *Kiev* was being built.

10
France and the Indian Ocean

Jean-Pierre Gomane

Prior to any analysis of French external policy, it is necessary to specify some special features of political life under the present system of government. Understanding the complexity of the decision-making process and the perspectives of the decisionmakers will help us see how foreign policy is elaborated, planned, and managed.

Who Makes Foreign and Overseas Policy in France?

Gen. Charles de Gaulle, the founder of the Fifth Republic, was much more interested in worldwide affairs than in internal problems. That is why as far as external policy was concerned the two ministries officially entrusted with its care were gradually deprived of their powers—the Ministry of Foreign Affairs (Quai d'Orsay) and the Ministry of Cooperation (rue Monsieur) were more or less put under the direct rule of the Elysee, the president's residence. Since de Gaulle, external problems have been usually known as the *domaine réservé*.

The Ministry of Cooperation—its field restricted to a few friendly African states—and the Direction des Affaires Africaines in the Ministry of Foreign Affairs used to act under the unofficial but efficient control of the Secrétariat Général de la Présidence de le République pour les Affaires Africaines et Malgaches, one of the branches of the Elysee staff, headed under General de Gaulle by Jacques Foccart. Subsequently Pres. Georges Pompidou put this special agency at some distance from his own presidential office, and Pres. Valéry Giscard d'Estaing later abolished the post. Still, Giscard d'Estaing has appointed a special adviser for African affairs, René Journiac, formerly Foccart's right-hand man.

We can notice the same kind of direct intervention as regards the armed forces, at least for operations on the African continent. There is, for instance, a special agency called the Secrétariat Général de la Défense Nationale attached to the prime minister's office. To complete this survey of the machinery existing inside the French government for international matters, we must make a short reference to the agencies that deal with information and intelligence, and they have the same multiplicity and complexity, not to mention the same possible rivalries.

One may ask whether the executive is influenced by domestic factors when conducting its external policy. The constitution of the Fifth Republic has considerably restricted the power of the Parliament, and the Senate and the National Assembly are rarely involved in foreign policy issues. As far as public opinion is concerned, it generally is rather indifferent to overseas ventures and is only sensitive with regard to financial consequences or military deeds. Today, the press, and the other mass media even more, are partly under the government's influence. They usually keep a low profile on overseas events or present them in a very favorable light. Some French people, however, seem to be bored with external actions. A few years ago, a newspaperman by the name of Raymond Cartier won popularity when he promoted a new brand of isolationism known in France as *Cartiérisme*.

During the colonial era, three lobbies were the strongest supporters of overseas actions: Christian—mainly Catholic—missionaries; the navy and, to a certain extent, the army, reinforced by nationalistic circles; and, more cautiously, the business world. Today, the first no longer exists, and the third is slowly shifting its interests from black Africa to Arabian countries, especially those that export oil. Only the nationalist lobby remains fully devoted to the French presence overseas, especially in Africa. This presence is considered a sacred chapter of de Gaulle's testament since, under his leadership, France tried to build up a kind of commonwealth named *communauté* and to gather the totality of the French-speaking populations in the world (most of them living in Africa) under the banner of *Francophonie*. Today, President Giscard d'Estaing, taking some liberty with Gaullist dogma, especially in European matters, is obliged to give some compensations to the heirs of de Gaulle's policy. Paradoxically, Gaullists and Communists often share the same nationalist attitude on external problems, particularly when anti-U.S. feelings are involved.

If we leave out European matters, we can say that because of relatively limited means, either economic or military, France is able to have a permanent and coherent policy only in Africa—for historical, sentimental, and political reasons—and in the Arabian world, for economic ones. Everywhere else in the world, the French presence is very discreet. The African and Arabian concerns have a deep influence on the way France conducts its policy in the Indian Ocean—the subject to which we now turn.

France and Its Former Colonial Territories

Off and on, some territories in the Indian Ocean were part of the French colonial empire between the seventeenth and the twentieth centuries. Because of this background, France tries to keep special links with them, even though they are now independent.

Until the Treaty of Paris in 1763 and the Congress of Vienna in 1815, France managed to balance British dominance in India and the Indian Ocean. French ships cruised throughout the ocean, and fear of French ambitions was one of the main reasons why Britain settled the western coast of Australia 150 years ago. French settlements were scattered all over the area. As a result, countries such as Mauritius and the Seychelles are partly French speaking and keep some special feelings toward France in spite of over a century of British rule. (Mauritius, in fact, was called Ile de France from 1715–1814.)

As soon as those two countries became independent, they joined the organization of French-speaking African states, called the Organisation Commune Africaine et Malgache (OCAM), which was organized for the purpose of economic and cultural cooperation. For a while the group became the OCAMM (the second M was for Mauritius) but returned to the name OCAM after the withdrawal of the Malagasy Republic (Madagascar) in 1974. France is not an official member of the organization but is deeply influential in its activities.

Both in Mauritius and the Seychelles, some French-speaking people are left-wing oriented.[1] In Mauritius they are members of the opposition. Power is shared by moderate Creoles and Indians in spite of a deep disagreement that occurred in 1973 between Prime Minister Sir Seewosagur Rangulam and the then minister of foreign affairs, Gaetan Duval—the latter was dismissed because he was making some approaches to Paris, supposedly about facilities to be offered to the French navy. In the Seychelles, the first president after independence was James Mancham, a moderate favorable to the British. One can understand then that France was at first very fond of France-Albert René, who succeeded Mancham after a June 1977 coup. The new leader was a sympathizer with French language but at the same time was a radical leftist. No one could even hint that France had a part in the change of regime, but the result is that in the Seychelles today France plays as prominent a part in the linguistic and cultural area as the USSR does in the political one.

To end, and not to forget any place where France governed in the past, we must mention that from 1763 to 1956, there were five settlements on the Indian coast that were French overseas territories. They were given back to the Republic of India between 1951 and 1954, an action that was formalized by a treaty of April 28, 1956. This arrangement stipulated that some linguistic and cultural privileges be preserved to the benefit of France in the five territories, but because of the opposition of French nationalists, this agreement was not ratified by the French Parliament until 1962.

Generally speaking, in spite of the dramatic exceptions of Indochina and Algeria, the movement for independence of the French colonies developed in a rather peaceful, gradual, and contractual manner. Such was the case, in the early 1960s, for all the new states in Africa and, as far as the Indian Ocean is concerned, for Madagascar.

The first president, Philibert Tsiranana, had been a schoolteacher and a rather moderate political leader during the period of French rule. His most intimate adviser was a French *gendarmerie* officer, who had to flee when Tsiranana was overthrown by Tananarive rioters in May 1972. On that occasion, Paris refused to commit French troops stationed on the island to rescue the unfortunate president, in spite of his urgent appeals. He had been one of de

Gaulle's devoted admirers, but President Pompidou was much more cautious regarding military involvements overseas. In Madagascar the transitional power of Gen. Gabriel Ramanantsoa did not fundamentally change relations with France, but from 1973 on, the new regime began to turn to socialism in economic matters and to local traditionalism in matters of language, culture, and administration. The main consequences for France were the exit of the new Malagasy Democratic and Popular Republic out of the franc monetary zone, a nationalization of most French interests and companies, approaches by the Malagasy Republic to other countries – not only socialist ones – for economic and financial help, and a reduction of French cultural cooperation. French residents had been very numerous during the Tsiranana era, but in 1973 most of them began to leave the country because they could no longer work there freely.[2] Last but not least, France was obliged to withdraw its military deployment and to evacuate the important Diégo-Suarez naval base.

According to the constitution of the Fifth Republic made by and for de Gaulle in 1958, two former French colonies in the Indian Ocean decided by a huge majority to choose the status of *territories d'outre-mer*: the Côte Française des Somalis (Djibouti) and the Comoro Islands. Both of them are very poor, but they both occupy a most important geostrategic position, one on the south outlet of the Red Sea and the other in the northern mouth of the Mozambique Channel. The populations in the two territories are not ethnically homogeneous, but practically all of them are Muslim.

Because of religious as well as geographical solidarity, some Arab and African leaders attacked France in international forums like the Organization of African Unity and the UN Decolonization Committee. Moreover, the internal stability of the territories was precarious; in 1966, General de Gaulle's visit to Djibouti took place in a turmoil. Consequently, the name of the territory was changed to Territoire Français des Afars et des Issas after the names of the two main ethnic groups competing for influence. Since the Issas are related to the Somali, France seemed to favor the Afars; when, under growing external pressure, Paris decided to grant independence on June 27, 1977, power was cautiously balanced between the two groups. In the capital city, the situation is different because the city is mainly populated by people of Issa or Somalian extraction, the latter being aliens. The present regime of the new République de Djibouti is rather weak, but thanks to a series of bilateral agreements, France is still very much present. French armed forces are still stationed there, theoretically in order to protect the new state against external dangers from its neighbors, Somalia and Ethiopia. Djibouti itself has a small indigenous army of about 1,500 men.

In the Comoro Archipelago, there are rivalries among the four islands, and the personality of each of them is quite unique, especially in Mayotte because its population is ethnically different and because its political status was separate from the other islands before the period of French rule. This special identity of Mayotte was the occasion for a show of peevishness in the French Assembly on the part of the Gaullist group. Prior to the 1974 referendum on independence, that group introduced an amendment to have the polls counted separately for each island. The results of the December 22, 1974, poll were 65.3 percent against independence on Mayotte and less than 1 percent opposed on the other three islands. As a result, Mayotte remains a French territory.

In response to this maneuver, and without any further negotiation with Paris, the local authorities made a unilateral proclamation of independence for the three islands of Grande Comore, Anjouan, and Moheli on July 6, 1975. In spite of this serious incident, relations were not too bad between the new republic and France until, a few weeks after independence, Ali Swali replaced Ahmed Abdallah as the head of state in a coup probably perpetrated with the help of Tanzania. Nearly three years later, a quick countercoup led by mercenaries ousted Ali Swali, to the satisfaction of the French government. The returning leaders have good connections with France, while the late Ali Swali, on the contrary, had close ties to radical Arab and African countries.

Today, the last two states to receive their independence from the former French colonial empire have close relations with the former dominating country. At the same time, both benefit from a large amount of financial help from Arab countries. Djibouti has joined the Arab League, and the Comoros are now officially called an Islamic republic.

The Means of French Policy

When a developed country decides to cooperate with a developing one, it is partly because of a feeling of human solidarity. But there are also political aspects to this kind of intervention. Such is the case for French policy in the Indian Ocean with respect to the Malagasy Republic, Mauritius, the Seychelles, the Comoros, and the new Republic of Djibouti. In those countries we find, parallel to the regular diplomatic mission under the Ministry of Foreign Affairs, an office called Mission d'Aide et de Coopération that is directly subordinated to the Ministry of Cooperation. This office is in charge of economic and administrative help, as well as educational and cultural cooperation. It is, however, under the nominal authority of the ambassador.

France continues to be a dominant force in Djibouti and the Comoros. Each country is weak from many points of view—population, economy, defense, and national unity—and moreover, they are still dominated by traditional social structures. The Malagasy Republic, Mauritius, and the Seychelles, on the contrary, are much more independent of French influence, and they have economic and political relations with many other countries. For these last three states, the main instrument of French presence is the language. The French government gives a high priority to the sending of educational personnel and material to those states and to the distributing of travel grants and scholarships.

Finally, France's cultural influence is not totally limited to the Francophone world; some cultural cooperation agreements have been signed with other countries all around the Indian Ocean in order to improve the diffusion of the French culture and language.[3] The nucleus of a French university in the Indian Ocean has been implanted in Saint-Denis-de-la-Réunion; a venerable French institute in Pondicherry is still active; and French researchers are dispersed all over the Indian Ocean area under the auspices of the Centre National de la Recherche Scientifique (CNRS), the Office de la Recherche Scientifique et Technique d'Outre-mer (ORSTOM), and the ancient and most famous Ecole Française d'Extrême Orient (EFEO). Finally, French broadcasting from Réunion covers all of the southeastern Indian Ocean, and television from Réunion reaches the surrounding islands, including Mauritius and northern Madagascar.

Besides its former colonies, which became independent in the course of the 1960s and the 1970s, France is still holding under its rule some territories in the southwestern and southern parts of the Indian Ocean. Let us make an inventory of these "confetti"—the expression of a French newspaperman because all of these lands have a very small surface and look like scattered spots on the map. All of them are under the authority of the Secrétariat d'Etat Chargé des Départements de Territoires d'Outre-mer.

The first group, whose name is Terres Australes et Antarctiques Françaises, is composed of lands very distant from each other, all located south of the 40th parallel. The administrator's office is in Paris because there is no permanent population in these territories; there are only scientific missions sent there for a few months or some rare fishermen who call at these very windy, freezing, inhospitable places when they cannot help it. On the Antarctic continent at the southern boundary of the Indian Ocean, we first find the Terre Adélie; proceeding northward, there are three archipelagoes, namely—from west to east—the Crozet Islands, the Kerguelen Islands, and the Saint-Paul and Amsterdam islands. Some Soviet ships and personnel can be met in these waters and islands, particularly because there are some joint Franco-Soviet scientific research programs on oceanography and on atmospheric and space studies.

At a more accessible latitude, there are several islands in the vicinity of Madagascar: first, Mayotte and then, unquestionably the most important French territory in the Indian Ocean, Réunion Island. It has a surface area of 2,500 square kilometers, and its population numbers almost half a million. The population descends from French, African, Indian, and Chinese immigrants. The possession of this island is no asset for the French economy because its only significant product is sugarcane. The financial cost is rather heavy for the French budget since France tries to raise the standard of living there to the average metropolitan level. (Despite these efforts, there is a permanent emigration to continental France where about 50,000 *Reunionnais* are presently living.) This situation helps explain why there is no real independence movement in spite of acute criticisms about French "colonialism" on Réunion.[4]

To end this inventory, we must mention the *iles éparses*. Three of them are located in the Mozambique Channel—Europa, Bassas da India, and Juan de Nova; the fourth one is actually a small archipelago, the Glorieuses Islands, not far from Mayotte; and the fifth one, Tromelin, is found half way between the north of Madagascar and Mauritius. Some of these small islands are used as meteorological stations, but they have no economic value in themselves. The administrative authority for these islands was transferred from the high commissioner in Madagascar to the *préfet* of Réunion before the Malagasy accession to independence in order to keep them under French dominance. This point is the object of a standing dispute between Tananarive and Paris—and, to a lesser degree, between Port Louis and Paris. The Malagasy government has recently given up its claims to Tromelin Island in favor of Mauritius, trying by this maneuver to spoil relations between France and that rather moderate state.

The French army has, on the metropolitan territory, a special force (the Eleventh Paratroop Division) whose mission is to be ready to operate in overseas territories or countries. As far as the Indian Ocean is concerned, however, air transport capacity is not sufficient and sea transport is too slow. Therefore about 5,000 troops are permanently stationed in the region. After the withdrawal of the French armed forces from the Malagasy Republic following the change of regime in 1973, some of those troops were moved to Djibouti, where they are still garrisoned in that newly independent state by virtue of the defense assistance agreement signed immediately after independence. The other troops are stationed on several islands, principally on Réunion. There are detachments of the Foreign Legion on Mayotte and on three of the *iles éparses*. On Réunion, moreover, the national draft system applies, even though, when adapted locally, it fits more with economic and educational aims than with military ones.

Some transportation and liaison aircraft and helicopters are based on Réunion and in Djibouti, and a flight squadron of Mirage IIIC with about 1,000 men is in Djibouti. The permanent strength of the navy consists of four or five combat ships of destroyer class and about the same number of logistic ships. This standing force is supported by a periodically relieved task group of two frigates and occasionally one aircraft carrier, which are detached from the home fleet. About 3,000 men comprise the permanent French naval presence in the Indian Ocean.

For the navy, the main constraint is the problem of a base. In colonial times and during the first twelve years of Malagasy independence, Diégo-Suarez, a huge natural bay in the north of Madagascar, was the support and command base of French naval forces in the Indian Ocean. But in 1974 the French had to evacuate that base.[5] Unfortunately Réunion has no naturally favorable place in which to install a naval base. Mayotte, a coralline island, has good shelters, principally in Dzaoudzi Bay, and some observers have hinted that France wishfully encouraged the *Mahouais* secession for that reason. But it seems that the French government, both from political and financial points of view, is not anxious to be more involved in Mayotte's affairs. Djibouti has rather poor naval facilities (there is no dockyard for careening), but the French ships can use them. At any rate, the French navy shares the same preoccupation of all other navies in the world, namely, looking not so much for permanent bases ashore as for mobile, less-vulnerable logistic support at sea. That is why the French naval force in the Indian Ocean is composed equally of logistic and combat ships. France maintains standing naval forces in the region, despite not having any real base ashore. Facilities and moorings are available, however, at Saint-Denis and Le Port on Réunion, at Dzaoudzi on Mayotte, and in Djibouti.

Still, it seems that there is no opportunity for French military assistance today, except in Djibouti. In June 1979, however, France sent a patrol craft to the Seychelles, perhaps in the hope of starting some sort of cooperation. In Malagasy Republic, an important team of French military advisers was dismissed by the new regime and replaced mostly by North Koreans. Joint maneuvers take place annually in the western Indian Ocean in order to test the efficiency of the military setup. Also, French naval ships cruise along the East African coast, and occasionally one of them might be in the northern or eastern parts of the Indian Ocean. The official calls at littoral countries mostly have the character of formal relations, in order to show the flag.

French Interests in the Indian Ocean

One may rightly wonder why France continues to have such a concern for the western Indian Ocean. What are the most important interests that France wants to safeguard in that area? France is vitally dependent upon foreign countries for raw materials, especially energy supplies. Poor in coal, natural gas, oil, and lignite, France has exhausted its hydroelectric potential and has decided to hurry up its nuclear program in spite of the risks of that undertaking. But for the next few years, the French economy will still be heavily dependent on oil, and about two-thirds of the petroleum that France needs comes from the Middle East. In addition, the French oil companies—the state-owned Elf-Aquitaine and the partly private Compagnie Francaise des Pétroles—operate in the Gulf area and off the Indonesian coast.

Before 1967, oil was shipped to France via the Red Sea. During the long period when the Suez Canal was closed, the oil tankers went around Africa by the Cape of Good Hope, and the increasing draft of the tankers made it impossible to use Suez again when the canal was reopened in 1974. Thus an umbilical cord links the Gulf to Europe through a long and vulnerable passage along the western coast of the Indian Ocean. One of the main reasons officially given to explain the permanent cruising of French naval ships in the area is the protection of the shipping trade, especially the oil tanker traffic that is so vital to France.

Oil imports are a common top-priority item in the economy of all Western countries, including the United States and Japan. Western countries are also buying other raw materials and commodities from many countries around the Indian Ocean, and France is no exception. It imports tin, timber, rubber, and manioc from Southeast Asia; various minerals from South Africa; and iron ore from Australia. France is thus concerned about the freedom of navigation and trade in the Indian Ocean as a whole and is reluctant to support the neutralization of that ocean as endorsed by the UN General Assembly in 1971.

One remark must be made concerning the structure of French international trade: Its most important clients are developed countries, with the Common Market countries being by far the most important. The volume of its exports is therefore relatively small to countries bordering the Indian Ocean. Most of France's European partners are more involved there—Britain, because of the Commonwealth network, and countries like West Germany, Italy, and the Netherlands, because of their ancient trading traditions. From the French perspective, African states are, with the notable exception of South Africa, rather poor trading partners. That is why, despite extensive Third World criticism, Paris maintains good relations with Pretoria. For years France carried on a huge and profitable arms trade with South Africa. That trade has been embargoed since 1977, but France continues to have substantial commercial ties with South Africa.

In order to balance the increasing amount of their oil expenditures since the 1973–74 oil crisis, French business circles, stimulated by the government, have been anxious to spread their activities on a worldwide scale. Industrial fairs took place in Kuala Lumpur in 1973 and in Jakarta in 1978, and France has been very successful in promoting arms sales. In the Indian Ocean region airplanes have been sold to India, Pakistan, Iran, Australia, Kuwait, and the United Arab Emirates. Saudi Arabia has bought armored equipment, and Pakistan, Malaysia, and Indonesia have bought ships. France also sold airplanes and other military equipment to South Africa until 1977. Recently, in spite of cool relations, the Malagasy Republic bought a landing ship. (Malagasy's current leader, Pres. Didier Ratsiraka, is a French-trained naval officer.) Although its investments are small, France is a member of international consortiums for financial loans to India, Pakistan, and Indonesia, and in 1970 France joined the Asian Development Bank. In addition, France is involved multilaterally in the area through the European Economic Community (EEC). France participates in the Lome Convention, which links the EEC with about fifty developing countries, including several in the Indian Ocean region, and France also contributes about one-third of the European Development Fund, which provides loans and grants to many Third World countries.

We therefore confront the paradoxical situation of France being the only European country to keep up a military apparatus in the Indian Ocean in order to protect trading activities that, with the notable exception of oil, are of secondary importance to that country. But since the primary importance of oil trading is not solely a

French concern, it has been suggested that the protection of merchant traffic in the Indian Ocean should be assumed collectively by Western countries, under a military alliance yet to be defined.[6]

After World War II, France was weakened by the 1940 defeat, German occupation, and internal rivalries, and it was not able to resist the worldwide movement of decolonization. Having lost first Indochina and then North Africa, it tried to maintain special links with French black Africa, even after independence was granted in the early 1960s. Simultaneously, France promoted a Western European community built around French-German reconciliation. Thus France appears today as a regional power in a Euro-African geopolitical framework.

On the other hand, General de Gaulle revived French national ambitions, and France sometimes thinks that its historical worldwide vocation is not completely outdated. Such desires are naturally held by statesmen who want to be considered as de Gaulle's heirs, but this consciousness of a very special role in world history is also deeply and commonly rooted in French thinking. For more matter-of-fact reasons, the business people think that the French economic involvements must be spread all over the world, instead of remaining focused only on the Euro-African area. One thus notices a contradiction between worldwide ambitions and an active policy geographically limited to Europe, the Middle East, and Africa (known in France as *trilogue*).

As far as the Indian Ocean is concerned, France's position remains delicate for three principal reasons. Its policy seems too favorable to South Africa, it is accused of colonialism because of its continued presence on Réunion, and it is criticized because the independence of the Comoro Islands was not extended to the archipelago as a whole in accordance with OAU recommendations.

Following the new definition of the "exclusive economic zone" as suggested by the new Law of the Sea Conference, France considers itself the third country in the world as far as the extension of its maritime domain is concerned—11 million square kilometers, of which 3 million are in the Indian Ocean and the Antarctic. New surveys off Réunion give hope for new wealth in polymetallic nodules while, for the present, the more traditional activities such as fishing are in the hands of foreigners, principally the Japanese.

Finally, we must not forget that the Indian Ocean is one of only two routes from Europe to the Far East and the Pacific, and France has another important maritime domain in the Pacific, from New Caledonia to Polynesia. Thus the Indian Ocean is part of one of the two compulsory ways of transit between continental France and its possessions in the antipodes, and the only route on the high seas for its full length. By the westward route, one must enter foreign waters in the Caribbean and transit the Panama Canal or brave the hazardous waters of Cape Horn.

The Future of French Policy in the Indian Ocean

In the early 1970s, some people in Parisian political circles thought that a slow and prudent reduction of French presence in the Indian Ocean would not substantially harm the country's interests. General de Gaulle and his ideas of "grandeur" were no longer in vogue, President Pompidou seemed to be much more pragmatic, oil was abundant and cheap and there was no definite threat concerning its supply, and the prospect of using the sea as a source of raw materials was considered remote.

Today, it seems that President Giscard d'Estaing would like to take a global view of the world situation, even though France's material means are no stronger than during Pompidou's time. But the internal balance of political power obliges the president to concede some satisfactions to his conditional Gaullist supporters.[7]

Besides this political conjuncture, there are two permanent reasons for France to maintain its presence in the Indian Ocean. France intends to keep at its exclusive disposal the whole new maritime domain allotted to it by the Law of the Sea Conference, and a noticeable part of the new domain is located in the Indian Ocean. Second, France is anxious to be present and ready for any necessary action along the oil lifeline that originates at the Strait of Hormuz. For these reasons, one can be sure that France will go on playing an active role in the Indian Ocean, even at the price of some minor concessions, like giving Mayotte back to the Comoro Republic.

Acknowledgments

I wish to thank a team of Indian Ocean researchers based at the Centre de Hautes Etudes sur l'Afrique et l'Asie Modernes (CHEAM) for their advice on this chapter. They are: Andre du Castel (economic problems), Raymond Delval (insular states), Alain Lamballe (Indian subcontinent), and Georges Malecot (Horn of Africa).

Notes

1. The ultra-leftist Mouvement Militant Mauricien (M.M.M.) was founded by a young student, Paul Berenger, who had participated in the May 1968 protest at the Sorbonne.

2. During the Tsiranana era, French people living in Madagascar were called Vahaza, and they were familiarly presented as the "nineteenth" tribe (there are eighteen principal, indigenous ethnic groups).

3. Bilateral cultural agreements have been concluded with Egypt, Sudan, Saudi Arabia, Iran, Pakistan, Malaysia, Indonesia, Kenya, and Tanzania. Cultural centers have been opened in Jakarta, Surabaya, and Nairobi. Less has been done as far as broadcasting, linguistic research, and publications are concerned. On this matter see A. Bellamal, "Pour une politique française dans le monde malayo-indonésien," *France-Asie*, no. 2 (Paris 1979).

4. An associated reason is that the present prime minister in Paris, Raymond Barre, was born on Réunion and that Michel Debré, the prime minister under de Gaulle, is the representative of one of the three constituencies of that overseas *département*.

5. For a transitional period, the shipyard was put under a purely industrial status, and a team of French civilian technicians stayed there to cooperate with new local authorities.

6. Alliance problems are very controversial in France since its military experts are mostly concerned with European defense. Very few seem to be concerned about protection of the sea-lanes and maritime approaches to Western Europe. On this problem see Adm. J.R.J. Lannuzel, "Exposé devant l'Institute des Hautes Etudes de Défense Nationale," *Défense Nationale* (October 1978):31-38. Admiral Lannuzel is the number one naval officer in the French navy.

7. In recent French national polls, the balance is close between the present right-wing majority in power and the opposition. In this situation, electors from the overseas territories are considered an important help. Réunion has three representatives and two senators.

Part 3

International Organizations in the Indian Ocean

11
The United Nations Ad Hoc Committee on the Indian Ocean: Blind Alley or Zone of Peace?

Philip Towle

The proposal to establish a Zone of Peace in the Indian Ocean (IOPZ) has become a hardy United Nations perennial, like proposals to ban nuclear weapons tests or the production of chemical weapons.[1] In part the IOPZ proposal is designed to isolate the area from the cold war, but as its name suggests, it was also intended to enhance the prospects for peace in the Indian Ocean. The two goals have not been distinguished; indeed, according to nonaligned doctrine, they are indistinguishable. The IOPZ resolutions passed annually at the United Nations by sweeping Third World majorities suggest that if the bases and naval forces of the great powers were removed from the Indian Ocean, the area would become a Zone of Peace. A few of the littoral states, notably Pakistan and Sri Lanka, have pointed out that there are other ways of enhancing the prospects for peace and stability in the area, but their views have received little overt support in the Third World.

The original proposal for an IOPZ made by Sri Lanka at the United Nations in October 1971 appeared to apply as much to the naval forces of the littoral states as to the forces of the outside powers.[2] It would have demilitarized the ocean outside the territorial limits, except for the right of transit. However, the stronger littoral states brought pressure on the Sri Lankans behind the scenes to angle their resolution exclusively against the great powers. Accordingly, the Sri Lankan representative stated, "In the course of our consultations it became apparent that the members of the [UN

First] Committee were not ready for such a comprehensive scheme for the demilitarization of the Indian Ocean. . . . Our proposal and our approach have therefore undergone a radical change in deference to the reservations expressed by our critics."[3]

Consequently the 1971 and all subsequent IOPZ resolutions have been aimed entirely at the military activities of the great powers. They seek to eliminate from the Indian Ocean "all bases, military installations and logistical supply facilities, the disposition of nuclear weapons and weapons of mass destruction and any manifestation of great power military presence conceived in the context of great power rivalry."[4]

Since 1972 the IOPZ proposal has been kept alive in the Ad Hoc Committee on the Indian Ocean established by the United Nations. The committee has twenty members from the littoral states, and China, Greece, and Japan have also joined as great powers or major maritime users of the area. The committee held eleven meetings in 1973 alone, and it has prepared the annual resolutions so assiduously passed by the UN General Assembly. In 1974 the resolution called for the convening of an international conference on the Indian Ocean. So far this proposal has had no effect because the United States and the Soviet Union have shown little enthusiasm for convening a conference designed to criticize their activities, and without their presence, the other states could make little progress.

From 1977 to 1979 the pressure on the great powers to agree to an IOPZ was reduced because the United States and the Soviet Union were conducting bilateral negotiations on limiting their forces in the area. In March 1977 President Carter announced that he had proposed to the Russians that the Indian Ocean should be "completely demilitarized." However, a few days later he told the United Nations, "We will seek . . . to establish Soviet willingness to each agreement with us on mutual military restraint in the Indian Ocean"—a very different and much more limited goal.[5] It was on this more limited basis that the United States and the Soviet Union held discussions in Moscow in June 1977, in Washington in September 1977, and in Bern in December 1977 and again in February 1978. The Pentagon's director of policy plans, James Thompson, suggested in October 1978 that "a general framework or format" had been worked out for an agreement covering the Indian Ocean but that no agreement had been reached with the Russians on the number of ships that the two powers could keep there, nor on the geographic area covered by the hypothetical agreement.[6] Subsequent reports become more pessimistic.

There were two main reasons for this change. On their side the Russians were expelled from Berbera in Somalia in November 1977, because of the support they were giving to Ethiopia in the Somalian-Ethiopian war.[7] They towed the floating dock, which they had previously stationed at Berbera, to Aden, but the Russians no longer had the use of any naval facility in the Indian Ocean to compare with the U.S. establishment on the island of Diego Garcia. Consequently any stabilization agreement would preserve the U.S. advantage. On its side, the United States has consistently tied progress on naval talks with the Russians to the preservation of stability on the littoral.

The Carter administration became less and less sympathetic toward the idea of force reductions as the shah's regime in Iran began to collapse, threatening to usher in an era of even greater instability in the Middle East. In the early months of 1979, U.S. spokesmen began to talk of strengthening U.S. forces in the area to compensate for the troubles in Iran. The U.S. defense secretary, Harold Brown, toured friendly states in the Persian Gulf in February 1979 and was quoted as saying subsequently that "the willingness to upgrade Diego Garcia indicated abandonment of the Indian Ocean arms limitations talks."[8]

Brown's comments and others of the same nature reflected divisions within the U.S. administration. Other U.S. officials still mentioned the Indian Ocean as one area where President Carter hoped for an agreement with the Russians when the president was in Vienna in June 1979 for the signing of the second Strategic Arms Limitation Treaty.[9] But at the same time, U.S. statements about the establishment of a quick-reaction force for military actions in the area and particularly in the oil-producing Persian Gulf area became more frequent. Speculation had also begun again in the United States about the possibility of using force to prevent an Arab boycott of the Western world following OPEC insistence that the price of oil should rise substantially in 1979.[10] While such speculations were continuing, the Russians sent an aircraft carrier into the Indian Ocean for the first time. The *Minsk*, like its sister ship the *Kiev*, had been built in the Black Sea and had then sailed through the Dardanelles in breach of one of the very few existing naval arms control agreements, the 1936 Montreux Convention.[11] The convention bans the passage through the straits of "surface vessels of war, whatever their displacement, designed or adapted primarily for the purpose of carrying and operating aircraft at sea." The *Kiev* passed through the Indian Ocean in April 1979 on its way to Vladivostok, which seems likely to be its home port. However its transit through the Indian Ocean appeared to many of the littoral states to reflect the general superpower buildup in the area.

It was against this background that forty-four littoral and hinterland states held a major meeting on the Indian Ocean in New York in July 1979. The idea of convening such a meeting had been endorsed by the UN General Assembly, and preparations had been made at the three previous sessions of the Ad Hoc Committee on the Indian Ocean. China, Greece, and Japan sent delegations, and twelve major maritime users of that ocean also sent observers.

Before the meeting began it seemed that the Pakistani delegation might lead it in a new and more constructive direction, which would not require the concurrence of the superpowers. Since 1973 Pakistan had been calling for the littoral states to agree to respect the sovereignty and territorial integrity of their neighbors. At the UN Special Session on Disarmament held in New York in May 1978 the Pakistani delegation had proposed that "the littoral and hinterland states of the Indian Ocean should reach agreement at their forthcoming meeting on measures, such as a commitment to settle outstanding disputes by peaceful means, the renunciation of nuclear weapons and the maintenance of a reasonable military balance amongst themselves, in order to promote conditions of security within the Indian Ocean region."[12]

The Pakistani proposal would be extremely difficult to implement, however, even if it were not implicitly aimed against India. India does not want to see a balance emerge between its forces and those of Pakistan, and Indian officials argue that they are justified in seeking superiority since it is Pakistan that has repeatedly tried to change the status quo over Kashmir. Moreover, even if there were agreement that a reasonable military balance was a desirable aim, it is very difficult for potential enemies to agree how such a balance can be achieved (as the European nations have discovered at the interminable mutual balanced force reduction [MBFR] talks in Vienna).

Thus the Indian delegation at the UN special session dismissed the Pakistani suggestions, and subsequently the Indian government showed little sign of relenting.

Despite these setbacks, the Pakistani delegation was particularly active at the ad hoc committee meetings that prepared the way for the July 1979 meeting. However, given the general background, it was almost inevitable that the meeting would concentrate on the great power threats, and the Indian delegation found it easy to gain support for its insistence that regional arms control initiatives should be blocked. All the Pakistani delegation was able to achieve was an agreement to call for the "strengthening of international security through regional and other cooperation in the context of the implementation of the Declaration of the Indian Ocean as a zone of peace."[13]

The one Pakistani proposal that was fully accepted was that the area covered by the IOPZ should be extended to include the littoral countries as well as the ocean itself. Ironically, this caused the most problem for Australia, because since Pakistan's decision to leave CENTO in March 1979, Australia is the only littoral state that is avowedly and explicitly aligned with a great power. As a result of the ANZUS alliance, Australia has several U.S. bases on its territory, and because of the Pakistani proposal, they were all brought within the area covered by the Zone of Peace. Previous documents outlining the ideas behind the zone have suggested that bases and military installations "conceived in the context of great power rivalry" should be removed from the area. However, the Iraqi delegation insisted that this phrase should be dropped and that all bases should be removed. This made the situation even worse for the Australians, who might otherwise have claimed that since the bases were used to verify the strategic arms limitation agreements, they were the result of collusion rather than competition between the great powers. The general nonaligned support for the Iraqi stance made such a claim impossible.

Ironically, the Western countries have sympathized with the Pakistani efforts to institute measures intended to reduce tensions and violence on the littoral. But the combination of the Pakistani proposals to extend the area covered by the IOPZ with the general nonaligned insistence that all great power bases within the zone be removed persuaded the Australian delegation to reject the conclusions reached at the July 1979 meeting. At the same time the Australians implicitly endorsed the Pakistani concern about violence among the states in the region and criticized the July meeting for failing to face up to the responsibility for this violence. Australia rejected the suggestion that

> the present level of Great Power military rivalry in the Indian Ocean is the only threat to the maintenance of peace and security in the region. . . . A major responsibility for the maintenance of peace and security . . . lies with the countries in the region itself. . . . In recent years, the security of the region has, on several occasions, been jeopardised by developments which did not arise as a consequence of Great Power military rivalry.[14]

Australian delegates to the meeting also suggested that it was unlikely that the Indian Ocean would be declared a Zone of Peace unless the littoral states renounced the production of nuclear weapons by adhering to the nuclear Nonproliferation Treaty. Press reports suggested that this was a veiled attack on Pakistan, which is believed to be developing nuclear weapons.[15] In the past, however, the Pakistanis have called for the establishment of a nuclear-free zone in South Asia in order to embarrass the Indians, and any stress on nonproliferation still probably irritates the Indians more than the Pakistanis.

The Indian delegation found it difficult during the 1979 conference to accept the suggestion that "the littoral and hinterland states of the Indian Ocean should agree not to acquire or introduce nuclear weapons in the Indian Ocean themselves or to allow their introduction by an external power." The Indians did accept, however, the suggestion that the states in the area should "uphold the fundamental objective of non-proliferation of nuclear weapons and reaffirm their conviction that production, acquisition and stockpiling of nuclear weapons . . . are detrimental to the maintenance of peace and security."[16]

The most active role at the July meeting was played by Iraq, which obviously saw the meeting as an occasion for reemphasizing the purity of nonaligned doctrine and for blaming the great powers for all the disputes and wars in the area. This has long been a prevalent Third World view. As one Indian writer has argued,

"Asian people have always attributed their conflicts to the machinations of 'imperialism' meaning the powers of West Europe and the United States. With every local conflict in Asia and Africa since the era of independence one or more colonial powers have been associated. The only exception is the Sino-Indian border conflict."[17]

In practice it is very difficult today to substantiate that thesis. The British intervened on the Indian Ocean littoral to protect Kuwait against a possible Iraqi invasion in 1961 and to protect three East African governments against mutinies among their own troops in 1964. The Russians have also intervened by force in support of Ethiopia and against Somalia. Otherwise none of the great powers have been involved directly in any of the wars in the area since most of the countries in the area achieved independence. Violence in the Indian Ocean area is essentially an indigenous phenomenon, the product of innumerable border, racial, and ideological antagonisms in the area. The great powers may sometimes have made the problems worse; by helping the weaker of two regional powers they may have prolonged a conflict, and by supplying arms they may have inadvertently encouraged a revisionist state, such as Somalia, to try to change the status quo. But the great powers have themselves almost always preferred the preservation of the status quo to any hypothetical gains that might occur from tensions or violence in the area.[18]

Moreover, when they wish to interfere on the littoral, the great powers find that their naval forces (against which the IOPZ proposal is mainly aimed) are an extremely blunt instrument to achieve their ends. The supply of arms, advisers, and finally auxiliaries or "volunteers" are much more effective and less risky ways for the great powers to support their friends on the littoral than using their naval forces in the area. Only in the case of minor mutinies, such as those put down by the British in East Africa in 1964, are amphibious forces likely to be adequate to protect a littoral government against internal unrest. In the case of a major revolution, like the one in Iran in 1979, naval power cannot preserve the existing regime. Similarly, when a friendly state is under attack by the army of another littoral country, the supply of arms and advisers is the preferred counteraction normally employed by a great power. On the other hand, the most likely form of intervention againt a littoral government is by subversion or by support for rebel forces. Neither of these forms of intervention would be prevented by the establishment of an IOPZ.

The littoral states would only be directly threatened by the superpowers if the Russians extended the Brezhnev doctrine to the Third World or if the Western states intervened by force against another OPEC oil boycott. The first case may have been made more likely by the Vietnamese decision to join the Council for Mutual Economic Assistance (COMECON) in 1979. Other Third World states may follow the Vietnamese example in order to obtain any benefits that membership in COMECON might bring, and experience shows that the Russians are prepared to use force to prevent states withdrawing from such organizations. But in Eastern Europe the Russians were very careful to mobilize massive military forces before they intervened to overthrow the established governments in Hungary and Czechoslovakia, and even then they were surprised by the levels of resistance to their invasions. The Russians are still very far from achieving that level of power in the Indian Ocean area, and above all they lack an effective carrier to provide air cover for invading troops. The vertical-takeoff Yak-36 aircraft on the *Kiev* and *Minsk* have not proved very successful and would be completely outclassed by the land-based planes of a medium-ranked power such as Pakistan.

The possibility of intervening by force to prevent an Arab oil boycott of the West was discussed in public by Dr. Kissinger and Pres. Gerald Ford in 1974. It was also extensively analyzed in the U.S. press. However the idea was widely criticized on the grounds that the oil-producing countries would be able to destroy their oil wells and refineries before the invading forces arrived and because, even if such destruction were avoided, guerrilla resistance would make continued supply hazardous. Moreover public opinion in the West would be very divided about such an operation. Rapid and successful military operations might be accepted, but if, as would be almost certain, the operations dragged on, resistance to the war would increase. Consequently military intervention is not likely to be undertaken by the West, and the possibility of such intervention has never been taken seriously in Japan or Western Europe, which are even more dependent on the Persian Gulf oil than is the United States.[19]

Despite the limited utility of naval power in the Indian Ocean area, the IOPZ proposal has focused almost entirely on such forces. Although the export of armaments is a much more effective and widespread way in which the great powers assist friendly states, the littoral states have been opposed to any discussion of conventional arms transfers. They feel the need for armaments to maintain internal stability and to deter attacks upon them. Thus the U.S. suggestions that the Conference of the Committee on Disarmament should discuss the problems presented by conventional arms transfers have been blocked, as have the Japanese proposals that the United Nations should consider the question.[20] Above all the developing countries resent the suggestion that they are unfit to possess the weapons maintained by the developed states. The other important way in which the great powers intervene in the area was also ignored by the July 1979 meeting. The presence of 50,000 Cuban auxiliaries in Africa, armed and supplied by the Russians, went unmentioned, although the Cuban forces have already had far more impact on African politics than all the superpower navies in the Indian Ocean put together.

Another reason sometimes given for the establishment of a Zone of Peace in the area is that the presence of Soviet and U.S. navies might involve the region in a war between NATO and the Warsaw Pact. However it is doubtful whether an IOPZ would protect the region from such a war. In the event of a full-scale nuclear war, the area could be severely damaged by nuclear fallout if the prevailing winds brought the fallout in a southerly direction. Such targets as there are for nuclear weapons in the area would not add substantially to this fallout. Most of the targets are "soft" and could be destroyed by conventional or small tactical nuclear weapons, and there is no way an IOPZ could protect the area from a major threat from drifting radioactivity. As the Yugoslavs pointed out at the United Nations in the 1950s, "The smaller powers, like Yugoslavia, which had no weapons of mass destruction, would nonetheless be annihilated by them if they were used."[21]

In the event of a conventional (or tactical nuclear) war confined to Europe, the Indian Ocean would escape damage because of the nature of the war, not because of an IOPZ. In the event of a worldwide naval war, the area would almost inevitably become embroiled, whether or not an IOPZ had been established. The Russians could not be expected to allow tankers carrying oil vital to the

Western war effort to pass unmolested through the Indian Ocean. They could argue that the West had breached the IOPZ agreement by sending nuclear submarines into the area in preparation for an attack on the Soviet Union, and it would be impossible to disprove their claims. If Russian submarines in the Indian Ocean began attacking Western tankers, the NATO navies would send warships into the Indian Ocean (when they could be spared from more important areas, such as the North Atlantic) in order to try to convoy the tankers to safety. On the other hand, if the oil-exporting countries cut off supplies to the West in anticipation of a Soviet attack on their tankers or territory, the West would regard this as an unfriendly act and would intervene when forces became available to protect the West's supplies. An IOPZ would not be an adequate protection against such actions.

The IOPZ debates at the United Nations have been occasions for scoring political points rather than for examining the premises upon which the proposal is based. Chinese spokesmen have argued, "The root cause of the prolonged disturbance and instability in the Indian Ocean region lies in the two Super Powers aggressive expansion and contention."[22] In fact the Chinese know perfectly well that the superpowers are not primarily responsible for the wars in the area. When the Chinese first took their seat at the United Nations and listened to the Sri Lankan proposal for an IOPZ, they were the first to point out the irony that such a proposal should be made when India and Pakistan were locked in conflict. Admittedly the Chinese claimed that the Soviet Union supported India's "attack" on Pakistan, but the main target for their criticism at the time was undoubtedly India.[23] At the littoral and hinterland states meeting in 1979 the Chinese kept up their attacks on the Soviet Union, and it is partly because the Russians make themselves vulnerable to such attacks that the Chinese have taken an interest in IOPZ meetings in recent years.

The Russians appeared more sympathetic toward the IOPZ idea after they were expelled from Berbera. Previously they had occasionally praised the idea on the conditions that it did not affect their naval activities in the Indian Ocean and that it led to the removal of all Western bases. But it was not until the Russians no longer had the use of the facilities of Berbera that they voted for the IOPZ resolution at the United Nations. Delegates to the July 1979 meeting were therefore surprised by the hardness of the line taken by the Russian delegation. Despite the fact that they had only observer status, they intervened several times in the discussions to protest against the language in the final document, which they felt was directed too explicitly against Soviet activities in the Indian Ocean area. They also demanded the right to reply to the Chinese, and they made clear that their attendance at future meetings would depend on the way the negotiations progressed.

The United States took a more self-effacing line. In his address to the opening session, the U.S. observer said that he was opposed to the area becoming the scene for an arms race. More significantly, he supported the suggestion made in the original IOPZ resolution in 1971 that the area should not be used for "any threat or use of force against the sovereignty, territorial integrity and independence of any littoral or hinterland state of the Indian Ocean in contravention of the purposes and principles of the Charter of the UN."[24] Critics of the United States would no doubt argue that it had indeed been threatening the littoral states by discussing the possibility of intervening to break an Arab oil boycott. But the littoral and hinterland states could build upon the U.S. statement and ask for a Security Council resolution embodying that declaration, along the lines of the Security Council resolution on security assurances that was made to back up the nuclear Nonproliferation Treaty.[25]

Apart from asking the great powers for such a commitment to respect their sovereignty, at their future meetings the littoral and hinterland states should ideally concentrate on minimizing the indigenous threats to stability. If the Americans and Russians can agree to stabilize their military presence in the Indian Ocean they will do so in their bilateral committee. A multilateral agreement limiting naval forces in the Indian Ocean would imply that the littoral states have the right under international law to say how the seas beyond their territorial waters will be governed.[26] The Russians and Americans have consistently opposed any such implication. The nonaligned nations have already suggested that the Mediterranean should become a Zone of Peace, and all the countries on the southern littoral (except Israel) have at one time or another supported this suggestion. An IOPZ would only encourage states to press for naval limitations in an area that is far more important than the Indian Ocean for the major military alliances. Consequently, both superpowers will continue to prefer a bilateral solution of the Indian Ocean problem to a multilateral one. If they cannot reach an agreement, then the ad hoc committee will continue to make as little progress as it has made over the last seven years.

Western and Pakistani proposals for regional agreements among the littoral states offer a way out of the impasse. For example, the littoral countries could institute regional confidence building measures (CBMs) to reduce the prospects for wars in the area without waiting for the agreement of the great powers. Moreover such measures would strike far closer to the real sources of violence and tension in the area than the proposed measures for naval limitation. Admittedly CBMs have not been very successful in Europe, where the effects of the exchange of observers at military maneuvers have been severely limited by the Soviet Union.[27] Nevertheless several states, including Britain and the Federal Republic of Germany, have suggested that such CBMs should be instituted across the world.[28] Of course, in many areas CBMs would be unacceptable. In particular the black African states do not want to improve their relations with South Africa. This reflects the old arms control dilemma: In cases in which relations between states are good enough for CBMs to be negotiated, such measures may be unnecessary, and in other cases relations may be so bad that negotiations cannot even begin.

Nevertheless, there are a number of intermediate stages in which CBMs and other measures could be acceptable and could help enhance stability around the Indian Ocean. "Hot lines" could be established between potential enemies to avoid miscalculations in a crisis. Military missions could be exchanged, and advance notification of any important military movements could be given. Regional arbitration tribunals could also be set up. Already there has been friction between India and Bangladesh over oil prospecting in the Bay of Bengal, and many other disputes over fishing and mineral rights in the area appear likely. Regional arbitration tribunals could help solve these problems, just as the Anglo-French dispute over oil prospecting in the English Channel has been solved by arbitration.

The littoral states might also consider the possibility of limiting their arms imports. Regional agreements of this nature would not carry the imperialistic overtones that efforts by the great powers to limit the arms trade to the Third World inevitably involve. Admittedly regional efforts of this nature have not fared very well in recent years. The Declaration of Ayacucho by eight Latin American states in December 1974 looked forward to the establishment of conditions in Latin America that "will make possible the effective limitation of armaments and an end to their acquisition for offensive purposes, so that all possible resources may be devoted to the economic and social development of every country in Latin America."[29] Subsequently relations among several of the Latin American countries have deteriorated, and the Andean region has been particularly tense. Peru alone has placed an order for 200 Soviet T-55 tanks and 36 Su-22 fighter bombers. The Ayacucho Declaration is not quite dead however. Venezuela fought very hard and successfully for a favorable mention of the declaration in the final document of the UN Special Session on Disarmament, and Mexico and Venezuela have subsequently called for a conference on the transfer of weapons to the whole of Latin America.

If future IOPZ meetings were to devote themselves to this sort of regional measure, then for the first time, they could begin to make a constructive contribution to peace and security in the region. It may be too much to say that the effects of the IOPZ proposal have been entirely negative, since it has certainly called attention to strategic problems in the Indian Ocean. But it has undoubtedly focused that attention on the wrong issues. It is, of course, a convention at the United Nations and at nonaligned meetings that the great powers should be criticized, and it is easy to understand the historical and other reasons for that tendency. But the charade has gone on long enough. It is time for the littoral and hinterland states to face up to their responsibilities. Opportunities for strengthening peace and stability in the Indian Ocean could be in their hands if they wished to seize them.

Notes

1. For a summary of proposals for an IOPZ and comments on the proposal, see UN Document A/AC.187/70, October 6, 1977, prepared for the UN Special Session on Disarmament, p. 35 and passim. For an extended discussion of the themes in this chapter, see P. Towle, *Naval Power in the Indian Ocean: Threats, Bluff, and Fantasies* (Canberra:

Strategic and Defence Studies Centre, Australian National University, 1979).

2. United Nations, *Declaration of the Indian Ocean as a Zone of Peace* (A/8492), October 1, 1971.

3. Meeting 1834 of the UN First Committee, November 23, 1971. See also the Japanese comments at meeting 1841, December 1, 1971, and subsequent Sri Lankan comments at meeting 1842, December 1, 1971.

4. UN Resolution 2832, December 16, 1971.

5. U.S. statements are summarized in Rear Adm. R. J. Hanks, "The Indian Ocean Negotiations, Rocks and Shoals," *Strategic Review* (Winter 1978).

6. "US-Soviet Accord on Indian Ocean," *Canberra Times,* October 14, 1978. See also "Positive Talks on the Indian Ocean," *Daily Telegraph,* November 18, 1977.

7. "Americans Fly in as Russians Quit," *Daily Telegraph,* November 18, 1977.

8. "US May Upgrade Indian Ocean Base as Soviet Counter," *Australian,* February 28, 1979. Also see "US Task Force Poised as Iran Crumbles," *Australian,* December 30–31, 1978.

9. "Leaders Agree to Avoid War," *Canberra Times,* June 18, 1979.

10. See "US Plans Huge Force," *Canberra Times,* June 25, 1979; "Cartel in Command," *Wall Street Journal,* July 9, 1979; and J. M. Collins and C. R. Mark, *Petroleum Imports from the Persian Gulf* (Washington, D.C.: Congressional Research Service, June 4, 1979).

11. For comments on the Kiev class see "From Montreux to Kiev," *Defence* (September 1976), and J. N. Moore, "Not-So-Chicken Kiev," *Navy International* (November 1976).

12. *Programme of Action on Disarmament,* Pakistani working paper (A/AC. 187/92), January 24, 1978.

13. *Principles of Agreement for the Implementation of the Declaration of the Indian Ocean as a Zone of Peace* (A/AC. 199/L. 1./Rev 1), July 1979, Principle 6.

14. "Indian Ocean Points Rejected by Australia," *Canberra Times,* July 16, 1979. See also the Australian representative's speech of July 13, 1979, to the closing session of the meeting.

15. "Nuclear Weapons Bar to Indian Ocean Zone of Peace," *Canberra Times,* July 13, 1979.

16. See *Principles of Agreement,* paragraphs 17b and c.

17. Chanakya Sen, *Against the Cold War* (New Delhi: Asia Publishing House, 1962), p. 21. See also K. P. Misra, "Developments in the Indian Ocean Area: The Littoral Response," *International Studies* (January-March 1977):17.

18. For Third World criticisms of the conservatism of the great powers, see Mohammed Ayoob, "The Super Powers and Regional Stability," *World Today* (May 1979).

19. For the Kissinger and Ford comments see R. W. Tucker, "A New International Order?" *Commentary* (February 1975). Also see "Further Reflections on Oil and Force," *Commentary* (March 1975), and "Paper War on Oil Security," *Canberra Times*, July 16, 1979.

20. For the U.S. proposals on limiting the conventional arms trade see *Further Documents on Disarmament, 1966*, Cmnd. 3120 (London: Her Majesty's Stationery Office, 1966), p. 27. See also *Further Documents on Disarmament 1970*, Cmnd. 4725 (London: Her Majesty's Stationery Office, 1971), p. 53. For the Japanese proposals, see the letter dated December 9, 1977, from the permanent representative of Japan to the United Nations addressed to the secretary general, (A/AC.187/86), December 13, 1977.

21. Meeting 663 of the UN First Committee, November 12, 1953.

22. Statement by the Chinese representative in the UN First Committee, November 23, 1973 (reproduced in *Documents on Disarmament, 1973* [Washington, D.C.: Arms Control and Disarmament Agency, 1975], p. 823).

23. Meeting 1849 of the UN First Committee, December 10, 1971.

24. UN Resolution 2832, December 16, 1971.

25. The Security Council resolution is reproduced in Stockholm International Peace Research Institute (SIPRI), *Arms Control: A Survey and Appraisal of Multilateral Agreements* (London: Taylor and Francis, 1978), p. 87.

26. This is admitted by nonaligned supporters of the IOPZ proposal (see K. P. Misra, "Indian Ocean as a Zone of Peace: The Concept and the Alternatives," *Indian Quarterly* [January-March 1977]:23).

27. J. D. Toogood, "Military Aspects of the Belgrade Review Meeting," *Survival* (July-August 1978).

28. *Draft Programme of Action* (A/AC.187/96), February 1, 1978, paragraphs 111-116.

29. SIPRI, *Arms Control*, p. 121.

12
Demilitarization Proposals for the Indian Ocean

George W. Shepherd, Jr.

The widening arms race in the Indian Ocean has resulted in a number of proposals for unilateral, bilateral, and multilateral agreements for demilitarization. These have originated from the littoral countries as well as the major powers. Results have been few, and the times do not appear propitious; yet the circumstances could change, and therefore an analysis of the results and prospects is in order.

There are differing views of the origins and character of the competition between the global powers. Western authors on the whole have been reluctant to speak in terms of an arms race in the Indian Ocean and talk instead of the rivalry and conflict between powers.[1] This writer believes that the concept of an arms race is applicable to the situation in the Indian Ocean, in terms of a steadily escalating pattern of arms intrusion in which there is a clearly established action and reaction response between states. When used, the concept of an arms race should be limited to specifically defined actions and some empirical arms data to show the pattern of the escalating competition among the contending parties. The escalating pattern is not limited to the global powers but includes both littoral and hinterland states.

The question this chapter seeks to answer is, Can such an arms race and its regional dimensions be reversed or controlled by any of the existing proposals such as the Zone of Peace, bilateral agreements between the United States and the USSR, or the foreign policies of the littoral states? To answer this question, we have to deal with the nature of the global power rivalry. The traditional explanations of its nature and origins are simply either too biased or too limited to a paradigm that is inadequate.[2] The relationships of the arms race to conflict and to other factors have to be established as well. We can then go on to an examination of the relevance of the peace proposals to various types of situations involving all or part of the Indian Ocean states.

Structure of the Arms Race

The basic outline of the structure and content of the Indian Ocean arms race is presented in Tables 12.1, 12.2, and 12.3. Table 12.1 shows the major source of arms for the Indian Ocean states in the crucial decade under consideration, 1967–76. Table 12.2 shows the types of weaponry transferred by the great powers to the littoral states, and Table 12.3 gives a picture over time of the acceleration of U.S. arms transfers.

What comes through very clearly in all this data is a pattern of steady U.S. and USSR rival activity beginning about 1965 and continuing to the present.[3] At times, rapid escalation has taken place in certain parts of the Indian Ocean, related to conflicts in those regions. For example, high transfer levels were reached at the time of the first and second India-Pakistani wars in 1965 and 1971 (see Table 12.3). The Gulf became a major center of activity two years before the Arab-Israeli war of 1967, and that activity continued at high levels through the 1970s. The African regional arms races began in the late 1960s and continued through the 1970s. Activity in the Horn accelerated rapidly from 1970 to the Somalian-Ethiopian war of 1977–78, and has continued with the Soviet and Cuban airlifts. In southern Africa, the slow pace of the liberation activity of the 1960s suddenly intensified with the independence of Angola and Mozambique in 1974 and the liberation war in Zimbabwe throughout that decade.

Tribute System

The interrelationship of global power activity to this regional activity is best explained in terms of a political economy model that I call the tribute system. This tribute system is based on the ancient

Table 12.1

TOTAL ARMS TRANSFERS OF MAJOR SUPPLIERS FROM 1967-1976 BY RECIPIENT COUNTRY (MILLION CURRENT DOLLARS)

RECIPIENT	TOTAL	US	USSR	FRANCE	UK	PRC	CAN[a]	FRG	WTO[b]	OTHERS
Afghanistan	315	-	100	-	-	-	-	-	-	215
Bahrain	1	-	-	-	-	-	-	-	-	1
Bangladesh	65	-	35	-	5	-	-	-	-	25
Ethiopia	190	135	-	10	5	-	-	5	-	35
India	1681	40	1365	41	75	-	-	10	100	50
Iran	5272	3835	611	15	270	-	45	275	-	221
Iraq	2460	-	1795	95	5	5	-	35	150	375
Kenya	52	5	-	5	35	-	5	1	-	1
Kuwait	122	31	-	-	71	-	-	20	-	-
Mauritius	-	-	-	-	-	-	-	-	-	-
Mozambique	21	-	15	-	-	1	-	-	-	5
Pakistan	835	85	25	265	10	335	-	5	20	90
Oman	72	5	-	-	21	-	1	-	-	45
Qatar	5	-	-	-	5	-	-	-	-	-
Saudi Arabia	1438	671	-	225	451	-	-	11	-	80
Somalia	187	-	181	-	-	-	-	5	-	1
South Africa	501	30	-	365	10	-	5	-	-	91
Sri Lanka	16	1	10	-	5	-	-	-	-	-
(North) Yemen	78	1	35	11	1	-	-	-	-	30
(South) Yemen	163	-	151	-	1	-	-	-	-	11
Tanzania	123	1	30	-	1	75	5	1	-	10

a. Canada
b. Warsaw Treaty Organization members

Source: *World Military Expenditures and Arms Transfers 1967-1976* (Washington, D.C.: U.S. Arms Control and Disarmament Agency Publication 98, Released July 1978).

international principle that the strong protect the weak for a price. This principle has had various manifestations, from highly centralized empires to colonial systems and alliance systems. The modern global system, with its basic North-South division between the industrialized capitalist countries of the North and the less developed countries (LDCs) of the South, is a new version of the ancient tribute system. This consists of the two global powers acting as major patrons, providing protection and other services for the Third World client-states in return for trade, resources, and profits. The patron powers form the basic structure of the international order,

Table 12.2

ARMING THE THIRD WORLD: US AND SOVIET
WEAPONS EXPORTS, 1967-1976*

	AFRICA US	AFRICA USSR	EAST ASIA** US	EAST ASIA** USSR	LATIN AMERICA US	LATIN AMERICA USSR	NEAR EAST US	NEAR EAST USSR	SOUTH ASIA US	SOUTH ASIA USSR
Tanks, self propelled guns, artillery	249	2543	5861	6630	876	771	4662	11,916	30	2596
Armored personnel carriers/armored cars	112	1551	2927	500	1250	200	5724	4,249	321	544
Surface combatants	6	56	121	5	86	12	13	67	-	16
Submarines	-	1	2	-	20	-	-	5	-	8
Supersonic aircraft	41	328	403	280	16	44	1673	183	-	447
Subsonic aircraft	20	189	456	-	211	-	387	5	-	45
Helicopters	7	112	1257	47	174	41	389	130	-	116
Missiles	135	130	2373	7000	485	111	5512	470	-	324

*Includes Australia, New Zealand, Japan, South Africa, Israel.

**Does not include Soviet transfers to North Vietnam and US transfers to South Vietnam under the MASF program.

Source: U.S. Arms Control and Disarmament Agency. Published in The Defense Monitor (Washington, D. C., Center for Defense Information, January 1979).

Table 12.3

U.S. FOREIGN MILITARY SALES AGREEMENTS WITH THIRD WORLD REGIONS
(Million Dollars-Current Prices)

FY	East Asia & Pacific	Near East & South Asia	Africa	American Republics
1964	51.0	160.5	0.4	62.4
1965	51.0	160.5	0.4	62.4
1966	51.0	160.5	0.4	62.4
1967	149.4	338.4	0.2	71.7
1968	132.0	460.1	0.2	44.5
1969	160.7	355.9	0.1	39.0
1970	141.6	412.1	0.1	76.4
1971	141.1	725.4	16.3	76.9
1972	309.0	1,274.6	2.8	145.2
1973	299.8	3,095.4	2.6	198.5
1974	316.6	8,916.2	13.7	316.3
1975	665.3	7,685.0	27.4	282.6
1976	551.2	9,644.2	224.7	148.3
1977	130.5	8,487.7	113.9	149.4
1978	337.3	9,671.8	222.3	181.8
TOTAL	3,487.5	51,548.3	625.5	1,917.8

Source: U.S. Department of Defense, *Foreign Military Sales and Military Assistance Facts* (Washington, D.C., G.P.O., 1976-1978).

and the other Western powers, China, and Japan participate in subsidiary roles. The LDCs (the Third World) are divided into various categories of tributary states.

The system works through arms transfers and other protection the North offers the South in return for trade and profits.[4] The facts that the trade is unequal and that the major benefits of the system flow from the South to the North have been well established by several dependency economists, though a great deal of controversy exists over what the precise benefits are and what value is to be placed on protection.[5] International trade would probably not exist, as we know it, without the order imposed by the global powers and their arms and navies. Therefore, the new Third World elites, who benefit, are prepared to pay a very high price, and sometimes much higher than they calculate, for protection by the system.

U.S. and USSR Tribute Systems[6]

Since World War II and especially since the British withdrawal from east of the Suez beginning in 1968, the two global powers have been constructing tribute systems that link together the regions of the Indian Ocean. This does not mean that the other actors (France, the United Kingdom, Eastern Europe, China, and Japan) are unimportant, but they all reinforce the international order imposed by the new instrusive powers. These tribute systems consist of an arms transfer and strategic policy on the one hand and a trade and resources policy on the other.[7] Since the benefits of the systems are what interest the global powers primarily, we must start with an explanation of their economic interests.

The primary benefit to the patron powers is assured access to energy and resources and also to the advantages of unequal exchange. The U.S. requirements for oil imports are now more than 50 percent of consumption, and they are increasing annually. Of this supply, approximately 50 percent is imported from African and Arab states, particularly those in the Arabian Gulf. Even a shortfall of 5 percent has been disruptive to the U.S. economy.

Among the twelve most strategic and essential minerals the United States imports, it is especially vulnerable in its requirements for bauxite, cobalt, tin, platinum, manganese, and industrial diamonds from Indian Ocean and African countries.[8] The dependency of closely associated Western European economies on the same sources of supply is even greater.[9] Australia and South Africa hold the greatest reserves of these minerals with the exception of the United States and the USSR.

U.S. investments in the Indian Ocean region more than doubled between 1965 and 1974,[10] and U.S. oil companies in the Gulf, despite nationalization, continued to average returns of over 21 percent. The U.S. investment in South Africa more than tripled during the same period, and its trade in the Indian Ocean exceeded that with Japan. In Southeast Asia, oil, nickel, and tin became important, and Australian uranium, bauxite, and iron ore became significant to the United States.[11]

The USSR is much less dependent upon these resources, but it will need Middle Eastern oil in the 1980s. The Eastern European economies will have an even greater vulnerability, since they import most of their energy and minerals from the Soviet Union. Thus, the critical energy resources and strategic minerals of the Indian Ocean littoral are of great importance to the centrally planned economies of Eastern Europe.[12] The Soviet emphasis on the export of its manufactured goods to Third World countries has become an important aspect of Indian Ocean trade. The unequal exchange basis of many of the barter arrangements has been illustrated by Soviet trade agreements with India, Pakistan, Ethiopia, and the Sudan.[13]

Soviet trade with several Indian Ocean countries rose rapidly in the first five years of the 1970s but then declined (see Table 12.4). As an industrial society, the USSR has sought to improve its balance of trade by obtaining new markets for its products, and the establishment of new industries in Third World countries using Soviet and Eastern European machines is in its interest. Such activity is not on the scale of Western capitalism and allows for greater local control than that allowed by most Western multinationals, but it frequently results in an exchange that primarily benefits the industrial country.[14]

Although the Soviet Union does not make direct investments, it has made loan and technical agreements with a number of Indian Ocean countries, including India, Iraq, North and South Yemen, Ethiopia, Mozambique, and Tanzania (see Table 12.5). Trade and aid are used by the USSR to gain political advantage against the

Table 12.4

USSR-INDIAN OCEAN TRADE
(Million U.S. dollars)

	1971	1972	1973	1974	1975	1976	1977	1971	1972	1973	1974	1975	1976	1977
	Exports							Imports fob						
Indonesia	11	5	3	12	34	15	9	10	7	6	26	26	37	32
Iran	61	68	164	193	210	115	19	---	---	---	---	---	---	---
Iraq	70	47	72	99	94	67	64	3	1	---	---	---	---	---
Kuwait	6	5	10	15	5	8	15	---	---	---	---	---	---	---
Saudi Arabia	5	3	10	3	3	14	24	---	---	---	---	---	---	---
Afghanistan	37	39	17	67	117	128	140	37	36	49	92	136	150	163
Bangladesh	---	---	37	86	56	31	33	---	12	16	25	22	16	24
India	107	106	145	533	359	214	129	287	366	390	469	511	475	471
Pakistan	21	12	11	29	46	36	41	36	26	17	34	30	16	19
Sri Lanka	10	3	7	20	15	8	13	16	10	10	15	15	19	14
Ethiopia	2	2	2	4	4	4	4	3	3	3	2	1	1	1
Kenya	1	1	---	1	1	---	---	1	1	---	1	2	3	2
Somalia	4	7	11	14	11	12	13	2	3	3	3	5	5	6
Sudan	20	14	24	6	4	16	22	52	1	---	5	10	18	40
Tanzania	---	---	1	2	4	2	1	---	1	4	8	4	6	8
Zambia	1	2	1	---	---	---	---	---	---	---	---	---	---	1

Source: Direction of Trade Annual (DOT) 1971-77, annual publication of the International Monetary Fund, Washington, D.C.

Table 12.5

COMMUNIST ECONOMIC CREDITS AND GRANTS EXTENDED TO LDCs, 1954-1977
(MILLION US DOLLARS)

	USSR	EASTERN EUROPE	CHINA
Afghanistan	1263	40	76
Bahrain	n.a.*	n.a.	n.a.
Bangladesh	304	159	61
Ethiopia	105	42	85
India	2283	455	0
Iran	805	685	0
Iraq	704	443	45
Kenya	48	0	17
Kuwait	n.a.	n.a.	n.a.
Mauritius	0	0	35
Mozambique	3	15	59
Pakistan	652	124	573
Oman	n.a.	n.a.	n.a.
Qatar	n.a.	n.a.	n.a.
Saudi Arabia	n.a.	n.a.	n.a.
Somalia	154	6	132
South Africa	n.a.	n.a.	n.a.
Sri Lanka	100	73	158
(North) Yemen	105	13	107
(South) Yemen	39	24	79
Tanzania	40	13	362

* Information not available.

Source: Communist Aid to Less Developed Countries of the Free World, 1977: A Research Paper (Washington, D.C., National Foreign Assessment Center, Central Intelligence Agency, 1978).

West and to establish new political as well as economic links in Indian Ocean countries—i.e., in India in 1971 and Mozambique in 1974.

As indicated previously, the sale of weapons has become an important part of the balance of payments for the two powers. The United States recovers a great deal of currency from the oil states in this exchange, and the Soviets gain approximately twice the U.S. percentage in their balance of payments from the sale of arms.[15]

Thus, in the arms-goods cycle of tribute, the United States gains cheap strategic resources, and the USSR finds new markets for its industry. The Third World countries are caught (with the exception of the oil producers) in a deteriorating balance-of-payments and terms-of-trade position. They expend a high percentage of their budgets on importing arms, which means they have less money for the energy and machinery they need.

Not all of the deterioration of economic standards can be attributed to this unequal comparative-advantage trade system inherited from colonialism, because the Third World leaders themselves bear much of the responsibility for it. But, for the most part, the elites of those countries benefit from the existing arms-goods cycle. The economic gains are distributed heavily in their own favor, and they employ the arms system to maintain themselves in power. When a coup d'etat or change of government has taken place, as in Iran and India, there has been a shift of power to new elites that cannot be called a structural change. A revolutionary class change has rarely succeeded.

The attempts of the Indian Ocean countries to use the rivalry between the global powers to their own advantage have usually resulted in their becoming the victims, either through revolutionary change, as in the case of the shah's pro-U.S. supporters in Iran, or through suffering the agonies of defeat, as in the case of Somalia when it thought it could use Russian support against Ethiopia.

Strategic Policies in the Indian Ocean

There are three major priorities that the United States and the USSR share. The first is the promotion and protection of their new trading relations. This includes arms sales, which have become an important part of the balance of payments of each of the superpowers. The second is the extension of political control in the different regions through favored elites. And the third priority is to obtain bases and links that will improve the global strategic position of each power in terms of its own defense and strengthen the capability of each for exerting pressure on any conflict point in the region.

U.S. Policy

The U.S. policy has as its first aim the protection of the increasingly important trade and supply routes from the Gulf to the Cape and the Suez Canal. Until 1975 the U.S. bases and facilities in Ethiopia were closely related to the Arabian Sea and Gulf policies, as well as to surveillance over the Red Sea route to the Suez Canal.[16] In addition, the U.S. strategic decision to strengthen the military power of South Africa from 1960 to 1977 was closely tied to the U.S. trade and investment policy.[17] Despite denials, the transfer of major weapons systems to South Africa and the use of communication facilities there for observing the entire Indian Ocean and southern Atlantic must be seen as strategic support for a trade policy.[18] The withdrawal of the United Kingdom from east of the Suez, beginning in 1968, intensified the U.S. concern, and a similar weakening of the strategic power of both the United Kingdom and Portugal in southern Africa, dramatized by the coup in Portugal in 1974, added to the growing U.S. involvement.

In South Asia, periodic visits by task forces from the Seventh Fleet based at Subic Bay increased, and the visits in 1971, 1973, and 1979 were directly related to threats to U.S. interests, either in Pakistan, in the Arabian Gulf, or on the Arabian Peninsula. The three weeks required to pass through the Strait of Malacca and into the Indian Ocean led to a search for bases closer to the Indian Ocean. The immediate need was met with the development of the base at Diego Garcia.[19]

U.S. strategy is directed toward preventing Communist or unfriendly groups from coming to power, especially through the volatile means of war and revolution. A major instrument of this strategy has been the increasing activity of contingents of the Pacific-based Seventh Fleet. From time to time, aircraft carriers from Subic Bay in the Philippines, aided by support ships stationed in the Gulf and eastern Africa, have been dispatched to the Indian Ocean during a crisis. The most noted occasion was the Bangladesh crisis of 1971, but other visits were made during the Somalian and Ethiopian (1977–78) and the Iranian and Yemeni (1979) conflicts. The frequency of these visits has increased along with the number and intensity of the conflicts.[20] None has yet led to the direct use of force, but the threat is a real one, and it seems to have stimulated rather than deterred the Soviets, since the number and activity of their ships in the Indian Ocean increased from 1969 to 1974.

U.S. naval activity is periodic and limited to surveillance, but the U.S. navy has a considerable intervention capability, particularly since it acquired the Diego Garcia base. Until the shah was overthrown, it was thought that Iran might undertake the role prescribed by the Nixon doctrine of naval "policing" of the Indian Ocean. With the changed situation in Iran, the Middle East Force has been increased from three to five ships. The building of Diego Garcia provides a base for supporting a permanent U.S. naval presence, which could intervene in any of the four quadrants of the zone.[21] Explorations to find access to other facilities in Mombasa, the Gulf, Australia, and Singapore are under way, and the pressures continue for a Fifth Fleet to be based in the Indian Ocean.

A related aim of U.S. strategic policy has been the suppression of liberation movements throughout the zone. There has been considerable denial of this policy, but until the Carter administration, the evidence was overwhelming that it was a top priority in southern Africa and the Arabian Gulf. This activity has taken the form of counterrevolution, CIA subsidies of rival movements, assassinations, bribes, and clandestine arms shipments through third parties to Angola in 1974–75, Somalia in 1974–75, Oman and the Yemens from 1965–75, and to Iran from the anti-Mossadeq coup in 1953 to the 1979 revolution.[22]

A final U.S. concern is the international strategic missile competition. The United States has deployed a submarine missile capability (SSBNs) in the Arabian Sea, a deployment primarily of Poseidon submarines and missiles.[23] U.S. officials have usually denied the deployment of submarines in the Arabian Sea, citing the limited range from Guam of the Poseidon submarines. The Russians, however, believe that the submarines and their missile systems are there. Since the development of the new, larger nuclear submarine with greater range, the *Trident,* the U.S. priority for Poseidon deployment has been reduced.

With the revolution in Iran, the replacement of the United States by the USSR in Ethiopia, and the removal of Portugal from southern Africa, political pressures in the United States have increased for the expansion of the U.S. naval and military presence along the major trade routes, especially the oil tanker routes and the chokepoints. The Carter administration has rejected the idea of a Fifth Fleet, but it has increased the number of naval visits to the Indian Ocean by the Seventh Fleet, beefed up the Middle East Force (MIDESTFOR), continued the sale of arms to client states at a high level, and created the ominous Rapid Reaction Strike Force.

Soviet Policy

Soviet strategic policies stem from similar aims, which brings the Soviet Union into direct rivalry with the United States. Like the United States, the USSR had developed an entirely new trade dimension with various countries of the Indian Ocean. Although the Soviet economy is not as strategically dependent upon the resources of the Gulf and the Indian Ocean as are the economies of the Western powers, the exchange patterns have become very significant. Also important is the extensive shipping between Soviet eastern and western ports. The protection and development of the Soviet Union's interests against the pressures of Western dominance has been a Soviet strategic priority. In this connection, the Soviets have increased arms sales and military agreements with countries of the Indian Ocean littoral, and the Soviet Union also has skillfully used the conflicts of the several regions to obtain military and trade agreements. The India-China War and the Indian-Pakistani rivalry were the events needed to lay the groundwork for the Soviet-Indian Treaty of Peace, Friendship, and Cooperation in August 1971. In the Gulf, the Arab-Israeli conflicts and wars provided the USSR with the opportunity to develop close links with Iraq and, for a time, the UAR (United Arab Republic). With Nasser's help, the Soviets assisted with the emergence of the People's Democratic Republic of Yemen (South Yemen). In each of these cases, major military agreements were reached, giving the Soviets bases and facilities, for example, at Umm Qasr and Aden.[24] On the Horn of Africa, initial links with Somalia, begun in 1964, became entangled in the Ethiopian-Somalian wars, and a major switch resulted in 1977 with the Soviets withdrawing from Somalia and extending major aid to Ethiopia. The first introduction of Soviet military forces into an Indian Ocean country began with the airlift to Ethiopia in 1978.[25]

The increasing activity of the Soviet navy in the Indian Ocean has been the subject of much discussion. The Soviet squadron in the Indian Ocean was established in 1968, with three combatant ships and a supporting oiler. This was linked to the rapid expansion of the Soviet shipping through the Indian Ocean and to requests for military and aid ties from the newly independent states of the four regions. The total size and activity of the squadron has gradually increased to twenty to twenty-two ships on a year-round basis. The Soviet bid for a base for their "fishing fleet" in the Maldives, just north of Diego Garcia, was rebuffed in 1977. Berbera became an important base for the Soviet navy until 1977, when the Soviet Union shifted its interests to Ethiopia. Since that time, Soviet ships have been welcome at many ports from Bombay to Maputo, though no nuclear ships are allowed into Indian ports. The Soviets have not been given navy bases at Massawa or Assab, but Aden has become a base for TU-16 bombers and for Soviet surveillance of the Arabian Sea.[26]

The USSR is interested in influencing the policy of the major states of the region by establishing friendly links with them. The Sino-Soviet rivalry in the Third World has intensified Soviet aid programs to countries such as India, and China's activities have been directed at weakening Soviet alliances.[27] The important Soviet-Indian friendship treaty of 1971 was attributable, in part, to China's attack on India in 1962 and China's support of Pakistan in the 1971 war.[28]

Soviet support of liberation movements, especially in southern Africa and the Gulf, derives not only from revolutionary zeal but also from a desire to create independent states that will trade and have other relations with the Soviet Union. From the 1960s on, the Soviets have been the primary supporters, through funds and training for southern African liberation movements, from SWAPO in Namibia to the Zimbabwe African Peoples Union (ZAPU) in Zimbabwe. The African National Congress of South Africa has long been a beneficiary of Soviet assistance. Such aid led to a major confrontation in Angola in 1975, with the introduction of Cuban troops in support of the Popular Movement for the Liberation of Angola

(MPLA) against other movements backed by the United States and South Africa. The same pattern has begun in other major conflict areas, with third parties acting as surrogates for the global powers. The USSR has moved into a powerful strategic position in Ethiopia, where the Soviet Union provides training support for Cuban and liberation movements operating in southern Africa and is able to monitor its interests in the Arabian Sea and the Gulf.[29] The People's Democratic Republic of Yemen has been a primary recipient of substantial Soviet and Cuban military assistance, including military personnel.[30]

The global strategic issue worries the USSR, and its extensive activity on the Horn of Africa and in the Arabian Sea is owing in part to its concern about the nuclear submarine activity of the United States, in addition to maintaining surveillance over the Soviet Union's major shipping route through the Red Sea and the Suez Canal.[31]

All the objective indicators of arms transfers, bases, naval activity, and troop installations from 1968 to date show a rise in the scale of the race between the global powers in the Indian Ocean. Points of confrontation have appeared over Iran, Bangladesh, Yemen, Somalia, and Rhodesia, and any one of these points of confrontation could become a major crisis overnight.

Demilitarization Prospects

Bilateral and multilateral types of demilitarization proposals have been considered by different parties within the Indian Ocean zone. There has been very little realism about the origins of the conflicts and the kinds of interests that have to be met if the arms race is to be ended and if escalating conflicts throughout the zone are to be turned around. The best appraisal of the possibilities can be made within the framework of the North-South arms-goods cycle.

The proposals fall primarily into three categories. The first comprises the bilateral limitation agreements between the global powers over general arms supply and access to the Indian Ocean. The second is the Zone of Peace proposal originated by several of the Indian Ocean nations and adopted by the United Nations. And the third category includes a variety of self-reliance policies and cooperative agreements among individual Indian Ocean countries.

Strategic arms limitation proposals have been made by both the United States and the USSR at different times during the period 1960–79. The first proposal came from the Soviets in the early 1960s, suggesting that a nuclear-free zone be established in the Indian Ocean. The idea was to limit the spread of nuclear weapons development or introduction into the zone and to limit the access of nuclear powered submarines or other ships.[32]

The Soviet Union sponsored this policy as a part of their worldwide campaign for nuclear-free zones, which had found broad Third World support. Thus, the nuclear-free-zone idea was a counter to the deployment of U.S. nuclear submarines and aircraft in Indian Ocean waters in the 1960s. It was largely a propaganda proposal and was regarded as such by U.S. policymakers until the late 1960s, when the arrival of the Russian navy, the withdrawal of the British east of the Suez, and the accelerating arms race within the framework of Middle Eastern and South Asian wars aroused antiwar groups and congressmen to attempt to limit the expansion of U.S. power.

However, strong pressures against limitation agreements prevailed in the United States until the 1970s when discussions regarding possible demilitarization began between the two major powers. These discussions were pushed by a group of liberal congressmen who resisted the pressures for unlimited arms sales and the expansion of U.S. military bases and presence, as represented by the establishment of the Diego Garcia base.[33]

In 1976, the United States became seriously interested in a strategic arms limitation agreement that would curb the dangers of a naval arms race and lessen the prospects of escalation. This was a dual response, involving both people who reacted against the Vietnam War and people who feared the expansion of the Soviet and Cuban military presences in southern Africa and the Horn of Africa. The Russians were alarmed about Diego Garcia and appeared to be ready for serious negotiations. With the reestablishment of détente and the election of President Carter, the talks began in June 1977.[34] They were recessed in February 1978 because of the Soviet buildup in Ethiopia, and there have been no further meetings. Details of negotiations have not been published, but the basis of the bilateral negotiations was a proposal for a naval arms limitation treaty (NALT), which would cap 1977 levels. Initially, the United States was willing to limit Diego Garcia as a base in return for a reduction of the Soviet facilities at Berbera.[35] However, with the Soviet loss of Berbera, this exchange became impractical. The Soviets were eager to obtain a withdrawal of the nuclear submarines in the Arabian Sea, though the United States would not consider such a step outside of a strategic arms limitation treaty.[36] The United States has also been interested in placing some controls on the unlimited arms transfers into southern Africa, but the Soviets have refused to limit their options as long as they are able to take advantage of the vulnerability of the white-led regimes in southern Africa.

The NALT proposal represents the high-water mark of the Carter demilitarization policy. It is a rational scheme, which would limit and stabilize the types of ships of the two powers and their logistic support facilities in the Indian Ocean.[37] However, the proposal runs counter to the major arms-goods cycle and the naval arms race. The client-states are not anxious to see their patrons limit their supplies, and both global powers are attempting to improve their position in the highly volatile politics of the area.

Since the Iranian revolution, a belief has gained ground in the United States Congress and administration that any movement in the Gulf to shut off the vital oil flow from Iran, Saudi Arabia, Kuwait, or Abu Dhabi is unacceptable and must be resisted by force.[38] Therefore, the U.S. Senate has become more supportive of bases and an increased naval presence. A powerful political move is under way in the United States to rapidly and substantially increase the U.S. military presence in the Indian Ocean region, despite the possibility of Russian reciprocation. Indications of this policy shift can be seen in the fact that during the 1979 North Yemen crisis the administration quickly shipped $390 million worth of arms and 100 military advisers to that country.[39] The establishment of a Rapid Reaction Strike Force, including the 82nd Airborne, available for quick military action in the Indian Ocean to secure the resource supply is another dimension of this strategy. Finally, and most significantly, there is a growing pressure in Congress for the navy's idea of a Fifth Fleet, made up of ships from the Pacific Seventh Fleet and the Mediterranean Sixth Fleet, which would permanently station a large force in the Indian Ocean.[40] Singapore is considered the most suitable base for such a force, though Diego Garcia could be enlarged to service such a fleet. Such moves would undoubtedly trigger countermoves by the USSR, so it is in the interest of both powers to stabilize the naval arms race and limit their expansion of bases.

The USSR has repeatedly requested the resumption of the bilateral talks, but as late as October 1979 the Carter administration refused, citing South Yemen and Afghanistan as examples of bad faith. This refusal puts the United States in the position of being the spoiler. An agreement to limit the force levels between the powers would not threaten present access to resources or oil routes. Since the U.S. role is more predominant through the region, it would be to its advantage to limit the scope of its rival's intrusion by international agreement. The reduction of Soviet pressures in southern Africa and the Horn can only be in the U.S. interest. Similarly, the reduction of U.S. naval activity in the Arabian Gulf and at Diego Garcia is of interest to the Russians. Thus, diplomatic agreement is a possible alternative to increases in the arms race. The Iranian hostage crisis of late 1979 does not alter the situation, since global superpower cooperation in such a crisis is more important than increased force. Overwhelming force is no longer a guarantee of interests in these areas. Cooperation of other powers is a very important instrument for stabilization.

Zone of Peace

The Zone of Peace idea was developed by the Indian Ocean countries themselves, particularly Sri Lanka and India, and it was adopted by the United Nations in 1971. Sri Lanka and India had the idea of curbing the arms race in the zone by restricting the access of the great powers to the Indian Ocean, banning military bases of the global powers, controlling the transfer of arms from outside powers to the Indian Ocean states, and settling disputes among Indian Ocean states.[41]

These general goals have been subscribed to with differing degrees of enthusiasm by all the littoral states, including several of the primary client-states.[42] South Africa has, of course, opposed the Zone of Peace idea because it favors an increased U.S. presence. The Western powers have, in general, ignored or quietly opposed the idea. The Soviet Union has sought to present itself in favor of several of the proposals, yet it has constantly pursued policies that contradict them. Soviet spokesmen believe that their own proposal of a nuclear-free zone fostered the idea of a Zone of Peace.[43] The U.S. position all along has been that there is no major arms race in the Indian Ocean and that the United States is happy to cooperate with all nations in arms limitation agreements.[44] However, the United States stands firmly on the principle of a freedom of the seas and maintains that its only base in the region, at Diego Garcia, is on an otherwise uninhabited island and does not violate the territory of any country.[45]

The United Nations established an ad hoc committee on the Zone of Peace, and its primary function is to try to monitor the strategic activities of the major powers in the Indian Ocean and issue reports about those activities.[46] Its findings have generally been criticized by the principal powers because of differences of interpretation regarding the facts of actual presence.[47]

Although the reports are useful, the attempt to establish a universal agreement on strategic activities in the Indian Ocean on the basis of the UN 1971 resolution has produced very little. Not only do the global powers and the other northern powers resist the limitations, but also the littoral countries are divided over the application of the principles. Several of the littoral countries are obviously allied with the global powers, despite a nonaligned policy. If the Indian Ocean countries could get together and agree upon step-by-step ways in which they would collectively attempt to limit the activities of the northern powers, they might have some effect.[48]

The littoral nations do have a considerable power of restraint upon global power policy, especially when they act together. This has been most effective at a regional level.[49] The Arab state mediation of the North and South Yemen dispute in 1979 prevented a dangerous escalation of outside intervention. Neither Ethiopia nor South Yemen has given the Soviets the full naval base they would like in the region. The front-line African states have been a major restraint upon the tendency for outside intervention to escalate in the Rhodesian and Namibian conflicts, and the African, Arab, and Asian attitudes toward the Western use of South African bases such as Simonstown have been effective. Such achievements, though, cannot mask the divisions that have led to some escalation, i.e., Somalian and later Ethiopian openness to the Soviet and Cuban buildup as well as Pakistani support for Diego Garcia.

The problem is to devise methods for greater regional and zone cooperation. This can best be done if the littoral countries recognize that their power lies in limiting the access of the global powers to the resources and the trade the powers seek to preserve and extend. The suggestion that OPEC should cut off oil to any power that uses military might to obtain its supply carries considerable weight among the Arab and African states.[50] However, the northern policy of using the littoral states as proxies to obtain global power objectives makes this method difficult to apply.

This raises a last point about the importance of "collective self-reliance" for the foreign policies of the Indian Ocean states. The close links between the arms and security issues have been established, but to isolate an arms or a demilitarization issue from the problems of economic dependency is to deal with only part of the problem. The way out of the tribute system is through a policy of self-reliance and nonalignment in cooperation with other Indian Ocean countries. However, breaking out is not easy, as many Third World countries have discovered. It is a step-by-step process that takes a considerable amount of time. The beginning of wisdom is to break with the tributary system through nonalignment and through building alternative sources of arms and goods. Countries such as Tanzania and India have begun to do this. The Tanzanian acceptance of Scandinavian economic assistance and Chinese military aid rather than aid from the global powers is a step toward self-reliance,[51] as is the rejection by India of the Soviet proposal to help build extensive nuclear power facilities.[52]

Such steps need to be taken collectively across the Indian Ocean zone. The refusal of one country to accept a major offer of arms support needs to be reinforced by that country's neighbors rather than undercut. The horizontal pattern is most effective if it is integrated into collective agreements.

Conclusion

There are two possible ways to achieve demilitarization in the Indian Ocean. The first, and most unlikely, is an agreement between the global powers to limit their arms transfers and naval deployment in the zone. This is likely to occur only if both the global powers come to a realization that the arms race is endangering assured sources of strategic materials and damaging the prospects for their extended trade among the countries and regions of the Indian Ocean littoral. The rivalry and antagonisms between the two powers tend to veil this reality, and the tendency is for each of them to try to strengthen its military capability and to hold on to what it has, rather than to limit expansion. A real danger is that the arms race will escalate rather than stabilize. If wisdom prevails, both the United States and the USSR will see that it is in their interests to agree on NALT, to limit the access of their naval units, and to place restrictions on the amounts and types of weapons, especially nuclear weapons, that they will transfer to the countries of the Indian Ocean littoral.

Second, the countries and peoples of the zone have a major responsibility to stop the arms race themselves, and they may be able to do so if they will take matters into their own hands and build new nonaligned policies of self-reliance. Through international agreements, regional policies, and individual actions, they need to see the relationship between types of military economic activity and military power. They can do this only if they recognize the scope of tributary protection that has developed. They cannot overcome this system alone but need to cooperate in their resource bargaining agreements to limit the global power military activity. Their present division and the regional rivalries make them extremely vulnerable to continued exploitation by the global powers. An awareness of the need to have systems other than the tributary system of global politics is spreading, but that awareness has yet to be mobilized into an effective Indian Ocean policy for the peripheral states.

Notes

1. See Ferenc A. Vali, *Politics of the Indian Ocean: The Balance of Power* (New York: Free Press, 1976).

2. Alvin Cottrell and R. M. Burrell, eds., *The Indian Ocean: Its Political, Economic, and Military Importance* (New York: Praeger, 1972).

3. Much information is summarized in Dale R. Tahtinen, *Arms in the Indian Ocean: Interests and Challenges* (Washington, D.C.: American Enterprise Institute for Public Policy Research, 1977), pp. 15-27.

4. The author believes the level of analysis must be limited to interstate relations.

5. The most useful account is by Samir Amin, who demonstrates the unequal exchange between the core and periphery (see Amin, *Accumulation on a Global Scale*, vols. 1-2 [New York: Monthly Review Press, 1974]).

6. The contribution of Johan Galtung's work to this model is acknowledged.

7. Ali Mazrui has described this system: "Vertical linkages establish connections between the arms race of the Northern superpowers and the arms race in the Third World. Horizontal linkages establish connections between the arms race on one side and problems of competitive imperialism and general underdevelopment on the other" (*The Barrel of the Gun and the Barrel of Oil in the North-South Equation* [New York: Institute for World Order, 1978], p. 7).

8. Derived from calculations by Anthony Wilkinson, "Strategic Minerals and Metals: Western Dependence on African and Alternative Suppliers," (unpublished ms., 1978).

9. William Sneider of the Hudson Institute has calculated that the United States is 50 percent dependent on overseas oil, the OECD nations are 75 percent dependent, and Japan, 100 percent (*Mining Journal* 289, no. 7350 [July 2, 1976]).

10. From 1965 to 1974, U.S. direct investment in the Indian Ocean area increased (outside the Middle East) from $4.1 billion to $10.3 billion (see the U.S. Department of Commerce *Survey of Current Business* for the years 1965-1975).

11. *United States Foreign Policy Objectives and Overseas Military Installations* (Washington, D.C.: Congressional Research Service, April 1979), p. 87.

12. *The International Energy Situation: Outlook to 1985* (Washington, D.C.: Central Intelligence Agency, 1979).

13. *The Soviet Union and the Third World: A Watershed in Great Power Policy* (Washington, D.C.: Congressional Research Service, 1977).

14. Arthur Klinghoffer, *The Soviet Union and International Oil Politics* (New York: Columbia University Press, 1977), pp. 18-35.

15. Weapons sales were over 10 percent of total Soviet exports in 1976. Without its arms sales, the USSR would run a $1.2 billion trade deficit with the Third World (*Defense Monitor* [Jan. 1979]).

16. Thomas Farer, *War Clouds on the Horn of Africa* (New York: Carnegie Endowment for International Peace, 1976), pp. 111-113.

17. G. W. Shepherd, Jr., "The Advocat Communication Facility at Silver Mine Surveys Shipping in the Indian Ocean for NATO," in G. W. Shepherd, Jr., *Anti-Apartheid* (Westport, Conn.: Greenwood Press, 1977), pp. 91-93.

18. Sean Gervasi, *The United States and the Arms Embargo Against South Africa: Evidence, Denial, and Refutation,* Southern Africa Pamphlet, no. 2 (Binghamton, N.Y.: Brandel Center, SUNY, 1978).

19. U.S., Congress, House, Committee on International Relations, *Diego Garcia, 1975: The Debate over the Base and the Island's Former Inhabitants* (Hearings, 94th Congress, 1st Session, 1975).

20. The Yemen crisis of 1979 is described by David Frankel, "Carter Pushes Toward War in Yemen," *Militant* (March 23, 1979).

21. See Adm. E. R. Zumwalt in U.S., Congress, House, Subcommittee on the Near East and South Asia of the Committee on Foreign Affairs, *Proposed Expansion of U.S. Military Facilities in the Indian Ocean,Hearings,* 93rd Cong., 2nd sess., February-March, 1974.

22. See John Stockwell, *In Search of Enemies* (New York: Nelson, 1978), and Fred Halliday, *Arabia Without Sultans* (New York: Vintage Books, 1975).

23. Adm. Gene La Rogue stated, "It is likely that the U.S. Navy intends to deploy SSBNs in the Indian Ocean more frequently in the future as additional Poseidon submarines with long-range missiles enter the inventory" U.S., Congress, House, Subcommittee on the Near East and South Asia of the Committee on Foreign Affairs, 1974.

24. *New York Times,* April 22, 1979.

25. Z. Brzezinski announced that along with the airlift of 10,000 to 11,000 Cuban military to Ethiopia, the Soviets had sent 400 tanks and 50 MiG jets (*New York Times,* February 25, 1978).

26. *United States Foreign Policy Objective and Overseas Military Installations* (Washington, D.C.: Congressional Research Service, Foreign Affairs and National Defense Division, 1979), pp. 92-93.

27. Nader Entessar, "The PRC and Iran: An Overview of Their Relationship," *Asia Quarterly,* no. 1 (1978).

28. K. Subrahmayan, "The Interests of External Powers in Pakistan," *Institute for Defense Studies and Analysis Journal* (Delhi, January 1973).

29. "Soviet Weapons Exports," *Defense Monitor,* January 1979.

30. David Frankel, "Carter Pushes Toward War in Yemen."

31. Both Soviet and U.S. sources confirm this (see Dale R. Tahtinen, *Arms in the Indian Ocean,* and Sergi Vladimirov, "Indian Ocean: Dangers and Hopes," *New Times* [Moscow] no. 29 [July 1977]).

32. Kim C. Beazley and Ian Clark, *Politics of Intrusion: The Super Powers and the Indian Ocean* (Sydney: Alternatives Publishing Cooperative, Ltd., 1979), p. 113.

33. U.S., Congress, Senate, Committee on Armed Services, *Disapprove Construction Projects on the Island of Diego Garcia, Hearing,* 94th Cong., 1st sess., June 1975.

34. Daniel Southerland, "Indian Ocean: U.S. and Soviet Demilitarization Talks," *Christian Science Monitor,* October 5, 1977. The U.S. navy was apparently opposed to the talks.

35. The *New York Times,* February 10, 1978, reported on three earlier rounds of the talks in which "agreement seemed close on a formula for freezing the existing size of the navies." Agreement on bases was also near.

36. U.S., Congress, House, Committee on Armed Services, *Indian Ocean Forces Limitation and Conventional Arms Transfers Limitation,* 1979, p. 4.

37. Richard Haas outlines this scheme in "Naval Arms Limitation in the Indian Ocean," *Survival* 20, no. 2 (March/April 1978).

38. *Rocky Mountain News,* June 6, 1979.

39. *New York Times,* March 20, 1979.

40. "The Indian Ocean: The U.S. Response," *Africa Confidential* 20, no. 10 (May 9, 1979).

41. P. R. Chari, "The Indian Ocean: An Indian Viewpoint," *Iranian Review of International Relations* (Fall 1976).

42. Iran has been one of the primary supporters of the Zone of Peace. Yet under the shah, Iran fostered the U.S. military presence in the Gulf and the Indian Ocean by supporting Diego Garcia as a U.S. base and providing facilities in Iran (see M. A. Atashbarg, "Indian Ocean Review of Outside Powers' Presence," *Iranian Review of International Relations* [Spring/Summer 1977]).

43. Alexei Sergeyev, "Indian Ocean: Tension Area or Peace Zone?" *New Times* (Moscow), no. 51 (December 1976).

44. Paul C. Warnke speaking about the Indian Ocean negotiations with the Soviets, *New York Times,* February 10, 1978.

45. U.S., Congress, House, Subcommittee on the Near East and South Asia of the Committee on Foreign Affairs, *Proposed Expansion of U.S. Military Facilities in the Indian Ocean, Hearings,* 93rd Cong., 2nd sess., February/March 1974, p. 27.

46. United Nations, General Assembly, Res. 2832 (XXVI), December 16, 1971. It called on the great powers to inter alia consult with the littoral states with a view to "(a) halting the further escalation and expansion of their military presence in the Indian Ocean and (b) eliminating from the Indian Ocean all bases, military installations and logistical supply facilities, the disposition of nuclear weapons."

47. UN Document A/AC.159/1, May 3, 1974.

48. D. Kappler, "Possibilities and Problems of Regional Cooperation in the Persian Gulf and the Indian Ocean," *Iranian Review of International Relations* (Fall 1976).

49. K. R. Singh, "The Indian Ocean: The Need for a Community Ap-

proach," *Institute for Defense Studies and Analysis Journal* (April 1978).

50. Thomas I. Aberystwyth, "Kissinger's Arrogant Threats," *Afriscope* (March 1975).

51. S. S. Mushi "Tanzania Foreign Relations and the Policies of Non-Alignment, Socialism and Self-Reliance," in *Foreign Policy of Tanzania* (Nairobi: Heinemann Educational Books, forthcoming).

52. *New York Times,* May 3, 1979.

The Editors and Contributors

Editors

Larry W. Bowman is an associate professor of political science at the University of Connecticut in Storrs, Connecticut. He is the author of *Politics in Rhodesia: White Power in an African State* (Harvard University Press, 1973). He has written widely on southern African politics and on Western policy in the southern Africa and Indian Ocean regions. He is also the general editor of the Africa Profile Series for Westview Press.

Ian Clark lectures on politics at the University of Western Australia. He is the author of *Reform and Resistance in the International Order* (Cambridge University Press, 1980), coauthor with Kim C. Beazley of *The Politics of Intrusion: The Super Powers and the Indian Ocean* (Sydney: Alternatives Publishing Cooperative, Ltd., 1979), and contributor to such journals as the *Review of Politics*, *Orbis*, and the *Round Table*.

Contributors

Henry S. Albinski, professor of political science at Pennsylvania State University, specializes in the international politics of Australia and its regional environment. He has held a number of visiting appointments at Australian universities, has lectured extensively in Australia and in the Pacific area, and has held various Australian-related consultantships. His most recent book is *Australian External Policy Under Labor,* published by the University of Queensland Press. During 1978–79 he was visiting Fellow in Strategic Studies at the Australian National University and a senior Fulbright scholar.

Kim C. Beazley is a lecturer in social and political theory at Murdoch University, Western Australia. He is the coauthor with Ian Clark of *The*

Politics of Intrusion: The Super Powers and the Indian Ocean (Sydney: Alternatives Publishing Cooperative, Ltd., 1979).

Dieter Braun has traveled widely in the Southern Hemisphere under the auspices of the Goethe-Institute. Since 1969 he has been a senior staff member of the Stiftung Wissenschaft und Politik (Foreign Policy Research Institute), Munich-Ebenhausen, FRG. He has written widely, in German and English, on South Asia and the Indian Ocean region.

Jean-Pierre Gomane had a first career as a naval and intelligence officer in Paris and the Far East. He retired as a commander in 1974 and joined the Centre de Hautes Etudes sur L'Afrique et l'Asie Modernes (CHEAM) in Paris. He is a specialist on colonial and contemporary problems in Southeast Asia and director of studies at CHEAM.

Geoffrey Jukes was employed in the United Kingdom civil service from 1953–67; since then he has been a member of the Department of International Relations at the Australian National University. He is a specialist on Soviet military history and naval policy and on Soviet relations with the Third World. His publications include *Development in Soviet Strategic Thinking Since 1945* (Australian National University, 1972), *The Indian Ocean in Soviet Naval Policy* (London: International Institute for Strategic Studies, 1972), and *The Soviet Union in Asia* (University of California Press, 1973).

Ashok Kapur is associate professor in political science, University of Waterloo, Ontario. He is the author of *India's Nuclear Option: Atomic Diplomacy and Decision Making* (Praeger Publishers, 1976), and *International Nuclear Proliferation: Multilateral Diplomacy and Regional Aspects* (Praeger Publishers, 1979). He has published in scholarly and professional journals on Indian security policy, Asian international relations, and arms control and disarmament.

Joel Larus is professor of politics, New York University. He is the author of *Culture and Political-Military Behavior: The Hindus in Premodern India* (Calcutta: Minerva Associates; Columbia, Mo.: South Asia Books, 1979), and *Nuclear Weapons Safety and the Common Defense* (Ohio State University Press, 1967), and he has edited several books on international affairs: *Nuclear Proliferation: Phase II* (Regents' Press of Kansas, 1974) with Robert M. Lawrence, *From Collective Security to Preventive Diplomacy* (New York: John Wiley and Sons, 1965), and *Comparative World Politics*

(Belmont, Calif.: Wadsworth Publishing Co., 1964). He currently is working on a study of U.S.-Soviet naval rivalry in the Indian Ocean.

Rouhollah K. Ramazani is the chairman and Edward R. Stettinius Professor, Woodrow Wilson Department of Government and Foreign Affairs at the University of Virginia. He was formerly vice-president of the American Institute of Iranian studies; Visiting Aga Khan Professor of Islamic Studies, American University of Beirut; visiting professor, Cambridge University (England); and visiting professor of Middle Eastern studies, School of Advanced International Studies, Johns Hopkins University. His most recent books include *Iran's Foreign Policy, 1941-1973: A Study of Foreign Policy in Modernizing Societies* (University Press of Virginia, 1975); *Beyond the Arab-Israeli Settlement: New Directions for U.S. Policy in the Middle East* (Cambridge, Mass.: Institute for Foreign Policy Analysis, 1977); and *The Persian Gulf and the Strait of Hormuz* (Alphen aan den Rijn, the Netherlands: Sijthoff and Noordhoff, 1979).

George W. Shepherd, Jr., is a professor of international relations at the University of Denver. He is a specialist on African politics and on international race relations. He is founder and past editor of *Africa Today* and the author of many books and articles on African related issues. His most recent book is *Anti-Apartheid: Transnational Conflict and Western Policy* (Westport, Conn.: Greenwood Press, 1977).

Philip Towle is a senior research fellow in the Strategic and Defence Studies Centre of Australian National University where he specializes on arms control questions. His book, *Naval Power in the Indian Ocean: Threats, Bluffs, and Fantasies* was published by the Strategic and Defence Studies Centre in 1979.

Index

Abdallah, Ahmed, 194
Aerospatiale, 155
Afghanistan, 24, 26, 61, 98, 143, 150
  coup in, 28, 71
  Soviet invasion of, 1, 99
  treaty with Soviet Union, 71, 150
African National Congress (ANC), 236
Agnew, Spiro, 110
Akins, James E., 111–112, 118, 121
Algeria, 8
ANC. See African National Congress
Angola, 74, 75, 89
Anjouan, 194
Anthony, J. D., 73
ANZUS (a security treaty of 1951), 65–67, 73, 78, 80, 211
  Council meeting in Wellington, 66
Apartheid, 32, 33, 75, 76, 93, 99, 146
Aqaba, Gulf of, 8
Arab-Israeli war (1973), 12, 107, 158
  effect on U.S. policy, 117–119
Arafura Sea, 65
Arms control. See Naval arms limitation talks; Demilitarization
Arms race in Indian Ocean, 46, 52, 132–133, 223–224, 243

ASEAN. See Association of South-East Asian Nations
Asian collective security system, 17
Asian common market, 17, 23
Assab, 236
Association of South-East Asian Nations (ASEAN), 34
Australia, 110, 115, 140, 191
  aboriginal population of, 78
  American presence in, 62–70, 80
  American use of facilities in, 67–70, 74, 211
  interest in Indian Ocean, 59–60, 67
  lifting of ban on nuclear powered ships, 67–68
  policies on Southern Africa, 74–80, 80–81
  and Soviet presence, 60–61
  and trade with Iran, 72–73
  See also HMAS Stirling; North West Cape; Nurrungar; Pine Gap; Zone of Peace in Indian Ocean
Ayacucho, Declaration of (1974), 219

Bab el Mandeb, Strait of, 2, 8, 15
Bahrain, 17, 31, 73, 112, 116, 117, 119, 123
Baikal-Amur Main Line, 184

al-Bakr, Ahmad Hassan, 158
Bandung, 22
Bangladesh, 23, 26, 27, 48, 177
Barre, Mohammed Siyad, 162, 163, 165, 166
Basra, 185
Bassas da Inda, 197
Bell, Coral, 138
Berbera, 44–45, 46, 60, 62, 64, 91, 94, 96, 125, 216
Bhutan, 26
BIOT. *See* British Indian Ocean Territory
bin Onn, Datuk Hussein, 35
bin Said, Qabus, 12
Blechman, Barry, 167
Botha, Pieter, 92, 146
Brezhnev, Leonid, 144
Brezhnev doctrine, 214
British Indian Ocean Territory (BIOT), 43
British presence in Indian Ocean, 110–111
Brown, Harold, 14, 136, 209
Brzezinski, Zbigniew, 98–99, 138, 166

Cape route, 90, 96, 140. *See also* Oil; Simonstown; Southern Africa
Carter, Jimmy, 1, 9, 18, 19, 52, 53, 62, 72, 77, 92, 95, 131, 138, 209
Cartier, Raymond, 190
CENTO. *See* Central Treaty Organization
Central Intelligence Agency (CIA), 117, 139
Central Treaty Organization (CENTO), 110, 114, 123, 211
Centre National de la Recherche Scientifique (CNRS), 195
Chafee, John, 109
Chagos Archipelago, 43
Chah Bahar, 116
Chittagong, 177
CIA. *See* Central Intelligence Agency

CINCPAC. *See* Commander in Chief, Pacific
Clements, William, 122
CNRS. *See* Centre National de la Recherche Scientifique
Cockburn Sound. *See* HMAS Stirling
Cocos Islands, 69, 70
Cohen, Saul B., 140
Collective self-reliance, 21, 25, 142, 242, 243
Colombo nonaligned summit, 36 (n1)
Colombo Plan, 26
COMECON. *See* Council for Mutual Economic Assistance
Commander in Chief, Pacific (CINCPAC) 117
Commonwealth Secretariat, 79
Comoro Islands, 193, 194, 195, 201
Confidence building measures (CBMs), 218
Congress party, 23, 47
Constellation, 19
Council for Mutual Economic Assistance (COMECON), 9, 214
Crozet Islands, 196
Culver, John, 119

Darby, Philip, 110
Davies, Rodger P., 118
de Gaulle, Charles, 189, 190–191, 193, 201, 202
Demilitarization, 2, 3, 17, 18, 62, 95, 99, 208, 237, 242–243. *See also* Naval arms limitation talks; Zone of Peace in Indian Ocean
Desai, Morarji, 41, 50, 51, 52, 53, 55–56
d'Estaing, Valéry Giscard, 189–190, 202
Détente, 99, 109, 113, 131, 136, 142, 147
Dhofar, 12, 116
Diego Garcia, 43, 46, 47, 49, 61, 68, 70, 94–95, 113–114, 117,

Index

119, 135, 143–144, 175–179, 239
Indian response to, 44, 45, 49, 52, 54, 56
Diégo-Suarez, 193, 198
Direction des Affaires Africaines, 189
Djibouti, 89, 163, 193, 194, 195, 197, 198
Douglas-Home, Alec, 50, 55
Duval, Gaetan, 192

East Timor, 62–63
Ecole Française d'Extrême Orient (EFEO), 195
EFEO. See Ecole Française d'Extrême Orient
Egypt
 Peace treaty with Israel, 12
 treaty with Soviet Union, 153
Energy crisis. See oil
Enterprise, 48
Eritrea, 87, 159–160, 163, 168.
 See also Ethiopia; Horn of Africa
Ethiopia, 26, 32, 33, 89, 90, 99, 150, 177
 treaty with Soviet Union, 90–91, 150
 See also Eritrea; Horn of Africa; Soviet Union
Europa Island, 197

Five-Power Defence arrangement, 110, 115
 integrated Air Defense System of, 69
Foccart, Jacques, 189, 190
Ford, Gerald, 61
France, 92
 activity in Indian Ocean, 3, 195–198
 interest in Indian Ocean, 191–194, 199–202
 policymaking in, 189–191
Francophonie, 190
Fraser, Malcolm, 60, 62, 65, 67, 77, 79

French Institute (Pondichery), 195
Fulbright, J. W., 112

Gandhi, Indira, 34, 38(n 27), 41, 42, 50, 53, 55
Ghanam Island, 13
Glorieuses Islands, 197
Gorshkov, Sergei, 97, 176, 177
Grande Comore, 194
Gwadar, 46

HAL. See Hindustan Aeronautics, Ltd.
Hawker-Siddeley, 155
Hindustan Aeronautics, Ltd. (HAL), 151, 156
HMAS Stirling, 65, 68, 70. See also Australia; Western Australia
Hormuz, Strait of, 2, 8–9, 71
 blockage of, 11–14, 181–182
 Common Patrol Authority for, 7, 17–18, 19
 importance to Gulf states, 9, 15
 legal régime for, 16
 Omani-Iranian agreement on, 10, 16
 territorial sea limits in, 10
 vulnerability of, 7, 13
 See also oil; Soviet Union
Horn of Africa, 1, 55, 61, 63, 87
 and Soviet arms supplies, 71, 90, 95, 160, 161–168
 and Soviet-Iraqi relations, 159–160
 See also Eritrea; Ethiopia; Somalia; Soviet Union; United States
Huisken, Ron, 156

India, 22, 64, 140, 143, 177, 210, 212, 242
 bilateral cooperation with: Africa 31–33; Gulf Region, 23, 29–31; South Asia, 27–29; Southeast Asia, 33–36
 development assistance program, 25–26

domestic defense production, 156–157
economic progress of, 23, 24–25
Engineering Export Promotion Council of, 28
Engineering Projects of, 30
Industrial Bank of, 28
military relations with Soviet Union, 151–157, 185
national oil company of (ONGC), 33
and naval presence of superpowers, 41, 45, 46–50, 52–55
policy of arms diversification, 155–156
treaty with Soviet Union, 42, 48, 51, 150, 151, 235, 236
Indo-African Development Association, 32
Indonesia, 8, 62–63, 110
relations with India, 34–35, 153
Indo-Pakistani war, 1, 109
effect on U.S. policy, 48, 113–115
International Conference on Indian Ocean Studies (ICIOS), ix, x
IOPZ. See Zone of Peace in Indian Ocean
Iran, 2, 8, 10, 13, 14, 34, 112, 115, 118, 124, 143, 161
relations with India, 30
security perimeters of, 116
trade with Soviet Union, 9
Iranian revolution, 1, 10, 12, 14, 15, 17, 71, 98, 179, 213, 239
Australian reaction to, 71–72, 73, 80
Iraq, 8, 9, 30, 161, 177, 211, 212
economic ties with West, 9, 159
military relations with Soviet Union, 157–161, 185
policy of arms diversification, 160–161
relations with India, 30–31
trade with socialist states, 9, 159

treaty with Soviet Union, 150, 158
Ivan Rogov, 19, 185–186

Janata party, 23, 27, 34, 50–51, 53, 54, 56
Japan, 9, 61, 92, 110, 115
Johnson, Lyndon, 109
Journiac, René, 190
Juan de Nova, 197

Kampuchea, 34
"Kangaroo" exercises, 65
Kennedy, Edward, 119
Kennedy, John, 109
Kenya, 26, 32, 33, 91, 162
Kerguelen Islands, 196
Khomeini, Ayatollah, 147
Kiev, 209, 210, 214
Killen, D. J., 69
Kissinger, Henry, 98, 117, 118–119, 120, 121, 122, 136, 138–139
Kuwait, 8, 17, 30, 31, 73

Laird, Melvin, 117
Larak Island, 8
Law of the Sea Conference, 15, 201, 202
Learmonth, 68
Lenczowski, George, 158
Libya, 8
Lichtheim, George, 132
Lusaka nonaligned summit, 32, 36 (n1), 46

McIntyre, Thomas, 119
McNamara, Robert, 139
Madagascar. See Malagasy Republic
Malacca, Strait of, 8, 15, 63
Malagasy Republic, 191, 192–193, 195, 197, 198, 200
Malaysia, 69, 110
relations with India, 35–36
Maldives, 26, 236
Mancham, James, 192

Index

Mansfield, Mike, 119
Massawa, 183, 236
Mauritius, 24, 32, 46, 191, 192, 195
Mayotte, 194, 196, 198, 202
Mazagon Dock, 157
Mengistu, Haile Mariam, 91, 99, 164
Midlink 74, 123
Ministry of Cooperation (France), 189, 195
Ministry of Foreign Affairs (Quai d'Orsay), 189, 195
Minsk, 19, 185, 186, 209, 214
Mishra, Brahesh, 54–55
Mission d'Aide et de Coopération, 195
Moheli, 194
Mondale, Walter, 66
Montreux Convention, 11, 16, 210
Moorer, Thomas, 121
Mozambique, 33, 74, 76, 89
  treaty with Soviet Union, 92, 150
Musandam Peninsula, 12, 13

NALT. *See* naval arms limitation talks
Namibia, 74, 75, 79, 89, 92
NASA. *See* National Aeronautics and Space Administration
National Aeronautics and Space Administration (NASA), 141
Naval arms limitation talks (NALT), 52, 53, 63–65, 66, 95, 131, 137, 208–209, 217, 238–240, 243
  Carter's motives in opening, 144–145
  Soviet interests in, 145
  suspension of, 63–64, 71, 95–96, 126, 146, 179
  See also Demilitarization; Soviet Union; United States; Zone of Peace in Indian Ocean
Nehru, Jawaharlal, 22

Nepal, 23, 26, 27
Neto, Aghostino, 74
New Zealand, 67, 110
Nigeria, 8, 77
Nixon doctrine, 108–111, 115, 117, 119, 137, 234
Nogee, J. L., 139
Nonalignment, 33, 143, 242
  Indian concept of, 41–43, 47–48, 50–51, 53–56, 155
North Rumayla oilfield, 185
North West Cape, 64, 68, 70, 175
North Yemen crisis (1979), 239
Noyes, James H., 114
Nuclear-free zone in Indian Ocean, 17, 238
Nuclear Nonproliferation Treaty, 212, 217
Nuclear proliferation, 1, 134, 140
  and South Africa, 92
Nurrungar, 68
Nyerere, Julius, 38 (nn. 31 and 33)

OAU. *See* Organization of African Unity
OECD. *See* Organization for Economic Cooperation and Development
Ofer, Gur, 158
Office de la Recherche Scientifique et Technique d'Outre-mer (ORSTOM), 195
Ogaden, 87, 90, 91, 159, 165
Oil, 1, 8, 61, 126, 134
  dependence of LDCs upon, 9–10
  embargo, 12, 107, 112, 118, 119, 121, 122, 136
  tanker traffic, 2, 8, 10, 15, 16, 17, 199
  See also Cape route; Hormuz, Strait of; Organization of Petroleum Exporting Countries; Soviet Union; United States
OKEAN, 125
Oman, 2, 10, 12, 14, 16–17

Gulf of, 8, 116
 Iran's military assistance to, 12, 116
 and navigational safety, 13
Ombai-Weter straits, 63
ONGC. See India, national oil company of
OPEC. See Organization of Petroleum Exporting Countries
Operation Sandgroper, 66–67, 70
Organisation Commune Africaine et Malgache (OCAM), 191
Organization for Economic Cooperation and Development (OECD), 14–15
Organization of African Unity (OAU), 168, 193, 201
Organization of Petroleum Exporting Countries (OPEC), 1, 8, 9, 22, 112, 142, 209, 214, 242
 See also oil
ORSTOM. See Office de la Recherche Scientifique et Technique d'Outre-mer

Pahlavi, Mohammed Riza, 7, 23, 114, 116
Pakistan, 27, 28–29, 31, 71, 161, 210
Panikkar, K. M., 140
Papua New Guinea, 78
PDRY. See People's Democratic Republic of Yemen
Peacock, Andrew, 66
Pell, Claiborne, 119
People's Democratic Republic of Yemen (PDRY), 94, 99, 150, 235, 237
People's Republic of China (PRC), 34, 113, 131, 184, 216
 and Third World, 22, 142
Persian Gulf, 8, 14, 15
 regional cooperation in, 16, 18
 See also Hormuz, Strait of; United States
PFLOAG. See Popular Front for the Liberation of Oman and the Arabian Gulf
Pine Gap, 68
Pompidou, Georges, 193, 202
Popular Front for the Liberation of Oman and the Arabian Gulf (PFLOAG), 12
PRC. See People's Republic of China
Presidential task force on energy issues, 111

Qatar, 8
Quoins, 8

Racial conflict. See Apartheid
Ramanantsoa, Gabriel, 193
Rangulam, Seewosagur, 192
Rapid Reaction Strike Force, 12, 209, 235, 239
Ratsiraka, Didier, 200
Red Sea, 89
Regional arbitration tribunals, 218
Regional conflicts, 3, 90
 and external powers, 3, 87–88, 99–100, 134, 212–213, 241
René, France-Albert, 192
Renouf, Alan, 80
Réunion Island, 195, 196, 197, 198, 201
Rhodesian Information Center (Sydney), 78

Sadat, Anwar, 153
Saint-Denis-de-la-Réunion, 195
Saint Paul and Amsterdam islands, 196
Saudi Arabia, 8, 13, 14, 31, 72, 73, 115, 119, 123–124
Schlesinger, James, 118, 120, 121, 122, 123, 124–125, 136
Secrétariat d'Etat Chargé des Départements et Territoires d'Outre-mer, 196
Secrétariat Général de la Défense Nationale, 190
Secrétariat Général de la Présidence

Index

de la République pour les Affaires Africaines et Malgaches, 189
Selassie, Haile, 90, 99, 162
Seychelles, 32, 191, 192, 195, 198
Shaba province, 74
Shatt-al-Arab agreements
 Iraq's denunciation of, 17, 185
Silvermine communications network, 96, 141
Sim, J. P., 61, 82(n5)
Simonstown, 96, 241
Singapore, 68–69, 70, 110, 239
 Commonwealth Heads of Government Conference in, 47
 Strait of, 8
Singh, Swaran, 46–47, 49
SIPRI. *See* Stockholm International Peace Research Institute
Sisco, Joseph, 114, 124
Smith, Ian, 74
Socotra Island, 46
Somalia, 44, 45, 89, 90, 96
 treaty with Soviet Union, 150, 162
 See also Berbera; Horn of Africa; Soviet Union
Southern Africa, 1
 Western interests in, 77, 89, 90 91–93, 228–229
South-South relations, 21, 25, 31, 33
South West Africa People's Organization (SWAPO), 74, 79, 236
South Yemen. *See* People's Democratic Republic of Yemen
Soviet Union, 3, 34, 89
 arms supplies by, 19, 89, 92, 149–169, 232, 235
 future naval missions of, 180–187
 interdiction of Western oil supplies, 11, 14, 112, 125, 180–183
 naval policy, 173–175
 naval presence in Indian Ocean, 19, 44, 47, 94, 125, 175–179, 185–187, 235–237

oil shortage in, 9, 180, 229
policy in Horn of Africa, 98, 162–164, 183, 235–236
policy in southern Africa, 146, 236–237
 See also Berbera; Naval arms limitation talks; superpower interests in Indian Ocean; Zone of Peace in Indian Ocean
Spiers, Ronald, 111
Sri Lanka, 26, 27, 28, 207
Stalin, Joseph, 174
Stockholm International Peace Research Institute (SIPRI), 143–144
Submarine missile technology developments in, 178
Suez Canal, 89, 177, 199
Superpower interests in Indian Ocean, 93–94, 96–100, 107, 232–233
 parallelism of, 132–134, 137, 146
 See also Soviet Union; United States
Swali, Ali, 194
SWAPO. *See* South West Africa People's Organization
Symington, Stuart, 119, 122

al-Takriti, Saddam Hussein, 160
Tanzania, 26, 32, 33, 194, 242
Task Force, 74, 113
Tengah airfield, 69
Terre Adélie, 196
Terres Australes et Antarctiques Françaises, 196
Territoire Français des Afars et des Issas, 193
Terrorist attacks, 13–14
 See also Hormuz, Strait of
Thompson, James, 208
Tiran, Strait of, 8
Trans-Siberian Railroad, 184
Tribute system, 224–232, 242, 243
Tromelin Island, 197

Tsiranana, Philibert, 192, 193
Tsushima, Straits of, 173

UAE. See United Arab Emirates
Umm Qasr, 185, 235
UNDP. See United Nations, Development Programme
UNESCO. See United Nations, Educational, Scientific, and Cultural Organization, ix
United Arab Emirates (UAE), 8, 30, 31
United Nations
  Ad Hoc Committee on Indian Ocean, 208, 210, 218
  Development Programme (UNDP), 26
  Educational, Scientific, and Cultural Organization, ix
  Meeting of littoral and hinterland states of Indian Ocean, 2, 54, 210–213, 216–217
  Special Session on Disarmament, 210
  See also Zone of Peace in Indian Ocean
United States, 3, 7, 34, 89, 96
  arms sales by, 91, 99, 116–117, 123–124, 232
  functions of naval presence, 120–121, 122–123, 136–137
  military capabilities in Indian Ocean, 2, 14, 15, 19, 54, 94, 108, 118, 135–136, 209, 233–235
  oil imports by, 9, 112, 228
  policy in Persian Gulf, 11, 14, 94, 110, 112, 115–117, 120–124, 134–135, 214, 239
  policymaking process and domestic cleavages, 132, 137–139
  threats to interests of in Third World, 141
  See also Demilitarization; Diego Garcia; Naval arms limitation talks; Rapid Reaction Strike Force; Superpower interests in Indian Ocean; Zone of Peace in Indian Ocean

Vajpayee, Atal Bihari, 51, 52–3, 54
Vance, Cyrus, 66, 138
Venezuela, 8, 219
Vickers, 155
Vietnam, 24, 34, 109, 143, 146, 214
Vikrant, 156

Weiss, Seymour, 118, 120, 127 (n15)
Western Autralia, 59, 64, 68, 69, 70, 140
  See also Australia; HMAS Stirling; Learmonth; North West Cape; Operation Sandgroper
Wicker, Tom, 133

Yakutsk Republic, 180
Yamani, Ahmad Zaki, 13
Young, Andrew, 92, 98

Zaire, 74, 75, 98
Zambia, 26, 32, 33, 92
ZAPU. See Zimbabwe African Peoples Union
Zimbabwe, 74, 76, 89, 92
Zimbabwe African Peoples Union (ZAPU), 236
Zone of Peace in Indian Ocean (IOPZ), 3, 22, 46, 53, 54, 55
  Australian position on, 62, 211–212
  goals of, 207–208, 240
  Pakistani proposals on, 211–212
  Soviet attitude toward, 216–217, 240–241
  U.S. attitude toward, 217, 241
  weaknesses of, 17, 178, 214–216, 219, 241
  See also United Nations

Zumwalt, Elmo, 97